THE RULE
OF THE CLAN

THE RULE
OF THE CLAN

WHAT AN ANCIENT FORM
OF SOCIAL ORGANIZATION
REVEALS ABOUT THE FUTURE
OF INDIVIDUAL FREEDOM

MARK S. WEINER

FARRAR, STRAUS AND GIROUX   NEW YORK

Farrar, Straus and Giroux
18 West 18th Street, New York 10011

Image of the Macpherson crest on page 22 courtesy of
the Clan Macpherson Museum, Newtonmore, Scotland.

Library of Congress Cataloging-in-Publication Data
Weiner, Mark Stuart.
    The rule of the clan : what an ancient form of social organization reveals about
the future of individual freedom / Mark S. Weiner.
        p.   cm.
    Includes bibliographical references and index.
    ISBN 978-0-374-25281-6 (hardcover : alk. paper)
    1. Clans—Social aspects.   2. Clans—Political aspects.   3. Kinship—Social
aspects.   4. Kinship—Political aspects.   5. Customary law.   6. Law, Primitive.
7. Democracy.   I. Title.

GN487.7.C55 W45 2012
306.83—dc23

                                                            2012023468

Designed by Jonathan D. Lippincott

www.fsgbooks.com
www.twitter.com/fsgbooks • www.facebook.com/fsgbooks

1   3   5   7   9   10   8   6   4   2

For Stephanie
for every moment

The savage mind is the mind of mankind.
—Robin Fox

CONTENTS

PART ONE

THE CHALLENGE
OF THE CLAN

INDIVIDUALISM'S PARADOX

Imagine that one fine morning you are strolling down the sidewalk on your way to work. Suddenly, a young jogger wearing headphones turns the corner, running swiftly, oblivious to the world around him. He crashes into you and as you hit the ground you feel a sharp pain in your arm, which quickly begins to swell. It's broken. Soon after visiting your doctor, you contact your lawyer. He begins a civil suit against the jogger so that you can be compensated for your injury.

The case is open and shut. The jogger was clearly at fault and he will be held accountable for the harm he caused.

Next, imagine that you decide to open a small business, perhaps a bakery specializing in German-style breads. You rent the perfect building for the shop and visit your local bank for a loan. The loan officer reviews your excellent business plan and approves it. You sign your name to a stack of papers he slides across his desk and soon you have the capital you need to purchase ovens and other equipment. You are now responsible for repaying the loan.

Nobody could seriously question your liability or the bank's right to be repaid.

In both these cases, the law's basic focus, what social scientists call its framework of analysis or its "jural unit," is the individual rather than the family. In the case of the errant jogger, when your lawyer contacts the jogger's lawyer, he will make a claim against the jogger and not against the jogger's brother or sister, who are irrelevant to the suit. Likewise, your own brother or sister will have no claim to any settlement money you might receive.

In the case of your business venture, too, much as you might wish to do so, you can't foist your financial obligations onto others without their consent. By taking out a loan, you don't make your family members responsible for the success or failure of your bakery. At the same time, you needn't obtain their permission to take out a loan in the first place. The law makes you responsible for meeting your financial obligations and it also enables you to contract for them yourself, with your own signature.

This individualist focus is fundamental to the law of modern liberal societies. It lies at the core of nations that trace their democratic political heritage to the Enlightenment and their economic roots to the Industrial Revolution—and that hold individual self-fulfillment and personal development as a central moral value. Indeed, legal individualism is so basic to the social fabric of liberal societies that most of us who live in them take it as a matter of course.[1]

In an election, you cast your vote for yourself alone, rather than for your household, village, or tribe. Doing so would seem absurd—it would contravene the axiomatic principle of "one person, one vote." Nor does the head of your household, village, or tribe vote on your behalf.

When you enter into a marriage, you alone incur its benefits and obligations. A wedding may bind two families together in a metaphorical sense. But it doesn't establish a relationship between them as a matter of law, for instance by requiring them to come to each other's mutual aid or military defense.

If one evening you are watching a movie and a notorious thief, John "Quick Hands" Smith, steals your car, police will seek to capture and arrest John Smith. If instead the officers arrest his staid brother Jack, an accountant, explaining to a judge that after all Jack is related to John, the officers will be disciplined. Likewise, when you call the police station to report the incident, you will be asked for your street address rather than the name of your grandparents—your lineage is irrelevant to whether the state will protect you from crime.

Such individualism extends as well to the legal issues of property and inheritance. In liberal societies, land need not be owned in common by tribal groups or village associations, as it is in many parts of the world, with individuals having only a temporary and limited claim to its use, known as a usufruct interest. Instead, land can be held by individuals, who have a general right to do with it as they wish, including the right to exclude others from its benefits.

Similarly, in common law jurisdictions, people are free to will their estates to whomever they please (civil law jurisdictions impose some limits on this principle). Assuming they comply with technical rules for creating trusts, people may even decide that upon their death their assets will pass to their dogs or cats, as did the flamboyant real estate tycoon Leona Helmsley, who left twelve million dollars in trust for her Maltese dog, Trouble. Whether or not it results in wise or just decisions in any particular case—it often quite clearly does not—a person's wealth is deemed to be his or her own.

All these facts may seem self-evident, perhaps even obvious. But if one looks beneath them, they point to an essential paradox about individual freedom, a paradox that's illuminated by examining the subject of this book: the rule of the clan.

It's a common and understandable belief that liberty exists only when the state is absent or weak. Many people often imply that individual freedom flourishes in inverse proportion to the strength and scope of government. The argument is a perennial feature of American political discourse ("freedom means the absence of government coercion," asserts a prominent recent presidential candidate), though it is hardly limited to the United States.[2] A deep antipathy to the modern state was a core principle of the United States' longtime enemy Col. Muammar al-Qaddafi, who sought, in the words of his manifesto *The Green Book*, "emancipation from the chains of all instruments of government."[3] Likewise, guided by a compelling spiritual vision, Mohandas Gandhi advocated for a stateless society of local self-rule for postcolonial India, in which power would be radically decentralized to ancient village communities—*panchayati raj*. He and his followers campaigned for "as minimal a 'state' as possible," following the maxim "keep government to the minimum, and what you must have, decentralize."[4]

Yet, whatever form it takes, the belief that individual freedom exists only when the state is frail misunderstands the source of liberty. The state can be more or less effective in the pursuit of its goals—it can be stupid or smart—and it can be used for illiberal, totalitarian ends. But ultimately a healthy state dedicated to the public interest makes individual freedom possible.

This is the paradox of individualism. The individual freedom that citizens of liberal societies rightly cherish, even our very concept of the individual, is impossible without a robust state. Modern individualism depends on the existence of vigorous and effective government dedicated to the public interest, to policies that a majority of citizens would support without regard to their particular position in society at any given moment. It depends as well on the willingness of individual citizens to imagine themselves as members of a common public whose interests the state regularly vindicates.

The state maintains a system of courts to ensure that people play by the rules, rather than resorting to trickery or force to advance their interests. It provides professionally trained police to safeguard people from crime; fire protection to prevent collective disaster; and military power to defend against threats from abroad. It constructs roads and bridges, builds or subsidizes utilities, and supports mass education to encourage economic growth and foster human capital. To mitigate major social and economic risk in advance of calamity, it operates a wide range of regulatory programs, such as those that safeguard the public health or oversee financial instruments, and it provides security for individuals through various forms of welfare.

Most important, the state stipulates the receipt of these benefits not on a person's membership in an inescapable group but simply on his or her status as an individual.

Your ability to obtain redress for injury, to enter into contracts on your own terms, to use land and other property, to dispose of your wealth, to be protected from crime, and to access a range of goods and services all depend on the state treating the individual—*you*—as a member of a community of legal equals.

The legal status of the individual under a strong liberal state, in which healthy government and robust individualism go hand in hand, might be represented in simple visual form this way:

LIBERAL SOCIETY

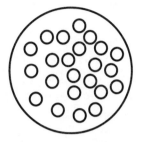

In a modern liberal society the state, represented by the large circle, is vigorous and effective, clearly demarcating and defining the community it surrounds. The discrete individuals living under the authority of the state, the smaller circles, are in turn equally vital and independent. An essential aim of the liberal legal tradition, as important as its goal of limiting state power—though we are often unmindful of its centrality—has been to build state capacities to ensure such vitality and independence.

By contrast, in the absence of the state, or when states are weak, the individual becomes engulfed within the collective groups on which people must rely to advance their goals and vindicate their interests. Without the authority of the state, a host of discrete communal associations rush to fill the vacuum of power. And for most of human history, the primary such group has been the extended family, the clan.

The clan is a natural form of social and legal organization—it is far more explicable in human terms than the modern liberal state—and people quickly, reflexively turn to it in the want of an alternative. Left to our own devices, we humans naturally build legal structures based on real or fictive kin ties or social networks that behave much like ancient clans. Our instinctual drives are not only psychological and sexual, but also legal. The impulse is part of who we are as human beings.[5]

•

In this book, I therefore invite readers to engage in what might seem to be a contradictory exercise: to consider what societies governed by the rule of the clan can teach citizens of modern liberal democracies. I believe that by examining the rule of the clan and understanding its legal and cultural architecture, including its many positive and compelling features, liberals can gain critical insights for liberalism (by "liberal" I refer to people committed to the values of individualism and the principles of liberal democratic government, regardless of party affiliation). This ancient form of social organization can sharpen our appreciation of the institutional and cultural values necessary to sustain our individualist way of life. We can also learn how best to assist native legal reformers abroad in turning their societies toward more liberal legal arrangements.

What exactly is the rule of the clan? When I refer to the rule of the clan, I mean three related contemporary phenomena.[6]

First, and most prominently, I mean the legal structures and cultural values of societies organized primarily on the basis of kinship—societies in which extended family membership is vital for social and legal action and in which individuals have little choice but to maintain a strong clan identity. Today these societies include many in which the United States and its allies have a major strategic interest, such as Afghanistan, Yemen, Nigeria, and Somalia, but they have existed across history and throughout the world. Sometimes they are described as "tribal," though I tend to avoid the term because in English it carries a host of negative and racialist connotations. This strict form of the rule of the clan also includes the traditional Hindu caste system and Indian joint family, despite the manifest great differences between tribal societies and rapidly modernizing democratic India.

Second, by the rule of the clan I mean the political arrangements of societies governed by what the *Arab Human Development Report 2004* calls "clannism."[7] These societies possess the outward trappings of a modern state but are founded on informal patronage networks, especially those of kinship, and traditional ideals of patriarchal family authority. In nations pervaded by clannism, government is coopted for purely factional purposes and the state, conceived on the model of the patriarchal family, treats citizens not as autonomous actors but rather as troublesome dependents to be managed.

Clannism is the historical echo of tribalism, existing even in the face of economic modernization. It often characterizes rentier societies struggling under the continuing legacy of colonial subordination, as in the Middle East and sub-Saharan Africa, where the nuclear family, with its revolutionary, individuating power, has yet to replace the extended lineage group as the principle framework for kinship or household organization. A form of clannism likewise pervades mainland China and other nations whose political development was influenced by Confucianism, with its ideal of a powerful state resting on a well-ordered family, and where personal connections are essential to economic exchange.

Third, and most broadly, by the rule of the clan I mean the antiliberal social and legal organizations that tend to grow in the absence of state authority or when the state is weak. These groups include petty criminal gangs, the Mafia, and international crime syndicates, which look a great deal like clans and in many respects act like them. Today corporate conglomerates and collectivist identity groups have the potential to transform into similar clanlike systems. In this respect, the rule of the clan is a synecdoche for a general pattern according to which humans tend to organize their communities.

Life under the rule of the clan is profoundly different from life in liberal societies. Most important, compared with modern liberal states, communities governed by the rule of the clan possess a markedly diminished conception of individual freedom. This is because under their legal principles people are valued less as individuals per se than as members of their extended families. The rights and obligations of individuals are fundamentally influenced by their places within the kin groups to which they inescapably belong.

The legal status of the individual under the rule of the clan might be represented like this:

THE RULE OF THE CLAN

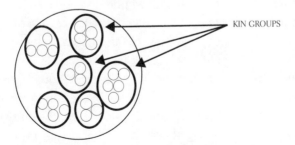

KIN GROUPS

Here, in the presence of a weak state, the individual is weakened and submerged in the more muscular corporate associations—kin groups—that maintain the society's political order.

•

The founding father of legal history and legal anthropology, Henry Sumner Maine, had an illuminating term for such communities. He called them societies of "Status," which he contrasted with communities he called societies of "Contract." According to Maine, the history of all "progressive societies," societies that had undergone a course of modernizing development, is a story of their transformation *"from Status to Contract."*[8] It is a formulation that sheds a good deal of light on a number of grave threats shadowing liberal societies today.

Born in 1822 and raised near London, Maine rose from relatively humble origins to the most influential heights of Victorian intellectual life. Strikingly, he brought together two professional paths that today might seem at odds: recondite historian of the ancient world and practical colonial administrator.

As a young man, Maine was a scholar's scholar. His raw intellectual talent as a student of classics at Pembroke College, Cambridge, was legendary—his academic achievements were "among the most impressive undergraduate records in the long history of Cambridge University"— and he was a masterful writer as well.[9] While an undergraduate he was the recipient of a prestigious prize in poetry previously awarded to Alfred Tennyson. Later, the future American president Woodrow Wilson would bestow upon him a compliment with which most of his admiring readers across the world would concur. He called Maine "a lawyer with style," one who "belongs by method and genius among men of letters."[10]

Like many an excellent student, Maine soon entered the professoriate, returning to teach at his alma mater at the tender age of twenty-four as the Regius Professor of Civil Law. He also began to teach civil law at the Inns of Court, the center of English legal education in London. The civil law tradition derives from the law of ancient Rome, whose principles provide the basis for the law of admiralty, the canon law of the Anglican and Catholic churches, and the doctrines of equity that were once the exclusive province of courts of chancery. Maine's first and greatest book, *Ancient Law* (1861), took the history of Roman legal ideas and used it to unravel the legal development of humanity as a whole.

One might have expected that after he published his illustrious study, the muttonchopped Maine would have retired into Oxbridge fustiness. Instead, he cast concerns about his frail health aside and set sail for India with his wife, Jane. There he worked for the British colonial government settling land disputes, reforming marriage laws, and codifying legislation, as well as serving as the vice chancellor of the University of Calcutta.

He served with distinction and, as luck would have it, his health improved and he greatly enjoyed himself. When he returned to England in 1869, he drew on his Indian experience in an important series of lectures and books. His writings on native law and society—particularly his observation that India possessed indigenous resources for self-government even as those institutions required western paternalist protection to survive—provided "the ideological linchpin" for Britain's distinctive mode of imperial rule.[11]

Maine's broad, comparative experience set him thinking in channels that were at once wide and deep. On one hand, he put a world-spanning range of societies into dialogue, often with surprising results. One of his characteristically intriguing observations, offered in *Lectures on the Early History of Institutions* (1875), was that modern India shared core legal ideas about marriage, property, and dispute resolution with medieval Ireland, as the two societies derived those rules from a common Aryan cultural ancestor. So outwardly different, the lands of Guinness and Gandhi are in fact genetically related in their legal principles, possessing a shared progenitor deep in the Indo-European past.[12]

But even more important, Maine used his knowledge to ask basic questions about a grand subject: legal evolution, the development of legal systems over time.

He explored two issues in particular. First, he sought to explain the mechanisms by which legal rules change in response to social pressure. What are the pathways of legal transformation? In biological evolution, as Charles Darwin had shown a few years earlier in *On the Origin of Species* (1859), the mechanisms of change include natural selection. Scientists now know they also include genetic mutation and genetic drift. According to Maine, *law* has only three methods of development, and in the last one hundred and fifty years, no one has effectively proposed another.

The first method is legal fictions, ideas that alter the substance of law without changing its letter. In the United States, for example, business corporations are viewed as "persons" under the terms of the federal Constitution, entitling them to due process of law and a host of other constitutional protections (including, controversially, protection of their political speech).

The second method is equity, the harmonization of existing law to higher bodies of principles external to the law itself, especially transcendent morals. The U.S. Supreme Court decision in *Brown v. Board of Education* (1954), which declared policies of racial segregation unlawful, did so on a slim constitutional basis but a firm moral one.

The third method is legislation, which changes law through the expressed will of the persons or institutions responsible for crafting rules. Such legal change takes place every day through the work of representative legislative bodies and administrative agencies.

In addition to exploring the mechanisms of legal change, Maine also asked whether those changes tended to move in a specific direction. By placing the laws of Rome, India, Ireland, and other societies side by side, could one discover whether legal evolution followed a particular trend or track? Maine's answer was a succinct theoretical formulation that has influenced the writings of legal historians and anthropologists for generations.

In Maine's view, the legal development of "progressive societies" follows a path *"from Status to Contract."*[13] The pithy phrase (the italics are his) was Maine's most important idea. In the words of one scholar, it "might well adorn the family crest of anthropology."[14]

One might say that it made Maine the Charles Darwin of jurisprudence.

By societies of Status, Maine did not mean societies that simply possess a sense of social rank or hierarchy. Instead, he meant those communities in which family groups serve as the primary basis for social organization and in which the law takes the extended family as its principal unit of concern. In these communities—societies governed by the rule of the clan—a person's social and legal role is determined by his or her place within the kinship group. For instance, the role of women in clan societies is to physically reproduce the clan itself and this role shapes all the legal rules affecting them, from their ability to sue or be sued to their property rights.

By societies of Contract, Maine meant societies in which law is oriented toward the individual rather than the group, and in which individual choice serves as the central value of the legal order. In such societies, individuals are no longer legally subordinated to their extended families. Instead, the legal order is directed toward fostering the ability of individuals to chart their own life course, economically, professionally, or personally, from enabling them to dispose of their assets through a will or charter their own corporations to permitting them to marry without regard to clan affiliation. Maine showed that this individualist orientation of societies of Contract was made possible by the growth of the state and its institutions.

According to Maine, the "progressive" societies of the world had been set on their course from Status to Contract through an internal force, an important social choice made in the ancient past, or by a unique accident of history. (Intriguingly, one of the first signs of the state's growth was the animal pound, where an individual's or family's most valuable property could be taken and held pending the adjudication of a grievance, a legal action known as destraint.) The task of the scholar was to chart this transformation and to discover what those forces, choices, or events were, discoveries which might then lead to practical insights for contemporary policy.

Maine was not alone in this aspiration, but he differed from a number of other important nineteenth-century scholars in a critical respect. Whereas Maine viewed a liberal society of Contract as an evolutionary endpoint, many of his contemporaries believed that Western nations had one more grand step to take—one that, ironically, would return society to its communal and egalitarian clan past. As we will see, this belief was essential to the development of the most important and compelling modern alternative to the liberal intellectual tradition, that of Marxism. As outlined by Friedrich Engels in *The Origin of the Family, Private Property, and the State* (1884), the goal of a communist revolution was to re-create the principles and conditions of clan society in a higher historical form.

Notably, another recent alternative to liberal society, political Islamism, makes an appeal to egalitarianism and social justice that is every bit as powerful as Marxism's. In doing so, it draws on a potent rhetoric of kin group solidarity (in Arabic, *'asabiyya*) that many Muslims use to understand their religious community. As Akbar Ahmed and Abdullah

Saeed each note, many Muslims view the global *umma* as one large clan, and thus interpret any assault on one of its members as a dishonoring of the group as a whole.[15] The genuine attraction of political Islam rests on a vision of legal and political community understood through metaphors of kinship drawn from deep in the Arabian past.

•

Understanding the rule of the clan—appreciating precisely how it works as a form of legal and social organization—is critical for liberals for a host of reasons. It is necessary to protect the social peace and national security of liberal states; to ensure political stability in vital regions of the world; and to effectively—and ethically—assist native liberal reformers abroad. Most of all, it is vital for attending to the stewardship of our own nations and protecting what matters most to us.

Yet the comfortable social and political conditions in which we live predispose liberals to neglect the rule of the clan's most distinctive and important features.

The modern liberal world—liberal modernity—has deep historical roots, but it is the immediate product of a group of interrelated changes that took place in the way people lived in the industrialized nations of nineteenth-century Europe and the Americas. These changes together unshackled the individual from various types of constraint.

Most strikingly, the vibrant economies of nations such as England, the United States, France, and Germany distributed unprecedented prosperity to a remarkably broad segment of their citizenries. Consider the historical trend of per capita gross domestic product (GDP). According to estimates made by the late British economist Angus Maddison, in the year 1000 the per capita GDP of the United Kingdom, calculated in 1990 values, was $400. In the following centuries, that figure slowly climbed, until in the Renaissance it began to increase at a rate of about $250 every one hundred years. In 1500, per capita GDP was $714; in 1600, $974; in 1700, $1,250; and in 1820, after some decades of economic expansion, it was $1,756. But by 1900, it had skyrocketed to $4,593. In the eighty years between 1820 and 1900, that is, per capita GDP in the United Kingdom grew by more than double the amount it had grown in the previous eight hundred years combined.

Statistics tell a similar story throughout Northern and Western

Europe, the British settler colonies, and in the United States (which in 1900 had a per capita GDP of $4,096). By contrast, in 1900 per capita GDP in China was $652; in India, $625; in Egypt, $509; and in Ghana, $462.[16]

This prosperity, and the personal freedom it supported, were underwritten by liberal advances in government, politics, and culture. In the realm of government, economic growth required the intervention of energetic states dedicated not only to expanding economic liberty, most importantly by making it easy for entrepreneurs to charter limited liability corporations, but also to furthering collective social development, for instance by policing public safety, advancing public health, and promoting public works. In time, states also fostered economic vitality through public education and secured the domestic peace, along with a more just political economy, through basic programs of social welfare.

In the realm of politics, similarly, the era witnessed the formal abolition of serfdom and slavery, while the gradual expansion of the franchise enlarged the influence of ordinary people in public life, making government more responsive to the common good.

Finally, in the realm of culture, popular and elite values alike were reoriented toward the individualist ideals of personal growth and psychological and emotional self-fulfillment. From the Evangelical revival in Protestant Christianity to the most important literary innovation of the era, the realist novel, the great drama of the self took center stage.

These changes brought extraordinary benefits to humankind, and the approach to law and government that made them possible—in which a strong, democratic state works on behalf of the public interest by expanding individual liberty, fostering economic prosperity, and enhancing the social conditions enabling personal freedom—ranks among the most liberating innovations in human history. For a citizen of a liberal democratic society, it thus would be easy to view societies of Status as remote, distant, and removed from one's own fate. Living in relative material comfort and political stability, a person could understandably isolate the rule of the clan at the margins of his or her attention.

But this would be a grievous mistake. Liberal societies and societies governed by the rule of the clan are inextricably connected, like two climbers together ascending the face of a mountain. Citizens of modern liberal nations can afford to ignore the rule of the clan as much as a climber can afford to ignore the partner tethered to the rope tied around his or her own waist.

In fact, I believe that if liberals fail to take to heart the lessons of the rule of the clan, particularly the lesson of individualism's paradox, our future will be a deeply troubling, literally "postmodern" version of our own clan past. If liberals lose the political will to maintain and nurture robust state institutions dedicated to the public interest, ignoring our human impulse to create clanlike forms of legal organization, it will spell the end of individualism as we know it. In a possibility Maine could not have imagined, our societies will move in historical reverse—from Contract to a new, terrible form of Status.[17] As various institutions rush to fill the power vacuum left by the state's decline, we will be over-taken by a new form of the rule of the clan.

Our future will look something like this:

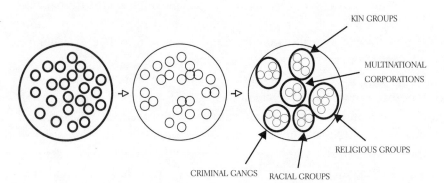

Here, as the liberal state is eroded, individuals begin to cluster into groups to protect themselves and assert their interests. Over time, these groups consolidate their power, becoming more important to the social order than the individuals the liberal state once nurtured.

In contemporary political discourse, one frequently encounters the warning of Alexis de Tocqueville, writing in *Democracy in America* (1835, 1840), that in the United States each person is "throw[n] . . . back forever upon himself alone" and that democracy may ultimately isolate the individual "entirely within the solitude of his own heart."[18] Many people fear that modern liberal society, not simply in the United States but wherever it is found, is threatened most by selfish individualism.

But from a legal and political perspective, rather than a cultural

and moral one, the major threat to liberal societies is precisely the opposite. It is that with the erosion of the state's capacities, the individual
will be submerged within corporatist groups that take the place of modern law. It is that the individualism we cherish will be lost as a result of
a deterioration of the state.

·

To understand the rule of the clan—where it comes from, what makes it
work, what it means for the people who live under it every day—this
book will examine a wide variety of clan societies across the world and
at different periods of history.

I wish to emphasize that this book is not a comprehensive survey of
clan societies past and present, nor is it a work of academic social science. There are many outstanding scholarly studies in the fields of law,
politics, history, anthropology, and literature that treat in detail many of
the issues I examine here. These works include, in particular, many specialized books in the fields of legal and constitutional history, the history of the family, and state formation. I greatly admire these studies,
and I refer to some of them in my notes, which I hope will be helpful for
readers who wish to pursue specific subjects in greater depth.

But this book is something else. Rather than a work of exhaustive
scholarship, policy prescription, or analytic theorization, it is a series of
narratives and reflections. It is a long essay, intended for a wider reader-
ship than most academic studies attempt to reach. Along the way, ac-
cordingly, I introduce a number of people from varying walks of life
who have important things to say about the rule of the clan and its
significance and whose often colorful stories I believe are important to
hear.

I begin in part II by describing the highly decentralized constitutional structure of the rule of the clan, in which legal and political
power reside not in a public authority but rather in numerous kinship
groups. To illustrate this decentralization, I examine three societies that
lie along a continuum of legal development. The first society is that of
the Nuer of early twentieth-century southern Sudan, a fully stateless
tribal community—known in technical terms as a segmentary lineage
system—which I consider by telling the story of the intrepid English
anthropologist E. E. Evans-Pritchard. The second society is medieval

Iceland, one of the most unusual polities of its age in that its government lacked an executive branch, making it a half-state in which kinship played an essential role. The third society is the contemporary Palestinian Authority, where the rule of the clan and a weak state exist side by side, hindering the development of the free, democratic government necessary for peace in the Middle East.

Next, in part III, I consider clans not in constitutional but rather in cultural terms. Specifically, I examine a range of contemporary societies to understand the rule of the clan's distinctive network of informal legal institutions: its values of group honor and shame, its jurisprudence of customary law, and the threat of blood feud. Group honor, custom, and feud provide the cultural connective tissue of the rule of the clan's decentralized constitutional structure. The rule of the clan's constitutionalism and its culture are inseparable—just as the liberal rule of law is inseparable from its own distinctive cultural foundations. I emphasize that it is a mistake to view feud as synonymous with anarchy; instead feud is a highly structured cultural practice that ingeniously maintains social harmony. The conditions necessary for feud to achieve this beneficial end, however, have been undermined by historical developments, especially by the proliferation of modern weapons.

In part IV, I draw lessons for the effective modernization of the rule of the clan from the story of two seemingly different medieval societies, Anglo-Saxon England and early Islamic Arabia. I consider how both societies developed a common, public identity that transcended particularistic kin affiliations and in the process adopted a concept of law fundamentally different from that of the customary legal principles of clan societies. I draw a number of lessons for today from this history, including the general principle that liberal reformers can be most effective in advancing their goals by working not against clans but rather with and through them to build modern states.

More specifically, I argue that reformers seeking to advance liberal values in clan societies can encourage the growth of a common, public life by looking to mechanisms that work both "from below" and "from above." I suggest, in particular, that liberals should encourage the spread of information and social media technologies in clan societies, predicting that in time social media will lessen the practical and personal importance of kin identity in much the same way as monotheistic religion did in the European Middle Ages. I also suggest that liberals should promote the development of the middle-class professions, which are the modern parallel to the Germanic ruling class within which a public identity in Anglo-Saxon England first developed.

In part V, I consider two different ways in which the rule of the clan is bound to remain an eternal presence in modern liberal societies—not shut off from view, but rather at the very center of our lives.

I begin by considering the surprising role the normative order of the clan plays in the modern liberal imagination—how after the clan's legal authority has vanished its cultural importance grows. (I anticipate this discussion immediately below, in chapter 2.) First, I consider what liberals' surprisingly romantic view of the clan reveals about the cultural values and social ideals that promote the rule of law and the individualist mode of life it enables. I argue that Walter Scott, who offered a vivid portrait of the Scottish clan past, best embodies the cultural foundation of a sustainable liberal constitutionalism. Scott's novels give voice to a historical and aesthetic sensibility that offers citizens the symbolic resources to imagine an abstract public identity beyond their specific social position or accident of birth, while also affirming the value of particularistic clan or clanlike affiliations as a powerful basis for personal identity.

In this light, I also argue that the valorization of the clan in cultural memory is often a sign not of an atavistic regression but instead of liberalism's legal advent—a phenomenon it is important for liberals to bear in mind as we observe the political development of societies abroad, especially in the Middle East and North Africa.

Finally, in my concluding chapter, I argue that the rule of the clan will always haunt modern liberal society as a postmodern threat: the threat of state erosion, constitutional decentralization, and cultural encrustation. I imagine the dystopian consequences of failing to meet this threat—of allowing the reemergence of a society of Status by failing to support a robust state—in a brief thought experiment.

Before considering these important matters, I wish in chapter 2 to draw attention to a curious phenomenon close to home, and then, in chapter 3, to consider in greater detail how clan societies challenge liberal interests and values from abroad. Doing so will deepen our appreciation of just what's at stake in our travels to come.

TWO

FROM CLAN TO CLUB

In the popular 2009 science fiction epic *Avatar*, the film's unlikely hero, Jake Sully, gives a rousing speech to the assembled members of the Omaticaya clan, one of the many scattered tribes of the blue-skinned Na'vi people of the planet Pandora. In the larger *Avatar* entertainment franchise other Na'vi clans include the Anurai, Li'ona, Ni'wave, Tawkami, Tipani, and the horse clans of the plain.

"The Sky People have sent a message that they can take whatever they want, and no one can stop them," cries Jake, referring to the capitalists who have come from Earth to extract Pandora's mineral wealth. "But we will send them a message. Ride out, as fast as the wind can carry you, tell the other clans to come . . . Fly now with me brothers and sisters! Fly!"

It is hackneyed stuff, a painful cliché—which is also why it reveals an important feature of modern popular culture. The fact is that in healthy liberal societies, clans—a deeply antiliberal social and legal form—are often portrayed in strikingly positive terms. Indeed, they are frequently romanticized, whether in Hollywood epics like *Avatar*, in popular books like Jean M. Auel's *The Clan of the Cave Bear* (1980), in the pervasive valorization of precontact Native American tribes, and even in the culture of hip-hop music and multiplayer video games, where groups of affiliated players are known as clans. High culture and the arts aren't immune from the tendency, either, for instance in the heroic Völsung clan in Richard Wagner's four-opera cycle *Der Ring der Nibelungen* (1848–74).

The roots of this antiliberal romance lie deep in our history. Jake

Sully's speech is the product of a centuries-long shift in the rules people use to organize their communities and of the psychological consequences of that evolution. Brush away the surface cliché in films like *Avatar* or books like *The Clan of the Cave Bear* and you will find a portrait of the personal and cultural effects of the legal development from Status to Contract.

The significance of the liberal romance with the clan was brought home to me one evening when I was strolling through the historic district of Savannah, Georgia. There, one can find a veritable monument to an antiliberal clan society of which many Americans feel rather fond—a memorial that's important precisely because of how common and unassuming a place it is.

The monument is a Scottish pub named Molly MacPherson's. It was founded in 2005 by two sisters, who named it in honor of their great-grandmother. The pub's website explains that Molly "led a wayward life in Scotland" (in what way we never learn, except that she "married young") and that after her husband died in the 1890s, she moved to Nova Scotia to raise her daughter. There, she opened a pub. When the two sisters created their own restaurant, they christened it after their brave ancestor and in proud recognition of their clan heritage—a heritage they put vividly on display. When patrons sit at the handsome oak bar at Molly's, their eyes wander naturally to a white marble fireplace at the center of the pub and to a red tartan banner hanging above its mantel. Emblazoned across the top of the banner is the name MacPherson, and in the center is the medieval crest of the Macpherson clan of Badenoch (capitalization of the clan name varies). The crest depicts a wildcat with sharp, threatening claws encircled by a strap and buckle, inside of which is written the clan motto: "Touch not the cat but a glove."

The ambiguity of the phrase—just what does it mean?—illuminates a great deal about what it took for Scotland to move from Status to Contract. Even more, it offers a window onto the changes which modern-day clan societies may experience in time, and which liberals should be prepared to recognize.

Centuries ago, the Macphersons and other Highland clans posed as great a challenge to state development as the *qaba'il* of Yemen, the *reero* of Somalia, or the many similar tribal or clan groups in the news today. It would be easy to overlook this fact in the warmth of a Savannah pub whose owners are proud of their heritage. It would be easy to do so in the countless other Celtic-themed bars and restaurants across the world where the walls casually display yellowing pen-and-ink drawings of handsome clan chiefs bearing swords. But the Macpherson crest and motto tell a story of kin loyalty and violence one could easily find in the pages of a twenty-first-century newspaper or blog, and the history of the Highlands contains striking parallels to the history now being told in headlines.

This resemblance is no accident. The very word English-speakers use to describe the social organization of some of the world's most precarious places derives from the Gaelic, from the word *clann*, which means children (and which is itself derived from the same Latin root as is the English word *plant*). Though Celtic society long centered on the family bond, the Highland clan system, well known from romantic movies such as *Brigadoon* (1954) and *Braveheart* (1995), is a product of the twelfth century. It was then that feudal institutional structures were wedded to Celtic family groups that had, over centuries, come to control various tracts of land.

Originally each of these groups, or clans, which took their names from a revered common ancestor, was an independent, self-governing community, with its own "unwritten law."[1] Notably, they were not strictly limited to blood relatives. Other families within a clan's territory often claimed membership in the group whether or not they had an immediate biological tie with its core members (such families are known as septs). Clans were led by a *toiseach*, or chief, who mediated disputes within the clan, led its members in battle, and received loyalty and tribute from his people. The Irish variant of the word, *taoiseach*, is still used in Ireland today to refer to the prime minister.

The Highland clans were not to be trifled with. For all their admirable features, such as their tight-knit social solidarity, political independence, and the captivating beauty of their poetry and music, they also had a well-deserved reputation for violence.[2] The Highlanders were especially involved in brutal intergroup feuds, often sparked by the theft of another clan's cattle for sale in Lowland markets, though other misdeeds were common enough to give regular cause for bloodshed. In the fourteenth century, the clans of Badenoch engaged in what one distinguished Scottish scholar calls "a career of pillage and extortion."[3] One of the resulting feuds, between Clan Kay and Clan Chattan, a federation that included the kernel of Clan Macpherson, was resolved in 1396 by a gladiatorial contest by the banks of the river Tay, thirty clansmen to a side, an event known as the battle of North Inch. After firing three allotted crossbow bolts each, the clansmen—who in one popular account were forbidden from wearing armor or using shields—hacked away at one another with axes, swords, and knives until only one member of Clan Kay and eleven members of Clan Chattan were left standing.[4]

Just as in weak or failed states today, the ferocity of Highland feuds was exacerbated by the absence of a central authority capable of maintaining order. Some very powerful clans could at times keep smaller groups in check and prevent conflicts from spinning out of control. In the fifteenth century Clan Donald imposed a dominion of this sort along Scotland's western coast. But the jealous independence of the clans prevented robust central authority from emerging from within, and Highlanders fiercely resisted English efforts to impose it from outside—in fact, it's often the case that external efforts to impose such order only intensify clan violence. Highland resistance came to a dramatic head in the Jacobite Rising of 1745, when clans rallied to the cause of Bonnie Prince Charlie and the house of Stuart. In this failed endeavor to unseat the Hanoverian monarch George II, the chief of the Macphersons, Ewen "Cluny" Macpherson, gathered an army of hundreds to fight against the English crown. In retaliation, the redcoats burned his home, seized his lands, and pursued him into the rugged hills of Badenoch.

Before he finally escaped to France, he hid for nine years in a cave in the face of Ben Alder, the highest peak of the region, aided by the local population. His dramatic flight would be memorialized in 1886 in Robert Louis Stevenson's stirring adventure novel *Kidnapped*.

The Macpherson crest and motto evoke this fearsome past. The lynx is the clan's totem animal, a symbol of its values, and the claws convey a threat: cross Clan Macpherson at your peril. If there were any doubt about the meaning of the image, one need only ask the twenty-nine clansmen who lay dead on the banks of the river Tay in 1396 after the battle of North Inch—the Macpherson crest and motto and those of Clan Chattan are the same.

•

Today, of course, membership in the Macpherson clan means something very different from what it did in the mists of Pictish Scotland, or in 1396 or 1745. No member of Clan Kay lives in fear of retaliatory violence from Clan Chattan and no one could reasonably accuse the Macphersons of engaging jointly in cattle rustling or its modern equivalent, stealing cars.

The clan still has a hereditary chief, its twenty-seventh, the Honorable Sir William Alan Macpherson of Cluny and Blairgowrie, TD. But his role is a symbolic one. Much as Sir William is respected, his word isn't law to those who bear his name—indeed, he formerly served as a judge of the High Court of England and Wales, where he was responsible for safeguarding the liberal laws of Britain, not those of his clan.

Clan membership instead provides an occasion for warm social gatherings in which people celebrate their common heritage. These gatherings are also remarkably welcoming to outsiders, including those whose roots extend far away from the mountains and lochs of northern Scotland. As I write, I am looking at photographs from a recent Macpherson gala, one of which shows a smiling participant whose ancestry is clearly South Asian. The home page of another clan features an image of a female reveler with deep ebony skin.

Clans have become clubs.[5]

The history of the Macpherson motto records the change, registering a profound process of state development in Scotland: the demise of the clan as an autonomous military and legal force. The original motto is "Na bean don chat gun làmhainn," a blending of Gaelic and French which roughly translates as "don't touch the ungloved cat" (the Gaelic word *gun* means *without* and *làmhainn* means *glove*). The glove to which the motto refers is the glove a cat metaphorically wears when its claws are retracted inside its soft paw. The phrase could be translated idiomatically as "beware of the cat's claw!"—or "beware of the clansman's sword!" But over time, the motto was altered through translation and became syntactically obscure.

In Scots, the word *without* can be rendered somewhat grandiloquently as *bot*. If you were to open one of the many scattered antiquarian volumes tracing the history of the Macpherson clan, you would quickly encounter early heraldic crests declaring "Touch not the cat bot a glove," a translation which would have made perfect sense in a country poised between English and Gaelic.[6] At some point, however, precisely when is difficult to say—both the curator of the Clan Macpherson museum and the greatest living expert on Macpherson heraldry generously owned that they are uncertain—the motto was transcribed fully into English as "Touch not the cat *but* a glove." While one can intuit the meaning of this phrase if one reads it rather swiftly and isn't a stickler for grammar, in fact it doesn't make much sense now that *but* and *bot* are no longer interchangeable, as they are in broad Scots. If anything, with the changing of the English language the motto now seems to counsel the beholder to avoid the claws of a wild animal by touching a piece of winter handwear.

This ambiguity is a product of the political development that makes modern individualism possible. Clan Macpherson is no longer the feared military organization it once was, nor does it possess an independent constitutional identity. If it did, the motto's frayed clarity would be as concerning to its members as it would be to any American if dollar bills suddenly began to circulate with the phrase "In God We Trustworthy" printed on the reverse of President Washington's portrait. But today, the Macpherson cat has been domesticated, so why be troubled by a colorful infelicity? What's imperative for the motto now is not that it intimidate potential enemies but rather that it conjure images of a heroic age of clan valor and solidarity. These are the values that make the crest a worthy object to hang above the fireplace of a Savannah pub. If anything, the motto's vagueness only enhances its talismanic power to summon a bygone era.

The transformation of Highland clans into objects of positive romantic memory reveals vital insights for nations in the throes of political modernization around the globe today. It suggests ways to tame the cat—or, more to the point, to enable its self-domestication—in Libya, Kenya, Nigeria, Pakistan, the Philippines, India, and many other countries. The history is also important for liberals, whose own nations are not nearly as far removed from the rule of the clan as we might like to think—nor incapable of returning to it.

I consider these issues in part V, but it's worth noting from the start that the transformation of Scottish clan identity was realized by Scottish writers, artists, and cultural activists of the nineteenth century who approached their work with a distinctively modern imaginative sensibility. Foremost among them was the novelist Walter Scott, author of the 1814 novel *Waverley*, set amid the Rising of 1745. In a fitting irony, however, Scott was inspired by the earlier writings of James Macpherson, a cousin of the very Cluny Macpherson who hid for nine years in a cave in Ben Alder. In 1761 James Macpherson published a large trove of ancient poetry he claimed derived from the ancient Gaelic poet Ossian. Though the authenticity of the texts is dubious, and was doubted by many at the time, his "translation" of the *Works of Ossian* became a touchstone of the Romantic movement, admired by Johann Wolfgang von Goethe, Scott, and many others, and it laid the foundation for the new Scottish national identity constructed after the clans' resounding military defeat. It was the most significant contribution of a Macpherson to modern Scottish history, dwarfing by comparison Cluny Macpherson's military adventures.[7]

In Scotland, the rule of the clan developed into the liberal rule of law in part through repeated acts of the imagination—through the development of new ways of approaching the past and new forms of literature and speech. Such acts of the imagination are critical for an effective transition to the liberal rule of law and it is necessary to consistently reaffirm them for liberalism to survive.

Among Celtic-themed eateries, Molly's is hardly unique in celebrating a heritage replete with bloody kin-based feuds. And in a nation where immigrants tend to shed the heaviest baggage of their past while retaining pride in their heritage, the ethnic Scots of the United States won't be the last people to open a restaurant centered on a clan theme. At least, one can hope.

A hundred years from now, if Somali food becomes popular across the United States, the great-granddaughters of a Somali refugee named Hirsi may open a restaurant in Savannah called Hirsi Hawiye's. In recognition of their ancestor's birthplace—by then a relatively stable, democratic society—the popular bistro will serve tamarind soda and chopped hamburger wrapped in canjeero bread, and above its fireplace will hang a decorative family tree tracing the Hawiye lineage, or perhaps a portrait of some long-forgotten leader of the United Somali Congress holding a rifle. The patrons will find the portrait genuinely charming, even if the ancestor after whom the restaurant is named, rejecting her own clan heritage, might have cringed upon walking through the door.

Just down the block will sit a Yemeni coffee shop called Jasmin Qabili's Mocha Paradise, which will proudly display a banner emblazoned with a calligraphed piece of slightly mistranslated Arabic tribal poetry.

If that happens, it will be but another instance of an essential modern irony whose roots I trace in the pages ahead: wherever one finds the liberal rule of law, one is surrounded by echoes of the rule of the clan. For modern liberals, the rule of the clan has been our secret sharer— our unacknowledged companion.

THREE

NATIONAL SECURITY AND CLAN HONOR

Across the world today, naturally, the rule of the clan is a great deal more than a romantic memory. In highly tribal societies like Yemen, semiautonomous tribal regions like Waziristan, weak states like Kenya or South Sudan, and even in the midst of more advanced democracies such as India and the Philippines, it is a basic fact of life. It is the primary source of people's values, it affects the choices they make every day, and it structures the operation of their major social and political institutions. Likewise, the principles of clannism influence nations that long ago ceased to be organized along tribal lines but that still afford a prominent role to lineage or ethnicity, such as Bosnia, or that hold patriarchal family authority in especially high regard, such as Egypt or China.

This makes it critical as a practical policy matter to understand how the rule of the clan works, in particular how its legal and cultural aspects are linked, and it makes failures to do so counterproductive to the interests of liberal societies.

Among other issues, if we overlook how the rule of the clan traditionally has maintained intergroup harmony and peace, most notably through the institution of feud, we will be unable to appreciate why today it creates the conditions for social instability and devastating conflict. Equally, if we lack an appreciation of the rule of the clan's genuine cultural appeal and why people would rationally adhere to its demands, we will obscure our understanding of the challenges that many nations face in governing democratically and of how liberals can best assist native reformers abroad. Relatedly, we will be unable to address the needs of immigrants from clan societies to liberal states. But most of all, if we fail to understand the rule of the clan, we will undermine our own national security by walking blindly in the geopolitical world.

Consider the following story from the American military detention facility at Guantanamo Bay. Two years after the September 11 attacks, the Department of Defense asked a young female scholar whom I will call Karen to lead the interrogation team interviewing detainees from Saudi Arabia.

The scholar and I are close friends, and though we have known each other since our first year of college, I learned of her work at Guantanamo only in early 2011, when she disclosed what she had really been doing during some otherwise mysterious years of her life. My wife and I had always assumed that she had been an intelligence agent, though in fact upon completing graduate school she was turned away from several three-letter agencies because, as a scholar with a PhD, she was considered overeducated and likely to be inept in an operational environment. She was turned away from the FBI in 2000 because, as a doctoral candidate at Yale, she had failed to accrue the two years of consecutive employment experience necessary to be hired. Between graduate degrees she had spent twenty-four consecutive months mastering Arabic—but the FBI considered that irrelevant.

After some months as a Department of Defense analyst, with a distinctly dreary assignment in Germany at an office that had no use for her skills, she was asked to become an interrogator. She jumped at the opportunity.

It was intense work, undertaken under enormous time pressure and in challenging physical conditions—her ramshackle working quarters were so decrepit, humid, and moldy that one afternoon she and her colleagues found a sizeable mushroom growing out of the wall.

Karen does not conform to the image most people have of a Guantanamo interrogator. She is nonjudgmental, emotionally perceptive, modest, and kind. An active environmentalist and a dedicated cyclist, she is devoted to recycling and to her garden. She puts on educational puppet shows for children. During her interrogations, she brought detainees tea in china cups and greeted them with the heartfelt words, in Arabic, "peace be upon you." When I once asked her what most of the detainees she knew were like as people, her instant, passionate reply was: "intensely human."

She is also a highly trained academic, and she knows a great deal about the society and politics of the Arabian Peninsula.

This knowledge enabled her to spot a variety of weaknesses in the detention process that were the result of a widespread failure to appreciate the radically different cultures of the detainees—a "lack of interest," as she explained it, "in local culture, including tribal identity."

The military she encountered was in many respects still fighting the Cold War. It was caught in the mentality of "how to win the Fulda Gap," the famed probable route of a Soviet tank invasion of Western Europe—a phrase Karen often heard during her training. Though there were individual exceptions, as an organization the military didn't seem to recognize that today's Fulda Gap is cultural.

A small but telling instance was the early detainee database. Like similar databases in domestic facilities, the Guantanamo tracking program contained slots to enter a person's first, middle, and last names. "That's just dandy for Mark S. Weiner," Karen explained to me one afternoon, sketching out the problem on a piece of paper, "but for a name like Abu Maryam Khalid Muhammad bin Sayf al-Utaybi it doesn't work" (the name is invented).

As Karen interviewed the Saudi detainees and raced to find information that could prevent future terrorist attacks, she soon made a critical discovery. Because the Arabic and Latin alphabets are so different, transliteration from Arabic into Latin script is a complex business. Even a very simple Arabic word can be rendered into Latin script in multiple ways. The Arab equivalent of a common name like "Smith" can be transliterated as "Smith," "Smithe," "Smyth," "Smeeth," "Smeath," "Zmith," "Shmit," "Shmish," "Schmit," "Schmidt," or "Szmeath." ABC News once recorded 112 different spellings of the name of former Libyan leader Col. Muammar al-Qaddafi.[1]

At Guantanamo, transliteration practices had not been standardized, and so detainees' names had been transliterated in "wildly inconsistent ways." Karen made attempts to standardize the system, but the scale of the problem was far-reaching.

Around the same time, she also began to prepare to brief then–Brig. Gen. Jay W. Hood, commander of the Joint Task Force Guantanamo.

General Hood requested that interrogation team leaders be prepared to tell him not simply about individual detainees, but rather about the detainees as a group.

Karen noticed that many of the detainees behaved in ways that didn't make sense within the standard account of captives motivated by Islamic fundamentalism. Some threw urine and feces on guards—conduct well outside the bounds of strict Islamic norms. Others asked for pornography. One detainee asked Karen if during his next interrogation she could bring him a beer.

This was not simply the global *umma* fighting the infidel. Islamist ideology explained only a part of their behavior. Clearly many more factors were at work.

Then Karen had what she described as an "aha moment."

As she prepared to brief General Hood, she looked through all the detainee profiles. She then looked at their transliterated names, one by one. The chaotic transliteration made a search for common names almost futile. But then, when she looked at the detainee names in the original Arabic and made a determined effort to make sense of the Latin script transliterations, a pattern emerged.

Two names stood out.

About a dozen of the detainees—about one in ten of Saudi detainees at Guantanamo—were from two extended families: the Qahtanis and Utaybis. (This information is now available in unclassified material online.)

From her readings in Saudi history, Karen knew that the Qahtanis and Utaybis are two especially powerful, influential tribes, each hailing from a particular region of the Arabian Peninsula. She also knew that both tribes have been locked in a conflict with the house of Saud and its allies since the 1700s. To note just a few recent examples, the 1979 seizure of the Great Mosque in Mecca was led by Muhammad bin Abdullah al-Qahtani and Juhayman al-Utaybi. The four men who were part of a high-level escape from Bagram detention center in 2005 included Muhammad Jafar Jamal al-Qahtani. Among the detainees at Guantanamo was the alleged twentieth hijacker of the September 11 attacks, Muhammad Mana Ahmed al-Qahtani.

For these dozen men, then—those whose tribal affiliations could actually be discerned—it seemed that the Islamist war against the United

States conveniently advanced their cause in a complex domestic tribal feud. As Karen explained, "for some of the detainees, Islamist ideology came onto young minds already in a disposition of wanting to reclaim family and tribal honor. The Islamist ideology added a global, even cosmic, significance to the centuries-long tribal feud, plus an excuse to pursue it with even more zeal than usual. But we Americans were stuck in our own cultural mindset of a liberal rule-of-law society, and we were analytically ill-prepared to make sense of the tribal signals we were seeing."

The dozen men Karen spotted, she explained, "are just the ones who had some indication of a tribal affiliation in the Western-centric name slots. Because of the first-middle-last-name structure of our database, vital information contained in a truly full name, such as tribal affiliation, was sometimes lost entirely."

When we fail to understand the clan heritage of a great many of our enemies, their motivation for taking up arms against us in the first place will remain obscure.[2]

We also find ourselves in a far weaker position when we engage them in battle. In the aftermath of the 2003 invasion of Iraq, for instance, winning the support of Iraq's scores of individual tribes was vital to the success of the war effort—each tribe that supported al-Qaeda in Iraq or the larger insurgency substantially diminished the likelihood of a coalition victory. The Albu Fahd, Albu Mahal, and Albu Issa were particularly significant to coalition efforts in al-Anbar province, which includes the city of Fallujah, site of one of the bloodiest battles in the war. Given the complexity of Iraqi tribal alliances, one might have expected that American knowledge of the tribes and their individual social and political characteristics would have been encyclopedic. Instead, one of the earliest Department of Defense efforts to come to grips with the strategic value of Iraqi tribes was completed a full three years after the war began.[3]

When we intervene militarily in nations like Iraq, or Libya, or Afghanistan, we need to be at least as informed as the leaders we are fighting.

Indeed, when we are, the results can be astonishing. When Saddam Hussein went underground after the invasion of Iraq, he was captured after military analysts constructed "link diagrams" of his tribal network.[4]

The American military has since sought to reckon with the importance of tribal and clan affiliation through programs such as the Human Terrain System, which embeds social scientists with military units on the ground. And, increasingly, military scholars identify the goal of their counterinsurgency and democratization efforts as "a healthy marriage of kinship politics and the modern nation-state."[5] But an organization the size of the American military is naturally slow to change. And such a reckoning has been sorely lacking in our political and public discourse.

•

To remedy this situation, liberals can begin by recognizing a key fact about clan societies: that their law and culture work together in a unique way. Specifically, the rule of the clan melds a decentralized constitutional organization with a culture of group honor. These are the topics, respectively, of parts II and III, but it will be helpful to consider the issue from the start—doing so will also highlight yet another way the rule of the clan implicates our practical interests.

From a constitutional perspective, clan societies are highly decentralized systems of government in which power is dispersed among a multitude of kin groups. I use the term *constitution* in its original, English sense, to refer to a structure of government, whether or not it is established by a single written document. In the terms of medieval Scotland, power in clan societies rests chiefly with the Macphersons, MacDonalds, MacKays, and many other discrete clans rather than with a body or institution common to them all. Clans possess the authority to discipline their members in accordance with group norms—they maintain their own law—and they are the basic institutions people rely on to assert their rights and interests.

To describe clan societies as cultures of group honor, by contrast, is to speak not in terms of structure but of values. In honor cultures, a person's social worth, including his or her self-worth, is inextricably bound to the perceived honor of his or her extended family and each of its members. By the same token, members of the family are held collectively liable for the wrongs of any member. Honor cultures are societies in which members of a kin group are deeply dependent on each other for their general social standing.

This value system supports a decentralized constitutional structure for two reasons. First, it fosters the ability of kin groups to enforce their own internal rules—it exerts a powerful pressure to conform. Second, it helps diverse kin groups within a single region to coexist in some measure of harmony.

Consider the following analogy. In a clan society a person's social worth—his or her honor—is bound to the honor of each of the separate members of his or her family. Now imagine that your personal *financial* worth were structured on the same terms. This would mean that the funds in your retirement account or your ability to obtain a mortgage would be tied not only to your own personal earnings, but also to the investment decisions and reputation for financial probity of every one of your cousins.[6]

In such circumstances, you surely would do whatever was necessary to ensure that your cousins maintained an unassailable reputation for fiscal trustworthiness. After all, your own financial power would depend on it. If one of your cousins were acting irresponsibly, you and your siblings and other cousins would use the utmost social pressure, and perhaps even physical force, to keep him in line and protect your interests. In clan societies, likewise, each member seeks to ensure that every other member of his or her clan acts honorably. The principle of group honor thereby strengthens the internal cohesion of family groups, enabling their autonomy and independence, which in turn promotes the decentralization of authority.

Now let's extend the analogy a bit further. Recall that in honor cultures members of a kin group can be held liable for one another's misdeeds. In our analogy, this would mean that if one of your cousins presented the member of another family with a bad check, the brother of the person to whom he presented the check would be entitled to attach a lien on *your* home. No doubt your cousin would think more than twice before perpetrating such a fraud, knowing the possible consequences of his behavior—including your wrath at being drawn into the mess he created. Collective liability thereby moderates infractions against other clans, enabling kin groups to coexist peaceably despite being autonomous and responsible to themselves alone.

Yet this link between honor culture and decentralized constitutionalism, which otherwise guarantees interclan harmony, also creates extraordinary potential for instability. As a result, clan societies can desta-bilize regions that are vital to the strategic interests of liberal states.

The trouble arises when a member of one clan wrongs a member of another clan. In honor cultures, such conflicts can be resolved in a number of ways. To begin, the elders of each kin group can try to reach an equitable agreement to redress the problem. Let's again consider an analogy involving money. Imagine that John Smith embezzles five hundred dollars from your brother and then spends it on a new stereo. Your father and Smith's father might come together over lunch and agree that the Smith family, which may lack cash on hand, will give your family their motorcycle, which is worth about five hundred dollars.

In the event that the elders of the two clans are unable to reach an agreement, a cool-headed mediator might be brought in to resolve the matter. If your father and Smith's father can't abide being in the same room together, their mutual friend Jones might convince Smith's father that in the interest of neighborhood peace he ought to write out a five-hundred-dollar check to atone for his son's misbehavior. Clan societies are notable for producing such mediator figures.[7] The most famous me-diator in world history was Muhammad, who even before his years as Islam's prophet was celebrated for his ability to settle conflicts among Arabian tribes.

Finally, if no such mediation is possible, then the principles of clan society demand vengeance. A well-placed act of vengeance generally renews intergroup peace almost as well as an equitable agreement be-tween clan elders. This is because when retribution is proportional to the original offense, it reestablishes equilibrium in the economy of group honor—it makes the groups even-steven.[8]

Humans have a deep and likely innate sense of balance, and so ven-geance typically is proportionate to the wrong that inspired it. To return to the example of John Smith, to exact the value of five hundred dollars in embezzled funds you might feel justified lifting a five-hundred-dollar watch from the Smith family jewelry store, but you probably wouldn't feel right swiping a twenty-thousand-dollar Rolex. The giving of gifts is governed by the same principles of proportionality. In the office, cowork-ers generally give each other holiday presents of equal value—a Christ-mas bauble one year is reciprocated with a Christmas candle the next; a box of birthday chocolates is reciprocated with a bouquet of flowers. If you give a coworker a box of chocolates one year and the next year he or she gives you a trip to Paris, you will probably feel some basic norm has been violated.[9]

But sometimes, whether by accident or design, retribution is not proportionate to the original offense. Imagine, for instance, if in response to Smith's action your hotheaded brother decided to burn the Smith family store to the ground. In such cases, the reciprocal exchange of violence between clan groups can swiftly escalate, and, in the absence of a central authority more powerful than the clans themselves, it can spin out of control. This is the logic of feud, and it is the Achilles heel of clan-based government.

Such a logic determined the unhappy fate of a society I discuss further in the pages ahead: medieval Iceland. After it was settled in the late ninth century, Iceland was governed peaceably under the highly decentralized leadership of about three dozen local chieftains, or goðar, who came together yearly in an islandwide assembly known as the Althing. But when Iceland collectively converted to Christianity in about 1000, the existence of a newly powerful Catholic Church initiated a cycle of competition between chieftains for ever greater authority. In time, this process consolidated land and power in the hands of five or six major families, or clans. These clans then began to fight each other in a grand series of feuds and, because no central government existed to stop the violence, in the early thirteenth century the country descended into all-out civil war. This period of Icelandic history is known as the Age of the Sturlungs, one of the great families of the time. Eventually, the violence led the country to place itself under the authority of the king of Norway.

Tired of ceaseless warfare and feuding, and eager for someone to maintain the peace that had been utterly destroyed, Iceland's leaders chose to submit to King Haakon's rule in 1262–64. As a result, Iceland was governed by the central authority of Norwegian and Danish monarchs for almost seven hundred years.

The memory of the incident runs deep. During the financial crisis of 2008, Icelanders often compared their bankers to the powerful chieftains who had brought their country to its knees centuries earlier.

Today, in our deeply interdependent world, clan feuds are fought not with spears, arrows, and clubs, but with automatic rifles. Many countries through which oil flows, along whose coasts container ships sail, and which are otherwise necessary to the economies of developed nations, are territories governed by an ancient form of government but awash in modern weapons. They are medieval Iceland plus Kalashnikovs. Colonialism also frequently left in tatters the traditional legal institutions and cultural values by which clan societies had long imposed restraint on individual behavior.[10] As a member of the Kalenjin tribe of Kenya put the matter in 2009 in the face of a scheduled election: "Before we were using bows and arrows to fight the enemy but changed to guns . . . because we realized, compared to guns, the arrows were child's play."[11] The fate of liberal societies now substantially depends on whether the people of such countries can secure stability by developing forms of government that can conquer the terrible logic of feud.

Naturally, if they are to succeed, they must do so on their own terms.

In addition to being sources of regional instability, clan societies also provide safe-havens for a wide variety of militant groups waging war against liberal democracies and other modern governments.

This is partly because clan societies are typically found in regions with weak or nonexistent states, where law enforcement is minimal—thus the Haqqani network of insurgents finds security in the Federally Administered Tribal Areas of Pakistan. More important, clan societies are organized around a powerful division between what social scientists call in-groups and out-groups, insiders and outsiders. Militants who either belong to a particular clan or who can claim its loyalty are protected throughout its sphere of influence and granted nearly impenetrable shelter (for the same reason that members of the Irish Republican Army found New York and Boston amenable places to hide). The Taliban in the Paktia province of Afghanistan, for instance, are supported by the Ghilzai tribe, which has long been at war with the Durrani, the tribe of President Hamid Karzai. The shelter clan societies offer is especially potent when those in hiding are Muslim and the nations seeking to capture or kill them are not.

The wide gulf between clan in-group and out-group likewise hinders the assimilation of immigrants from tribal cultures into liberal democratic societies. For instance, the challenges Europe faces today with its Muslim immigrants will be seen in time to arise less from religious differences than from differences in family structure—differences between the nuclear family and the extended-lineage group—and from the generally skeptical attitude toward government immigrants learned under the rule of the clan.[12] It is not Islam but rather the social and psychological importance of extended kinship that typically hinders assimilation into liberal society.

Finally, the rule of the clan implicates citizens of liberal democracies not only as a matter of our practical interests. It also deeply implicates our values, because the rule of the clan diminishes the status of the individual that our own societies are devoted to advancing. This is not to deny that clan societies possess many positive features.[13] Indeed, I believe the future of liberal society depends on our ability to recognize the ways in which clan societies meet certain basic human needs more effectively than liberal nations. But at bottom, clan societies oppose the principles of individualism to which liberal societies are fundamentally dedicated. These principles are justified not by a particular cultural tradition or religious revelation but rather on the universal grounds of human dignity and reason.

Liberals thus have an ethical stake as much as a strategic interest in advancing their ideals of individual freedom and in assisting indigenous reformers who are seeking to do so at great personal cost.

•

The anti-individualism of the rule of the clan burdens each and every member of a clan society, but most of all it burdens women. The fate of women lays bare the basic values of the rule of the clan and, as outsiders, citizens of liberal states often find their own values clarified when they confront the lives clans afford their female members.

The nature of this ethical encounter was made vivid to me one afternoon during the sweltering August of 2010, when I was having lunch in New Jersey with a young civilian analyst for the United States Central Command. Steve, whose name I have changed, was telling me a story about one of his tours in Afghanistan. A commanding officer had invited him to attend a council of local elders, a *jirga*, which was adjudicating a case of murder. Steve pulled on his flak jacket, for such councils can turn violent, and piled into an armored vehicle. After a dusty ride, he arrived at the gathering, where it turned out that the case concerned a young man who had killed another in a fit of anger. The details are unimportant; there is probably a young man in prison in your own community right now for a similar crime.

Steve is an easygoing fireplug of a man in his late twenties whose love of life and natural good cheer earn him friends wherever he goes, the kind of person everyone calls a "great guy." He can wax poetic about spicy meals he ate years ago in low-down restaurants, and his stories of travel misadventures keep listeners in stitches for hours. But Steve's joviality masks a deeply thoughtful personality that shows itself in occasional flashes of melancholy. I saw one such flash as he told me this story, and something about it, and about the memory that brought it on, has returned to my mind regularly ever since.

Pashtun tribal elders are, like most of our own mediators and judges, very good at what they do, and the ones presiding over the murder case Steve witnessed soon convinced the victim's family not to exact violent retribution against the perpetrator or his relatives. But though they managed to avoid a blood feud, they were unable to convince the victim's family to accept monetary compensation for their loss. The family simply refused to allow the murder of their son to be absolved by a cash payment. Something more was needed to make things right. Of course, prison was not an option in this community, far removed from the authority of Kabul, not to mention from our own standards of criminal justice. So what to do? The case was at an impasse.

Then, after much deliberation, the elders came upon a solution everyone agreed was equitable and wise. Rather than making things right with money, the perpetrator's family would give their youngest daughter in marriage to the brother of the victim. Steve gestured emphatically as he repeated the sentence: the sister of the killer would be forced to marry the brother of the man he had murdered. By giving away their youngest daughter, the perpetrator's family would pay a restitution that was more valuable than money, and the families would now be bound together. Naturally, the young woman had no choice in the matter. Her brother's actions had condemned her to a kind of exile. Like many married women in traditional societies, she would be cut off from her own family. But she would also be held at arm's length by her new family as an everlasting reminder of the murder of one of their cherished members.

The customary practice is known as *swara*.

Steve stared straight at me, eyes fixed, with a look of indescribable sadness about what he had seen—and a look of something else, too, which I struggled at the time to discern, but which I later realized was a look of profound self-reflection. "Can you believe that?" he asked, shaking his head. "Can you believe that?"

I have thought a lot about Steve's story since then. His encounter with the rule of the clan seemed to clarify for him the values and underlying political commitments of the modern liberal society in which he was raised. A similar recognition takes place wherever liberal citizens encounter the rule of the clan, whether in traditional societies abroad, in the history of state development, or within liberal nations themselves. For both practical and ethical reasons, it is essential to make this encounter. This book is thus in some respects a response to Steve's story—perhaps a surprising one—from my perspective as a scholar of legal history and constitutional law.

PART TWO

THE CONSTITUTIONAL ORDER OF THE CLAN

For most citizens of modern liberal nations, the state is like gravity. Its presence and effects are everywhere, yet because it is largely invisible, we tend to forget that it makes our entire world possible.

In examining the constitutional structure of clan societies—the subject of the following three chapters—my hope is to enable readers to appreciate this otherwise invisible force and so to view their own societies differently. I hope readers might see their societies with the eyes of an immigrant for whom life under a liberal state is a new experience.

Most liberal citizens in fact "see" the state every day. A fire truck races down the street, sirens blaring. A soldier in uniform walks down the aisle of a train. The cashier at the local grocery store hands you a receipt with the word *tax* printed at the bottom.

Yet the most profound effects of the state are imperceptible. Just as few people, other than perhaps some physicists, contemplate the existence of gravity when they climb a set of stairs or drive their car to work, so few people—other than lawyers, law professors, or immigrants from the rule of the clan—actively recognize how much the state provides the underlying structure for their daily lives.

As we have seen in the case of the errant jogger, in modern liberal societies the property people own, the professional agreements they make, even the intimate relations they form, are all predicated on the state's existence, which is assumed without a second thought.

The reason for this general neglect lies in the success of liberalism itself.

Over the past two hundred years, the United States, the United

Kingdom, and continental Europe have come to be guided by a liberal vision of the state that has also slowly spread across much of the world.

This vision is guided by two basic aims, both of which are intended to advance individual freedom. The first aim is to limit the power of the state in order to protect people from state interventions into their private affairs. The second aim is to develop the power of the state so that it can achieve public ends.

In the Anglo-American tradition, especially in the United States, liberals have often defined themselves in terms of the first aim, understanding their tradition as an ongoing struggle to limit the state's potential for tyranny. This effort is a noble part of our constitutional story, from Magna Carta through the modern fight against fascism and communism and varied efforts to foster the institutions of civil society.

But our constitutional tradition also involves the active construction of state power—and not simply to manage economic and political competition between particular interest groups but rather to vindicate the public interest at large. The story of the liberal state has never been a simple story of laissez-faire, even in the United States. It has always been one in which state capacities have been crafted over time to advance the general welfare and thereby to expand possibilities for personal self-fulfillment and individual autonomy.[1]

This generations-long state-building project has been so successful that many citizens have forgotten that building an effective state lies at the heart of the liberal tradition, just as much as the struggle against tyranny. They also find it difficult to imagine realistically the catastrophic consequences for individual freedom that would ensue if the political will to maintain an effective state were to be lost.

In this respect gravity and the state differ in a critical way. Whereas gravity will continue to operate whether humans pay attention to it or not, the state can waste away through neglect. It can grow anemic. It can even vanish.

When it does, the type of human life the state enables vanishes with it.

The reason is simple. Society abhors the absence of power as much as nature abhors a vacuum. In the absence of a democratic, liberal state devoted to principles of individual freedom, other institutions naturally grow to fill the void. And for most of human history, the primary institutions of legal and social order have been kin groups dedicated to principles of Status—clans.

If liberal nations choose to erode the state until it is a mere shadow of its former self, or to pursue a postmodern vision of a world "after the state," we will return to this antimodern world of diminished individual autonomy. Having forgotten the lesson of individualism's paradox, we will return to a society of Status—to the rule of the clan.

The great difference between the constitutional structure of the rule of the clan and that of liberal nations lies in its degree of centralization. Whereas political authority under a liberal state is comparatively centralized, under the rule of the clan it is dispersed among fragmented kinship groups and other informal patronage networks.

Clan societies differ among themselves, however, in the nature and intensity of their resistance to central authority. They exist along a spectrum. They range from stateless societies known as segmentary lineage systems to modern societies in which a weak state has difficulty containing the forces of clannism. In some circumstances, they even exist in developed, centralized states.

Here, I consider three societies along that spectrum.

I begin with the Nuer of East Africa in the early twentieth century, a people once organized entirely in the absence of a state. Next, I examine medieval Iceland, where the state was, by modern standards, radically incomplete. Finally, I turn to the case of the Palestinian Authority, a society in which modern conceptions of government and clannism compete for dominance—a clash characteristic of many societies today.

The constitution of the rule of the clan: When did this distinctive type of legal organization develop? Why has it proven to be such a powerful and enduring way of organizing society? What does it mean for the people who live under it today? And what does it mean for the people—for us—who might live under a novel and fearsome version of it tomorrow?

FOUR

LAW WITHOUT A STATE
THE NUER OF SOUTHERN SUDAN

In the world's newest sovereign nation, South Sudan, live a tall, slim, cattle-raising people known as the Nuer. Among observers of African politics, they are famous for their long-running battle with their cultural cousins the Dinka, who were themselves until recently locked in a decades-long civil war with the Arab-dominated government of Khartoum. The war, which raged especially in the region of Darfur, ended with the creation of the Republic of South Sudan in 2011.

Despite increasing links of interdependence, however, the conflict between the Nuer and the Dinka lives on.

In April and May 2011, for instance, 86 people died and 73 people sustained severe injuries when bands of Nuer from the state of Unity launched a raid against Dinka residents in the state of Warrap, attacking civilians and stealing their cattle. The comments on the *Sudan Tribune* website about the episode provide a chilling glimpse into the tribal dynamics of the region.

The first comment reads: "If Nuers don't refrain from such ugly behavior then all Dinkas must unite to avenge those innocent civilians." The second comment, posted eight minutes later by a user named Liberator: "Bring it on!!!!!!!!!! Nuer Warriors are just more than ready." The final comment, written after more than fifty furious prior postings, is a plea for reconciliation: "I hate tribalism. I hate aggression. I hate injustice . . . I love my motherland and crushed people. Let the Lord show us His Miracles."[1]

Much depends on whether this noble sentiment prevails. Together Sudan and South Sudan are the sixth largest producer of oil in Africa, churning out half a million barrels of crude every day.[2] A full three-quarters of the oil comes from the south, where the Nuer and Dinka reside. Under a 2005 power-sharing agreement, Sudan and South Sudan will equally divide oil revenues between their countries, but with oil counting for over 90 percent of total Sudanese export revenue, many observers wonder how long this agreement will last.

But while the Nuer are largely known today for the political role they will play in charting the course of a new nation, among anthropologists their fame rests elsewhere—in the work of an intrepid English scholar named E. E. Evans-Pritchard, who beginning in 1930 undertook a series of difficult expeditions to study this extraordinary tribal people.

The trilogy of books Evans-Pritchard produced now rank among the most important in the field. Interpretively careful and scientifically rigorous, they cover a wide range of topics, from the Nuer belief in sky spirits and their strict rules of exogamy in marriage to their methods of hunting fish, raising cattle, and growing millet. Most important of all, the books provide a window onto how societies without a central government maintain political order: through the principle—call it the constitutional mechanism—of kinship.[3]

They provide a framework for understanding communities that lie at the strongest end of the continuum of the rule of the clan.

•

The young anthropologist stood on the bank of the Bahr al-Ghazal, the Gazelle River, which flows hundreds of miles eastward through the wetlands of southern Sudan until at Lake No it joins the river Bahr al-Jabal and becomes the White Nile. The trip had been a difficult one. He had expected to collect his luggage in Marseilles, but it had been delayed by a storm. He had expected that his food stores would be forwarded from Malakal, but they never arrived. Someone had even neglected to tell his Zande servants to meet him.

Fortunately, Father Pasquale Crazzolara and the brothers of the Comboni mission had been kind after he landed at Yonyang. Now he stood here, along with two hastily engaged servants, members of the Atwot and Bellanda people, awaiting his carriers.

He waited nine days. By the tenth day, only four carriers had arrived. "If it had not been for the assistance of an Arab merchant, who recruited some local women," he explained a decade later, "I might have been delayed for an indefinite period."[4]

The year was 1930 and Evans-Pritchard, then in his late twenties, must have had a sinking feeling that this was going to be a difficult trip.

He had accepted his assignment—to conduct fieldwork among the Nuer people on behalf of the Anglo-Egyptian government—only "after hesitation and with misgiving," as he wrote in his classic *The Nuer* (1940).[5] The land of the upper Nile is rough country, awash in malaria, and the Nuer were notoriously hostile to outsiders. They also had special reason to be unwelcoming to an anthropologist from Oxford.

Just over thirty years before, British forces had marched southward from Egypt, defeated the Islamic Mahdi Army in Omdurman, and then brought French forces to a stalemate in Fashoda, now Kodok, about fifty miles downriver from Malakal. While London had secured the upper Nile from the influence of other European powers, it soon faced nationalist resistance from within Sudan, under the auspices first of the United Tribes Society and then of the White Flag League. The British had trounced a Sudanese military rebellion six years earlier, in 1924, and their efforts to ensure submission throughout the country were ongoing.

When Evans-Pritchard first met the Nuer, the tribesmen thus viewed him "not only as a stranger but as an enemy," and they "seldom tried to conceal their disgust at my presence."[6]

If Evans-Pritchard had any illusion that his trip would become easier once he had secured his carriers, he was quickly disabused of the fancy.

The next morning, after setting out for the village of Pakur, the carriers dropped his tent and goods "in the centre of a treeless plain." Despite his entreaties, they refused to carry the load a half-mile farther to an area with shade and water. Relief came after a boy named Nhial whom Evans-Pritchard had befriended "persuaded his kinsmen to carry my goods to the edge of the forest."[7]

But then his carriers grew nervous. Like many native Sudanese, they were terrified of the Nuer, and they spent "several sleepless and apprehensive nights"—after which they "bolted to the river to await the next steamer to Malakal." The Englishman and the boy were alone in Nuer country.

His writings reveal no trace of fear. Instead, Evans-Pritchard worried about language. The Nuer spoke no Arabic. Once his carriers had fled, he had no interpreter. And no serious Nuer grammar or Nuer-English dictionary existed. He couldn't communicate with the people he had been sent to study.

So he went about learning the obscure, dipthong-packed Nilotic tongue on his own. It was daunting work, its inherent difficulties compounded by the hostility he provoked as an outsider—and a representative of a colonial power. As he noted years later, "only those who have tried to learn a very difficult tongue without the aid of an interpreter and adequate literary guidance will fully appreciate the magnitude of the task."[8]

His fluency increased dramatically after he relocated to the lakeside settlement of Muot Dit. There he "made friends with many Nuer youths who endeavoured to teach me their language," and each day he "spent hours fishing with these lads in the lake and conversing with them in my tent." His time there was "happy," and he "began to feel my confidence returning." But government forces in the area were searching for two rebel leaders—prophets possessed by one of the Nuer sky spirits. One morning authorities surrounded the camp, took hostages, and "threatened to take many more" if the rebels weren't apprehended. Sensing that he "was in an equivocal position," he decamped for Zandeland (the Azande live primarily in the present-day South Sudan, the Democratic Republic of the Congo, and the Central African Republic).[9]

Evans-Pritchard returned to Nuer country the following year, staying for more than five months, and visited again in 1935 and 1936. Each journey posed its own peculiar difficulty. In his second expedition, he stayed in cattle camps on the Nyanding River. The choice of locale, he recalled later, was "unfortunate." In the Nyanding camps, "the water was scanty and foul, the cattle were dying of rinderpest, and the camps swarmed with flies. The Nuer would not carry my stores and equipment, and as I had only two donkeys, one of them lame, it was impossible to move."[10] Even worse, the Nuer by the Nyanding were yet more hostile than those he had previously encountered.

In fact, of all the difficulties he faced in all his visits to Nuerland, the greatest and most persistent was Nuer intransigence. Although Nuer youths were welcoming, adults barely spoke with him, and when they did, they "steadfastly stultif[ied] all efforts to elicit the simplest facts and to elucidate the most innocent practices."[11] They refused to play the role of passive anthropological informants for a colonial outsider's professional benefit. Here he recounts one of his conversations with a Nuer man named Cuol:

I: Who are you?

Cuol: A man.

I: What is your name?

Cuol: Do you want to know my *name*?

I: Yes.

Cuol: You want to know *my* name?

I: Yes, you have come to visit me in my tent and I would like to know who you are.

Cuol: All right. I am Cuol. What is your name?

I: My name is Pritchard.

Cuol: What is your father's name?

I: My father's name is also Pritchard.

Cuol: No, that cannot be true. You cannot have the same name as your father.

I: It is the name of my lineage. What is the name of your lineage?

Cuol: Do you want to know the name of my lineage?

I: Yes.

Cuol: What will you do with it if I tell you? Will you take it to your country?

I: I don't want to do anything with it. I just want to know it since I am living at your camp.

Cuol: Oh, well, we are Lou.

I: I did not ask you the name of your tribe. I know that. I am asking you the name of your lineage.

Cuol: Why do you want to know the name of my lineage?

I: I don't want to know it [Evans-Pritchard had clearly come to the end of his patience].

Cuol: Then why do you ask me for it? Give me some tobacco.[12]

When visiting Nuerland and associating only with Nuer, Evans-Pritchard joked, begging pardon for the pun, a person quickly displays "the most evident symptoms of 'Nuerosis.'"[13] "I have obtained in Zandeland more information in a few days," he wrote, "than I obtained in Nuerland in as many weeks."[14]

But in time his persistence paid off. The Nuer granted him a measure of acceptance, at first because they saw his kindness toward their children. Indeed, as he and the Nuer grew better acquainted, Evans-Pritchard encountered another, quite unexpected challenge to his work: the tribesmen began to speak with him *too much*. Once a person came to know them, the Nuer were decidedly voluble. Barely a moment of the day passed without some visitor in his tent, often several, joking, interjecting, and making pleasantries. He had no opportunity for confidential, one-on-one conversation or for recording extended reflections on Nuer society—he collected most of his information piecemeal and by observing daily village life through his doorway.

"The men came at milking-time and some of them remained till mid-day," Evans-Pritchard wrote of his time in a Nuer camp.

> Then the girls, who had just finished dairy-work, arrived and insisted on attention. Married women were less frequent visitors, but boys were generally under the awning of my tent if grown-ups were not present to drive them away. These endless visits entailed constant badinage and interruption and, although they offered opportunity for improving my knowledge of the Nuer language, imposed a severe strain. Nevertheless, if one chooses to reside in a Nuer camp one must submit to Nuer custom, and they are persistent and tireless visitors.[15]

The problem was a revealing one. Having been at least partially welcomed into the camp, he was now part of its garrulous family.

•

In their constitutional organization, the Nuer differ profoundly from two neighboring peoples, the Shilluk and the Anuak. The largely Christian Shilluk live today in a six-hundred-square-mile area in South Sudan on the Nile's west bank. The Anuak are agriculturalists located in southwestern Ethiopia and the eastern section of South Sudan's Greater Upper

Nile province. The Shilluk and the Anuak possess a political institution that the Nuer and their cultural cousins the Dinka lack.

The Shilluk and the Anuak have a king.

The significance of the contrast is not lost on any of the parties. For their part, the highly egalitarian Nuer deride their neighbors' political hierarchy, which they view as part of a culture of personal servility. The Nuer Evans-Pritchard knew rejected not only an executive office of king or president but the very social stratification a state needs to exist. "They have one big chief," a Nuer informant told Evans-Pritchard contemptuously, speaking of the Shilluk, "but we have not. This chief can send for a man and demand a cow or he can cut a man's throat. Whoever saw a Nuer do such a thing? What Nuer ever came when one sent for him or paid any one a cow?"[16] The Nuer have an ethic of personal independence reminiscent of the Argentinean pampas or the American old west.

The Shilluk and Anuak, naturally, view the matter quite differently. "I am deeply in love with the traditional system of governance [of the Anuak and Shilluk]," wrote a man on an Anuak community Web forum recently. "Before, during and after the civil war in the South, seldomly did we hear of deadly inter-sectional or clan against clan wars among the Anyuwaks, Azande or Cholos [Shilluks]. Why not? It is because they are bound together by common allegiance to the central authorities led by their majesties the Kings or Queens." This allegiance "is in sharp contrast to the likes of the Naath [Nuer] or Jieng [Dinka]," whose lack of central government authority "led to countless inter-sectional or clan vs. clan wars which became more destructive and deadly with the uncontrolled acquisition of modern, automatic firearms."[17]

But while the Nuer lack a central political power—the society is, in technical terms, acephelous, or without a head—they do not lack political order. The absence of a state does not create a Hobbesian war of all against all. Contrary to the implication of the Anuak Web forum participant, stateless societies like those of the Nuer or Dinka are often surprisingly stable. They exist in a condition that Evans-Pritchard described as "ordered anarchy," and that one scholar writing of a very different society (the Bedouin of Sinai and the Negev) calls "justice without government."[18]

From a liberal perspective this might seem like a contradiction in terms, but if so it is a contradiction by which humans have been governed for millennia.

The Nuer establish political order by a number of means—we might call them constitutional institutions. One such institution is known as the leopard-skin chiefs. These are not chiefs in the usual sense of the term—they are not tribal executives—but rather men whose religious role involves mediating conflicts between rival groups. In modern terms, each chief is like the director of a regional office of alternative dispute resolution, except that he wears a uniform, a leopard skin draped across his shoulders, and he is entitled to perform certain sacred cleansing rituals. Societies with weak or nonexistent states tend to rely on such offices or figures to resolve the prisoner's dilemma that results when hostile parties are structurally unable to reach a mutually beneficial accord on their own. I noted earlier that Muhammad played such a role in seventh-century Arabia.

More important, order among the Nuer is secured by the organization of their society into what anthropologists call a segmentary lineage system.[19] Thanks to Evans-Pritchard's studies, Nuer society in fact serves as an archetype of this ancient form of constitutional organization. Like many theories, the segmentary lineage model doesn't always fit neatly with the complexity of societies as they appear on the ground, and it has been the subject of heated controversy. Yet it remains useful for explaining what keeps societies like the Nuer from descending into chaos despite their lack of an executive authority. For in the segmentary lineage model, a community achieves social and political order not through a single figure or institution with whom the buck stops, but rather through its basic social structure.

Segmentary lineage societies are divided into tribes, which in turn are divided into smaller units, or segments. Each tribe originates from a single ancestor common to all members of the tribe under the rule of unilineal descent. Under the unilineal principle, community members trace their kinship through a single proscribed parental line, either their father's or mother's. Marriage rules, property ownership, inheritance rights, social status, and responsibilities are all based on a person's place within the descent group. More often than not, societies with a unilineal descent system are patrilineal, tracing descent through the father's line. But matrilineal societies or institutions are not uncommon. The famed

Hopi people of Arizona are matrilineal. The matrilineal Khasis of northeast India consists of more than a million members.

With each generation, the tribe splits into divisions, or segments, headed by the sons of the family heads of the previous generation. A father is the head of a lineage; his sons are the heads of their own sublineages; their sons are the heads of their own subsublineages, and so on. Each lineage is a box that holds many smaller boxes—sublineages—each of which in turn holds still smaller boxes. Sometimes groups can be incorporated into or united with a tribe outside their actual descent group, as in the case of septs of the Scottish Highlands, in which case they are said to share a "fictive" kinship.

Lineages are the basic political building blocks of most tribal societies, whether or not they conform precisely to the strict segmentary lineage model. From a constitutional perspective, tribal societies are loose confederations of their lineage units. If you are Christian or Jewish, or if you happen to have the holy book of either Christians or Jews at hand, you can quickly find a census of a famous tribal society subdivided on the basis of lineage that was held on the ancient plains of Moab—or you can type "Numbers 26" into your browser's search engine. If you are Hindu, you will be familiar with tribal organization from the *Mahabharata* and the Rigveda. The Qur'an 49:13 (The Private Apartments) likewise characterizes such tribal organization as a basic part of the social order and as part of God's larger plan of human brotherhood.

Or consider a modern tribal society, that of Waziristan, part of the Federally Administered Tribal Areas in Pakistan. The two main tribal groups in the south are the Wazir and the Mahsud. But each tribe is divided into numerous parts. The Mahsud, for example, are divided into three branches, the Alizai, Bahlolzai, and Shaman Khel. The Shaman Khel are divided into four parts: the Budinzai, Char Khel, Galleshai, and Khalli Khel. The Khalli Khel are divided into five branches: the Jandi Khel, Salimkai, Sar Sarmashai, Sikandar Khel, and Tor Sarmashai.[20] The region is a jigsaw puzzle of subgroups, with numerous clans intermixing within a single territory.

Likewise, in Somalia there are six major clans: the Darod, Dir, Digil, Mirifle, Hawiye, and Isaaq. The Darod possess five subclans: the Yusuf (Awrtable), Lel-Kase and, especially, the Harti, Absame, and Sade. The Harti are in turn divided into the Majeerteen, Warsangeli, Dhulbahante, and Dashishe. Clan members are typically able to trace their patrilineal descent back twenty generations or more to the founding figure of their group. Were the same lineage knowledge to be shared by citizens of the United States, most Americans would be able to recite the names of their paternal ancestors back in an unbroken chain until about the year 1500.[21]

The Bedouin of North Africa and Arabia have a similar form of social organization, which has left its deep impression throughout the cultures of the Middle East.[22] At its most extreme, Col. Muammar al-Qaddafi put their principles at the core of his tribal vision of Libya as a "stateless state."[23]

Many Native American tribes likewise were or continue to be organized along segmentary lines.

The origin of the lineage form of political organization lies deep in human history, in the transition between the Paleolithic and Neolithic eras. As humans shifted from hunter-gatherer to pastoral economies, communities grew in size and scale, which in turn necessitated new political arrangements. Small-scale bands became larger tribes.[24]

The tribal form has endured since time out of mind because of its inherent advantages. Like Neolithic physical technologies such as the polished stone axe, lineage organization has persisted and adapted to an endless variety of new circumstances. This is because lineages possess certain characteristics that make them as effective at maintaining order in tribal societies as the executive branch of modern states is at maintaining order in liberal democracies. One should as soon denigrate the use of lineage as a mechanism for maintaining social and political order as one should look down upon the modern axe you may have recently purchased and stored inside your brick house (another Neolithic development).

What makes lineage constitutionalism so strong?

For one, lineages tend to lay real or symbolic claim to particular bodies of land, frequently where their ancestors are buried. Just as the Macphersons are from Badenoch, so the Bang segment of the Gaawar tribe of the Nuer people has its particular migratory area between the Bahr al-Jabal and Bahr al-Zeraf rivers.[25] A lineage name is a primitive GPS device, and a rather precise one. Most modern Western names are much less accurate. This precision also establishes a generations-long symbolic communion between the living and the dead—the metaphysical foundation of clan solidarity. As one of my colleagues, an adventurous Italian anthropologist of Madagascar named Liliana Mosca, explained to me recently, for the Malagasy, as for many ancient peoples, "the purpose of life is to become an ancestor."

In addition, segmentary lineage systems and similarly organized tribal societies derive their strength from the principle of exogamy. Lineage members, that is, are required to marry outside their core lineage group. As a practical matter, the rule of exogamy forges complex links between lineage groups and the bodies of land they inhabit, creating a network of political alliances that contribute to social integration and stability in a given geographic area. The norm of exogamy also provides the basis for a lean anthropological definition of a clan, a term for which there are many conceivable meanings, namely: the largest group of lineage members to whom principles of exogamy apply. If as a Nuer man you are allowed to marry a Nuer woman, then by definition the woman is not a fellow clansman.

But most of all, lineage constitutionalism is so effective and enduring because its political divisions are mirrored in the structure of a member's emotional life, which channels conflicts in a constructive way.

In tribal societies the bonds of kinship are exceptionally strong. Members of a lineage possess powerful feelings of fellowship with each other—and under the principle of unilineal descent the lines and boundaries of solidarity are exceedingly clear. At the same time, members of distinct lineage groups that are related through a common ancestor will share strong feelings of *opposition* to any group to which they have mutual reason to be hostile. In theory each lineage group will join with all the other lineage groups to which it is related to fight against an enemy common to them all. Whatever lineage group is relevant at any given moment—tribe, lineage, sublineage, clan—thus depends on where within the crystalline tribal structure a conflict takes place or a threat exists. A famous Middle Eastern adage puts it this way: "I against my brothers; my brothers and I against my cousins; my cousins, my brothers, and I against the world."

Evans-Pritchard translated this bracing maxim into precise, technical terms in a chart, which is included on the next page. Although it may seem at first glance like a dry, scientific diagram, it can be understood as

something far grander. It is the unwritten constitution of Nuer governance—as clear, succinct, and elegant as the constitution of any liberal
democracy.

It's worth taking the extra effort of referring to the chart as Evans-
Pritchard elucidates its meaning. In the diagram, A and B represent two
segments of a larger Nuer group; X and Y represent segments within
group B; and Z represents a still smaller segment within group Y. "When
Z^1 fights Y^1," Evans-Pritchard explains, "Z^1 and Z^2 unite as Y^2." He
continues: "When Y^1 fights X^1, Y^1 and Y^2 unite, and so do X^1 and X^2."
Further: "When X^1 fights A, X^1, X^2, Y^1, and Y^2 all unite as B." And last
of all: "When A raids the Dinka A and B may unite."[26] Recall the
reader's statement in the 2011 *Sudan Tribune*, "If Nuers don't refrain
from such ugly behavior then all Dinkas must unite to avenge those innocent civilians"—if D attacks Z^1, then A and B unite.

A		X	Y	
		X^1	Y^1	
		X^2	Z^1 —————— Z^2	Y^2

With Evans-Pritchard's chart, we can quickly grasp why lineage
constitutionalism creates societies that are powerful and enduring, as
well as resistant to change. *When X^1 fights A, X^1, X^2, Y^1, and Y^2 all unite as
B*—the structure has all the strength of a diamond. For an indigenous
or, worse, an outside reformer, breaking it apart is well-nigh impossible
(not to mention being ethically dubious at best), and helping a society
replace it with a new form of political order is a monumental task.

The chart also suggests why such societies are so effective at resist-
ing outside military threats—especially when the opposing military fails
to appreciate the human environment in which its troops are operating.
When at the end of Evans-Pritchard's first expedition British government forces took hostages from Muot Dit in an effort to track down two

Nuer rebel prophets, what irked villagers was not so much that the government had taken hostages, but rather that the hostages weren't part of the rebels' extended lineage groups. The government "was looking at the affair in territorial terms, they in kinship terms on analogy with the conventions of a feud."[27] An invading army can attack Z^2 only if it is prepared to fight a ferocious battle with all of A and B.

Even more, the chart reveals why societies like the Nuer can maintain long-term harmony within their tribal groups despite the natural tendency of conflicts to arise. Small lineage units like Z^1 or Z^2 maintain good relations with each other because the groups possess very strong feelings of solidarity, which makes the settlement of disputes between them seem like a moral imperative to the participants. The number of people involved in any dispute will also necessarily be small. At the same time, serious conflicts with more distantly related groups tend to be avoided for more practical reasons: though feelings of solidarity are less intense, a serious clash has the potential to unleash a massive, bloody feud. The United States and the Soviet Union maintained a similar rough peace throughout the Cold War under the principle of mutually assured destruction. International relations between states generally operate under similar principles.

The entire system can be likened to the steel girders of a building, each pressing against the other and thereby holding the entire structure aloft. Far from living in a world of disorder, then, the Nuer live in a highly structured society—a society structured by kinship.

•

Although the attitude of modern states to tribal societies has historically been one of conquest and condescension, the stateless political structure of Nuerland has also struck liberals as admirable, at least in some respects. The Nuer are democrats, with all members of the tribe participating in common affairs. They are committed to egalitarian ideals, with no man acknowledging the superiority or inferiority of another. They share good things in common (as a result "no Nuer ever has a surplus"—an appalling yet often romanticized state of affairs).[28] And above all, they are remarkably independent, both personally and politically—what Nuer "ever came when one sent for him or paid any one a cow?"

But the independence and governmental simplicity of Nuer society also comes with a profound price. When political life is structured according to kinship, individuals are fundamentally submerged within their lineages. This phenomenon, it should be emphasized, is profoundly different from the influence families may have on their members in modern liberal societies. In liberal societies, every person naturally has a family and some families can exercise a powerful influence on their members. In Nuer society, however, belonging to a lineage is essential to being treated as someone worthy of any regard at all.

For example, once Evans-Pritchard asked a group of Nuer for directions, and he "was deliberately deceived." He returned to the camp, angry, and asked why the people had lied to him. One replied: "You are a foreigner, why should we tell you the right way? Even if a Nuer who was a stranger asked us the way we should say to him, 'You continue straight along that path,' but we would not tell him that the path forked. Why should we tell him? But you are now a member of our camp and you are kind to our children, so we will tell you the right way in the future."

"Either a man is a kinsman, actually or by fiction," observed Evans-Pritchard, "or he is a person to whom you have no reciprocal obligations and whom you treat as a potential enemy."[29]

Indeed, just as the Nuer draw a sharp distinction between those who are part of their kin group and those who are not, treating the latter with aloof disdain, so even within smaller groups of kinsmen all relationships are filtered through the framework of kin relations.

This phenomenon is present in Nuer law, which changes in application and force depending on the kinship distance between parties to a dispute. The leopard-skin chiefs can settle disputes within a village or district, but the farther outside a limited radius the dispute takes place, the less likely it is a settlement can be reached. In this light, Evans-Pritchard wrote that the Nuer in fact possess no real "law" at all.

The inextricability of the self from its lineage is present as well in the Nuer propensity to engage in feud—a subject I consider in chapter 8.

But most profoundly of all, the supremacy of lineage is present in the very way people apprehend each other as persons.

At the end of Evans-Pritchard's second expedition, he asked some Nuer in a cattle camp at Yakwac if they would carry his tent and belongings to the edge of the Sobat River. At the time, he was severely ill with malaria and soon to be evacuated by steamer. They refused. Instead, ailing, Evans-Pritchard did it himself, along with a Nuer youth.

When the anthropologist asked the young man why "the people were churlish," he tellingly replied in terms of a lineage relationship: "You told them to carry your belongings to the river. That is why they refused. If you had asked them, saying, 'My mother's sons, assist me,' they would not have refused."[30]

Even in rituals of civility and good manners, the self cannot be conceptually divorced from its family. For the Nuer, every person is always somebody's kinsman.

•

The Nuer as described by Evans-Pritchard—a fully stateless society in which political life is structured around internesting lineage units—exist at one end of a spectrum of peoples governed by the rule of the clan. But as we will see, other quite different societies, when understood in legal terms, exhibit the same underlying consequences for the individual. Appreciating this similarity is essential for understanding how the rule of the clan can be overcome, and why it remains a looming presence even within modern liberal states.

Unlike the stateless society of the Nuer, the European country I examine next possessed a state that was in many respects quite modern— but with one critical exception. The exception made kinship essential to its governance structure, and it allowed the country to slide into a devastating civil war.

FIVE

A STATE WITHOUT A KING

MEDIEVAL ICELAND

The first thing visitors tend to notice is the giant field of lava. That's the landscape that greets travelers who make the thirty-mile drive from Iceland's Keflavik International Airport to the nation's capital, Reykjavik. Nothing but semiporous, slate-gray rock to the left and right, stretching as far as the eye can see. Beneath the northern summer sun the vast expanse of volcanic detritus creates a vertiginous panorama of stark beauty.

The scene is a harbinger of sights to come.

Clamoring seabirds circle and nest along Iceland's rocky coasts; the glaciers of the interior are solid sheets of white unfurling into the distance; in the autumn the moss and lichen of the tundra mellow into a soft orange and brown. Drive down one of the island's pockmarked dirt roads and you might come across a scalding-hot geothermal pool steaming in the middle of a pasture. Many visitors call the landscape dreamlike, a description that captures something essential about the place. It's the world you know, but in a convex mirror.

Much the same thing could be said of the island's early legal history, especially during the Middle Ages, the touchstone of Icelandic national consciousness. Iceland's constitutional story is as unique and extraordinary as its natural environment and it casts a fresh image of liberal societies and the legal values they protect. Iceland's government possessed a sophisticated legislature and system of courts, but it lacked an executive authority to enforce legal judgments. In modern terms, it was an incomplete state. Like the Nuer as studied by Evans-Pritchard, Iceland reveals modern liberal values by setting them in sharp relief against the power that filled the vacuum created by the state's half presence: the rule of the clan.

Medieval Iceland and modern South Sudan—the two societies are different from one another in a host of ways. For one, their climates differ dramatically. Although in the early Middle Ages Iceland was significantly warmer than it is today, relative to east Africa it was, as the name implies, relatively cold. Moreover, Iceland was a country of sedentary animal husbandry and prosperous farms. It was a land of "pale fields and mown meadows" (the words are those of the hero Gunnar Hámundarson in *Njal's Saga* as he gazes wistfully back upon his homestead while contemplating his possible exile, in one of the most exquisite moments in Icelandic literature).[1]

Moreover, despite their Nordic egalitarianism, medieval Icelanders accepted a far greater degree of social and political hierarchy than the modern Nuer. Some Icelanders grew rich and powerful while others grew poor and weak; some were even slaves. Likewise, the foremost state structures the Nuer knew in Evans-Pritchard's day were those of their colonial enemies or the hated Shilluk and Anuak, whereas the state with which medieval Icelanders were most familiar was indigenous to their own Scandinavian people.

Most important of all, Icelandic kinship structures were much different from those in Nuerland. Whereas the Nuer trace their kinship unilineally through the father's line, and conform as closely as any society can to the model of a segmentary lineage system, medieval Icelanders understood kinship bilaterally—through both parents. When Iceland was settled Germanic kinship structures were in the midst of a centuries-long evolution away from the principle of patrilineality.[2] With kinship reckoned bilaterally, the bonds of kin solidarity in Iceland were neither so clear, so segmented, or so powerful as they were in tribal East Africa.

Yet it is precisely these differences that make examining medieval Iceland as critical for liberals today as knowing about the modern Nuer. As a society with a more developed but still incomplete state, Iceland stands at another point along the spectrum of societies governed by the rule of the clan. In this, medieval Iceland evokes many contemporary states that are struggling with the consequences of a weak or illegitimate central government.

The story of Iceland also reveals an unusual but highly instructive path a people can take toward a system of governance in which kinship plays a central role—for medieval Icelandic constitutionalism was the product of a deliberate, conscious *choice*. Liberal societies today stand at a similar point of decision. In the face of well-intended but misguided criticism that the state is inimical to freedom, we must choose whether to maintain the state as our most basic public institution or to let it degrade through lack of political will.

•

The Icelandic story begins in about the year 870, when the country was colonized by a group of bold settlers from western Norway—men and women commonly known as Vikings. They bore names like Helgi the Lean, Ketilbjörn Ketilsson, and Unn the Deep-minded, daughter of Ketil Flat-nose. As Norwegians, the settlers were a northern Germanic people, and they possessed a heroic Germanic worldview. Theirs was a free warrior society rooted in the principles of honor, courage, and fate. Two literary works inspired by their moody pagan mythology, Richard Wagner's *Ring* cycle and J.R.R. Tolkien's *The Lord of the Rings* (1954), capture the spirit rather well. Norse deities included Odin, ruler of Asgard; Thor, Odin's son, the hammer-wielding thunder god; Freyja, goddess of love, gold, sorcery, and death; and Loki, the shape-shifting trickster.

At the time of the settlement, Iceland was uninhabited, or very nearly so. Although a handful of Irish monks called the place home, they fled soon after they saw the prows of Viking ships glide over the horizon. They departed in such a hurry that, in the telling words of an early Icelandic record, they left behind "books, bells, croziers, and lots of other things."[3]

Their haste was wise. The first historian of Iceland, Ari Þorgilsson the Learned (1067/8–1148), dates his country's settlement to the year when the Viking leader Ivar the Boneless killed St. Edmund during the Great Heathen Army's invasion of England. Ivar's men strapped Edmund to a tree and shot him repeatedly with arrows "as if it were a game," until the martyred king "was entirely covered with their missiles just like the bristles of a hedgehog," after which they lopped off his head in a single stroke.[4]

Within sixty years, Iceland's population grew swiftly to between twenty and thirty-five thousand inhabitants. Nearly all modern Icelanders, who now number about 320,000, are descended from these first settlers, as well as from the Celtic women and slaves they fetched on their northwestward voyage.

Significantly, the form of government the settlers created reflected the reasons they left their homeland in the first place. In particular, the Norse sought to escape the power of King Harold Fairhair, who had recently unified Norway under his sole royal authority. In the battle of Hafrsfjord of 872, Harold had crushed the leaders of a cluster of smaller Nordic kingdoms and chieftaincies in the south, including Eirik of Hordaland, Sulke of Rogaland, and Kjotve the Rich of Agder. We know little about the battle other than it was "violent and long-lasting"; that King Kjotve's son, a berserker, fearlessly stormed Harold's ship; and that in the end Harold emerged victorious.[5] Among the upstart leaders, only King Kjotve remained alive, his men in flight across the lowland flats of Jæren. After many years of struggle, Harold had united his country.

He was part of a trend. While Harold was conquering the petty kingdoms of southern Norway, Alfred was becoming the first king to claim to rule over "the English people," or *Angelcynn*, a claim that was even more credible for his grandson, King Athelstan. About seventy years earlier, Charlemagne, the great leader of the Carolingian dynasty of the Franks, had been crowned emperor by the pope. Europe's royal houses were consolidating their power, often looking to the ancient Roman state as a model (on their coinage, for instance, Anglo-Saxon kings tellingly referred to themselves by the Latin term *rex*). Local sovereignty was giving way to greater central control—the medieval version of modernization.[6]

Many Norwegians chafed under the new regime. They resented not just Harold's vigorous leadership but also the structural principles of his rule. When the Norse set their sails toward Iceland, they were escaping a particular ruler, but they were also breaking free from the emergent ideal of kingship he represented.

They were refugees from political development.

The government they created gave full expression to their passion for decentralized rule. It was based on the regional leadership of about three dozen chieftains, known as *goðar* or, in the singular, *goði*. The term comes from the Norse *goð*, or god, and the *goðar* at one time likely held not only political power but also authority to conduct pagan rituals.

Each chieftain was the leader of a local group of yeoman farmers, who were in turn leaders of their own households. A yeoman provided a chieftain with muscle when he needed it and a *goði* in turn held various responsibilities toward a yeoman, including mediating conflicts and advocating for him in disputes.[7]

The institution of the *goðar* was peculiar in many ways. For one, the office itself was a species of property: it could be inherited, it could be given as a gift, and it could be bought and sold. Also, in theory farmers could choose with which *goði* they would affiliate, and if they were unhappy with their current *goði* they could freely change their allegiance, although in practice almost all farmers chose and remained with a chieftain nearby.

But most unusual of all was what happened when the island's chieftains came together. For two weeks each summer, the *goðar* convened in an assembly called the Althing, meeting at one of the most striking locations of northern Europe—Thingvellir. The Althing embodied Iceland's deliberate rejection of the modernizing constitutional development sweeping the Continent, and it is in the central role it established for kinship in Icelandic governance that it holds a convex mirror up to liberal societies today as they contemplate the future role of the state.

In a nation whose countryside is scattered with monuments to its medieval past, Thingvellir is the most famous, and with good reason. Several years ago I had the chance to see it, along with my wife, and we marveled at what we saw. As we turned our car off a misty dirt road, the national park unfolded before us like the long, slow storyline of an Icelandic saga. There was Thingvallavatn, Iceland's largest lake, deep and clear, shimmering atop an expansive plain of green tundra grass. Above was the dazzling summer sky, with its never-ending daylight.

And then there were the cliffs.

Located east of Reykjavik, Thingvellir is situated at the meeting point of the North American and Eurasian tectonic plates. Over millennia, the plates have been slowly drifting apart, which is a somewhat less alarming way of saying that the eastern and western halves of the country are steadily cleaving in two. For the most part this movement of the earth's crust is a source of trouble—one of its consequences is that the island is dotted with active volcanoes, whose periodic flare-ups can be devastating. An eruption in 1783 released a cloud of poisonous ash so wide that for years it altered the climate of Europe and ravaged its economy.

But at Thingvellir, the effect of the earth's drift has been a happy one. It created a canyon of jagged cliffs and rock formations that was an ideal spot for the central institution of Icelandic government.

In Old Norse, the word *þing*, pronounced *thing*, means assembly. Its roots lie in the proto-Germanic word for "appointed time," which is also the ultimate origin of the English word denoting an object lacking a specific name. Germanic peoples had a long tradition of small community councils in which local tribesmen came together to discuss their common affairs. Often such meetings were held under arms beneath the new or full moon. In Anglo-Saxon England, the assemblies were known as folkmoots.

Early Icelanders brought the tradition of local Germanic councils with them during the settlement. If one drives across the country with the exhaustive *Icelandic Road Atlas* in hand, one can find in every corner of the island quiet little spots with names beginning with *thing*. Today these places are often just expanses of fallow meadow, but a millennium ago they were the Nordic version of town halls. People met there at regular intervals to exchange views, to resolve conflicts, and to make decisions about their common life.

Beginning in 930, Icelanders also established a general assembly, an *al-thing*, that encompassed not just a small district but the entire island. Early historians assert that the institution was created at the urging of an especially wise settler named Úlfjótr. Whether or not Úlfjótr was the Althing's founding father (modern historians are dubious—the story seems a bit too patterned on the tale of Moses to be true), whoever chose the site for the gathering was brilliant. Thingvellir, the "assembly plain," lay at a meeting point of land routes across the island and it had plenty of fresh water.

And it had those cliffs. Gray and rugged, wrenched apart through ages of tectonic force, they formed a natural amphitheater. One particular jutting crag was designated the *lögberg*, or law rock, and served as a dais.

The Althing was the grand event of each year's calendar, where gifts were exchanged, alliances were forged, and people fell in love. But the main business there was law, which is why the site today is the unrivaled shrine of national identity. The modern Icelandic parliament is called the Althing—which in American terms would be like calling Congress the Folkmoot—and when the justices of the nation's supreme court go to work, they walk through a corridor designed to echo the shape of the Thingvellir cliffs.

Some Icelanders even call Thingvellir "sacred." The adjective in fact may not be far from the truth given how the island converted to Christianity—a story that, tellingly, also is a tale about the importance medieval Icelanders attached to law.[8]

The story takes place around the year 1000. Some years before an Icelandic convert had spread the gospel to a handful of goðar. Now, under orders from the devout king of Norway, two Icelanders had arrived with a priest to engage in a major evangelizing campaign. After establishing a church in the Westman Islands, the group rode on horseback to the Althing. There, they celebrated mass atop a gorge and paraded to the law rock dressed in vestments and carrying two life-size crosses.

After the men spoke of their Christian mission, the Althing broke into two loudly opposing camps, each viewing the other's beliefs as abhorrent—and each refusing to be bound by the other's rules.

In the midst of the quarrel, an unnamed man came running to announce that a volcanic eruption was about to engulf the home of one of the Christian chieftains.

"It is no wonder the gods are enraged by such talk," the pagans declared.

"What were the gods enraged by when the lava we are standing on here and now was burning," retorted one of the Christians.

According to a Christian source, the pagans then prepared to sacrifice two people from each quarter of the island by pushing them over a cliff, while the Christians began their own "sacrifice" of "liv[ing] better lives and be[ing] more careful to avoid sin than before."[9]

The community was splitting apart.

But as matters were coming to a head, the Icelanders decided to resolve the conflict through a traditional method of Germanic dispute resolution, one regularly used at the thing, as in all clan societies: they called in a mediator.

The man was a chieftain named Thorgeir—and he was a pagan.

Thorgeir lay down, pulled a cloak over his head, and lay still for the entire day and through the night. Whether he was communing with the likes of Thor in a pagan trance or merely finding some private time to prepare his speech we don't know, but today when Icelanders wish to mull something over they explain that they need to pull a cloak over their head.

When Thorgeir emerged from his reverie, he spoke to the assembly from the law rock.

"It appears to me that our affairs will reach an impasse if we don't all have the same law," he explained, "for if the law is split asunder, so also will peace be split asunder." He then exacted promises from both parties "to accept the law that I proclaim."

The assembly listened.

"This will be the foundation of our law," Thorgeir announced, "that all men in this land are to be Christians and believe in one God . . . and give up all worship of false idols, the exposure of children, and the eating of horse meat" (the last demand was in effect a prohibition on equine sacrifice). Pagan practices were to be overlooked for a few years if they were conducted in secret, but soon they were to be forbidden altogether.[10]

To show that he meant what he said, Thorgeir soon after took his own pagan idols and hurled them into one of the most exquisite waterfalls on the island, a place now known as Godafoss.

Through an arbitration at the Althing, Iceland peaceably became Christian and maintained its law intact.

•

From a modern liberal perspective, the structure of medieval Icelandic government resembles a car that lacks a steering wheel or a plane without wings. While much of it seems sophisticated and admirable, something also seems fatally flawed. It leads many people to wonder how such a peculiar institutional design could actually work—and, indeed, the Althing was as close to a laboratory experiment in political science as history will ever provide.

At the foundation of the Icelandic constitution were the local chieftains: thirty-nine of them spread across the island's four quarters. Each quarter was divided into three districts, each typically containing three chieftaincies.[11]

In the spring, the chieftains convened thirteen separate district-wide assemblies—the regional *things*. In the summer, all the chieftains of the island came together for the Althing.

At the Althing, each chieftain was accompanied by two yeoman farmers from his district. They were called *thingmen* and they were there to advise their chieftains.

When the chieftains, *thingmen*, the island's two bishops, and a few added representatives from less populated parts of the country sat together, they formed a congress of 147 men. This was the Icelandic legislature, the law council, or *lögrétta*—the core of the Althing assembly.

The legislature was a vigorous institution, and its members seem to have kept themselves busy. Initially Icelanders were governed by the Gulathing law of western Norway, but as the *lögrétta* added to this Norwegian foundation, Icelandic law positively swelled in size. The island's collected rules, codified in 1117, run to several hundred pages—the largest legal code in medieval Scandinavia. Charmingly, and for reasons that remain a mystery, the collection is known as the Gray Goose.

For anyone used to thinking of the Middle Ages as a benighted time, the scope, detail, and complexity of the Gray Goose can come as a surprise. "If two men own a horse jointly," explains one representative provision, "each may warrantably use it as need arises but neither may warrantably lend it to anyone else or hire it out without the consent of both. If one of them does hire it out, then his penalty is a fine, and moreover the man who hired it from him is under penalty for its use if he knew that both owned it."[12] The Icelanders were a people who took rules seriously.

Other sections of the Gray Goose cover land use, contracts, civil and criminal procedure, marriage, and various Christian duties. Want to know the rules for building walls adjacent to a communal pasture? About burning grass? Stray pigs? Exemptions from tithing? What happens when an outlaw fathers a child? How to put an attachment on someone's property? It's all there.

In addition to a busy and sophisticated legislature, the Althing possessed a judicial branch, whose judges were nominated by the chieftains. The judiciary included four distinct quarter courts, which dealt with disputes arising in the four separate quarters of the country. In time, Icelanders also created a fifth court, something like a court of appeals, with forty-eight judges. The Gray Goose provisions for the conduct of these courts read like passages from any modern procedural code.

But it's here that parallels between the Althing and the modern state strikingly end. For while the Althing contained a legislative and judicial branch, it entirely lacked an executive. There was no single person or institution in charge of enforcing law—no head chieftain, no prince, and certainly no king.

The closest thing the assembly had to a chief was the elected law-speaker. He presided over the gathering and, remarkably, was responsible for reciting the entire legal code from memory over a period of three years. But the lawspeaker had no special administrative authority.

Indeed, nobody did—that was the main reason they left Norway. Unlike anywhere else in Christian Europe, Iceland was merely a loose federation of chieftains.

As a litigant, then, if a legal judgment was rendered in your favor by one of Iceland's quarter courts based on the sophisticated law of the Gray Goose, you would be responsible for enforcing the judgment yourself.

Without an executive of any kind in charge of enforcing law, why wasn't legal activity viewed as an exercise in futility?

Sometimes, in fact, it was. The sagas are peppered with stories of men sentenced to exile, their goods technically forfeit, who hole up on their farms, armed to the teeth, and dare their enemies to make them move.

Likewise, in a telling passage from the great historical tale known as *Njal's Saga*, an important lawsuit is quashed on a mere procedural technicality. When the leader of the group bringing the suit, Thorhall, hears of the fatal outcome of his legal labors, he seizes his spear, drives it into his own leg to lance a boil that had prevented him from walking, and rushes to court. There he comes across Grim the Red, a member of the opposing party, and instantly thrusts his spear at him with such force that it splits Grim's shield in two and emerges from between his shoulder blades.

Thereafter, the Althing descends into uncontrollable violence.

But despite these shortcomings, Icelandic law in fact worked rather well at resolving disputes and maintaining order. A legal system does not need a strong executive branch to be successful—depending on how one defines success. Consider the European Union today, or the United States under the Articles of Confederation. The decentralized constitutional structure of Iceland was quite effective for three hundred years. Far from seeing law as futile, Icelanders positively loved their lawsuits, and their medieval literature is filled with stories of spectacular legal contests. Many of the sagas read like modern courtroom dramas.

How was this possible?

The reason can be glimpsed if we return to the story from chapter 1 of the errant jogger.

Imagine that rather than settling the grievance you had against him, the young man chooses to go to trial. He might believe he can convince a judge that you share blame for the accident, for instance because, late for a meeting, you were hurrying down the sidewalk. In the event of the trial, however, you emerge victorious, and the court declares that the jogger owes you five thousand dollars for your pains.

The next day your lawyer calls the jogger's lawyer and lets him know where he can send the check.

Now imagine that your own legal system, like medieval Iceland's, lacks an executive branch, and so like medieval Iceland has no police. What if the errant jogger ignores your request for the compensation to which your successful trial entitles you. What would you do?

The first thing you would probably do is call on other people for help. These people would include a prominent and respected man from your neighborhood. We might call him a *goði*. You would ask him to wield his influence on your behalf, and in turn you would owe a favor to him in the future. But perhaps the very first people you would call would be your family and those friends with whom your bonds are so close that you consider them to be "as good as family"—in anthropological terms, your fictive kin.

Together, you might then pay the errant jogger a visit at home or ask him to tarry a while in the midst of his morning exercise routine in some isolated corner of the local park. You would indicate that unless he paid the money, he might face a number of tough consequences, which the court's judgment would authorize you to exact. You might note that you admired his fine new car.

If your family looked sufficiently resolute and substantial, the jogger would probably pay up—but, in fact, in most circumstances he wouldn't wait to be threatened. Knowing about you and your respected family and friends already, he would have sent you a check soon after the court's judgment.

Icelandic law worked in a similar way. Its decentralized constitutional structure was predicated on the ability of litigants to draw on their kin in the course of resolving legal disputes. In the United States, the federal Constitution makes no mention of political parties, and yet they are essential to our political system. So in Iceland, kin relations were the unwritten third branch of government.

•

British Prime Minister Margaret Thatcher once famously asserted that "there is no such thing as society"—that there are only individual men and women and families. In many ways, medieval Iceland embodied this maxim.[13]

The term for clan in Old Norse, and in modern Icelandic, is *ætt*. Tellingly, the word is closely related to the Norse words for belonging, possession, and geographic direction. The clan was a community of kinship which provided your deepest sense of belonging, which you possessed and which possessed you, and which provided your overriding sense of place. We may approach the notion of family today with similar ideals, but in traditional societies those values are far more robust, different not simply in quantity but in kind, as the Norse etymology suggests. In Iceland, individuals were known and assessed not simply in themselves but in relation to their *ætt*.

It's for this reason that the Icelandic sagas invariably begin or introduce significant characters with extended genealogies (and why many ancient tales from other lands do the same). "There was a man named Ulf, the son of Bjalfi and of Hallbera, the daughter of Ulf the Fearless," begins the great *Egil's Saga*. "She was the sister of Hallbjorn Half-troll from Hrafnista, the father of Ketil Haeng."

Or from the *Saga of the People of Laxardal*:

A man called Ketil Flat-nose, the son of Bjorn Buna . . . lived in Romsdal in the Romsdal district, between South More and North More. [He] was married to Yngvild, the daughter of Ketil Ram, a man of good family. They had five children . . . One of their daughters, Thorunn Hyrna, was married to Helgi the Lean. Helgi the Lean was the son of Eyvind the Easterner and Rafarta, the daughter of Kjarval, king of the Irish. Another of Ketil's daughters, Unn the Deep-minded, was married to Olaf the White, [who] was the son of Ingjald, the son of Frodi the Valiant, who was killed by the descendants of Earl Sverting. Ketil's third daughter was called Jorunn Manvisbrekka. Jorunn was the mother of Ketil the Lucky Fisher, who settled at the farm Kikjubaer. His son was Asbjorn, the father of Thorstein who was the father of Surt, who was the father of Sighvat the Lawspeaker.[14]

If you wish to make a cultural comparison, ask yourself the following question about one of the United States' early national heroes: Who was George Washington's mother or father? What about Thomas Jefferson's?

The importance Icelanders attached to kinship also was reflected in their law, in explicit and implicit ways. In matters of inheritance, for instance, individuals were decidedly not free to dispose of their assets in a will however they wished—as one can generally do in liberal societies. Instead, strict rules of family inheritance were proscribed in advance. A property owner was even prevented from giving away his assets during his own lifetime.

Most of all, without a robust executive, kinship was essential to any significant social or legal action a person might undertake. The lack of central authority meant that the vindication of an individual's legal interests ultimately rested in the hands of his or her kin—and against the background threat of feud.

One should not dismiss such a constitutional arrangement lightly. Like the law of the Nuer or other societies in which kinship plays a constitutionally important role, Iceland maintained a system of governance worthy of respect. But from a liberal perspective, it came with a price.

In medieval Iceland, that price ultimately was the civil war of the Sturlung era, discussed in chapter 3, when the country divided into a handful of warring families, with no central authority to put an end to their violence. The civil war ended with the ceding of Icelandic independence to other powers for almost seven hundred years.

For societies today, we can assess that price, at once personal and societal, by considering how the rule of the clan operates in nations with a functioning executive authority. The rule of the clan can exist side by side and within the state, asserting its power where the state is weak, preventing democratic development, and inhibiting the growth of a common public identity. This widespread phenomenon, clannism, is illustrated in the cluster of contemporary societies to which I now turn, particularly one on whose future stability a great deal hangs in the balance.

SIX

CLANNISM AND DEMOCRATIC REFORM
THE PALESTINIAN AUTHORITY

Many liberal observers in 2002 watched in astonishment as the government of Turkmenistan officially renamed the first month of the year after its president for life, Saparmurat Niyazov.

In Turkmen the name for "January" had been Ýanwar. Now it was Turkmenbashi, after Niyazov's nickname, "leader of the Turkmen."

The government changed the names of all the other months of the year, too, as well as of the days of the week. September (Sentýabr) was renamed after the title of Niyazov's celebrated book of spiritual advice. It became Ruhnama. April (Aprel) was designated Gurbansoltan, after the president's mother.

Other months were renamed after figures from Turkmen history.

The incident was of a piece with political developments throughout Central Asia. After the fall of the Soviet Union, Turkmenistan, Kazakhstan, Kyrgyzstan, Tajikistan, and Uzbekistan all seemed to be sliding toward a future in which megalomaniacal rulers would erect towering statues of themselves in barren city centers. The postcommunist transition seemed likely to produce not capitalism, democracy, and cultural freedom but corruption, authoritarianism, and patriarchal repression.

The mood was adroitly captured in 2006 in Sacha Baron Cohen's mockumentary *Borat*, which had an unfair laugh at the expense of Kazakhstan (in fact the most modern and promising nation of the group). The film and its spin-offs follow the adventures of a "Kazakh" reporter as he travels through the United States and Britain flouting various liberal social norms, especially concerning women's equality.

Liberal anxiety about the future of Central Asia is understandable. But in the midst of our concern, we often fail to understand the meaning of events like the changing of the Turkmenistan calendar.

From a liberal perspective schooled on the history of Europe, any nation that renames the months of the year after the country's own president must be under the thumb of a government that is far too powerful. We view a leader like Niyazov as a Central Asian analogue of communist rulers like Erich Honecker of East Germany or Nicolae Ceauşescu of Romania—potent leaders in charge of a juggernaut state.

But in fact the case is precisely the reverse.

The rule of the clan can thrive within a weak state, resurfacing even after years of being held in abeyance, capturing the state's institutions and using them to advance narrow group interests above the public good.

As one distinguished scholar writes, "the supposedly 'authoritarian' rulers of Central Asia have all been functioning under conditions of actual *under-government*, which they lack the resources to correct." In particular, presidents like Niyazov are beholden to indissoluble power-sharing agreements with "powerful but largely invisible regional, clan, and economic power brokers." The Soviets had kept these clan networks at bay but never fully destroyed them, and when the Soviets left, the networks assumed a new importance.

Under these circumstances, changing the calendar isn't a sign of the strength of the state. It's a sign of the state's weakness. When rulers feel weak, they "resort to bluster and bombast" and "exploit national symbols" to "generate centripetal force" and increase their perceived authority.[1]

This gambit is rarely if ever successful. While leaders attempt to exert their influence, "clan networks infiltrate, penetrate, and transform the formal regime," in the words of another Central Asia expert. Clans end up holding sway and appropriating the power of the state for their factional interests.

This in turn makes democratization "unlikely," and it pits clan against clan in political conflicts over resources that may quickly turn violent.[2]

The condition of post-Soviet Central Asia exemplifies another manifestation of the rule of the clan: clannism. Clans can rule not only when the state is fully absent, as among the Nuer, or when the state is incomplete, as in Iceland, but also when the state is relatively developed and possesses a modern executive power. This is the challenging condition that today affects liberal reformers in the Palestinian Authority (also Palestinian National Authority)—and in a surprising array of the world's developing nations.

In sub-Saharan Africa, in the long wake of European colonialism, "tribalism" (the term widely used in Africa itself) is not confined to pastoral peoples distant from government authority. Because throughout Africa the state distributes benefits on the basis of personal favor rather than formal entitlement, merit, or the public good, clan affiliations are often strikingly important for members of the middle class who live in the administrative and economic centers of their countries. Tribalism is a modern, urban phenomenon. As one Nigerian scholar writes in an influential essay, "the degree and scope of tribalism in Africa are negatively correlated with the predominance of 'tribal' life."[3] What we tend loosely to call corruption is often the distribution of favors along clan lines.

Likewise in China, under very different political conditions, people frequently look to their extended lineage, *tsu*, for their personal identity—individuals develop their core sense of self in relation to the duties they hold within their family networks. More practically, lineage groups are inextricable from the social institution of *guanxi*, or personal relationships, through which the Chinese access economic resources and opportunities. Chinese clannism developed over centuries in the absence of an effective legal system and it was reinforced by neo-Confucian principles under which a well-ordered patriarchal family was viewed as the foundation of a well-ordered state. While modernization under communism reduced the functional significance of family lineage, the core ideals of the clan and its principles of Status are still influential.[4]

Most relevantly of all, clannism is an essential part of Arab societies, where, in the words of the *Arab Human Development Report 2004*, it forms a basic link in "the chain that stifles individual freedom."[5]

The origin of Arab clannism lies partly in the ancient tribal structures of Arab peoples and the historical ability of Islam to accommodate them. But more immediately, it lies in the way that European colonialism distorted traditional tribal forms by consolidating the power of tribal chiefs and other power brokers, for example by granting individual leaders personal ownership of land that previously had been collectively held by tribes. In the words of Palestinian intellectual Hisham

Sharabi, these and other colonial policy measures "had among [their] consequences *the juridical modernization of patriarchal structures in society*"—they updated the rule of the clan for the twentieth century. They amplified its power, made it urban, and severed it from most traditional communal restraints.[6]

This was the state of affairs many Arabs faced after winning their national independence, and in time it helped lock the Middle East and North Africa in a box of political and cultural repression. It now also confronts the liberal activists and reformers working in the glow of the sociopolitical changes sweeping the region.

Indeed, clannism poses a particular challenge in this moment of political transition. For the rule of the clan tends to assert itself most in the face of a deficit of public authority. As the *Arab Human Development Report 2004* puts it, in terms liberals ought to keep in mind as we contemplate our own societies:

> Clannism flourishes, and its negative impact on freedom and society becomes stronger, wherever civil or political institutions that protect rights and freedoms are weak or absent. Without institutional supports, individuals are driven to seek refuge in narrowly based loyalties that provide security and protection, thus further aggravating the phenomenon. Tribal allegiances also develop when the judiciary is ineffective or the executive authority is reluctant to implement its rulings, circumstances that make citizens unsure of their ability to realize their rights without the allegiance of the clan.[7]

Even more troubling, clan groups often find ways to coopt emerging institutions for their own ends.

In this light, the case of the Palestinian Authority is instructive. For while clannism has hindered social and political development across Arab societies, Palestinian clannism poses a significant obstacle to the growth of effective state institutions at just the moment when a viable Palestinian state is critical to the future of peace in the Middle East. As we will see in chapter 10, clans can participate in effective state modernization. They also can destroy a growing state in its infancy.

•

The challenge of clans in Palestine marks the convergence of the customary social organization of the Palestinian people and an ill-fated turn in their recent political history.[8] Traditionally, social and political power among Palestinians has been rooted in systems of lineage. These kinship systems include not only those of nomadic Bedouin tribesmen and the elite families who served as intermediaries between the Palestinian population and government administrators under the Ottoman Empire and British Mandate, but also hundreds of extended family groups, or *hamula*, tracing their patrilineal descent to a common ancestor. *Hamula* exercise only limited influence in shaping the mundane choices individual Palestinians make day to day, for instance in their career paths. But *hamula* continue to play an important part in Palestinian politics and the administration of justice.[9]

In particular, clans possess their own tribunals for resolving disputes within their lineage groups, and they abide by time-honored practices for reaching reconciliation and renewal (*islah*) between disputing groups under recognized principles of customary law (*'urf*). They also observe a strict code of honor (*mithaq al-sharaf*) that requires members to take revenge (*tha'r*) against those who have injured their kin.[10] The viability of a free and independent Palestinian state will depend not only on Israeli political will, but also upon whether these traditional systems of justice can be replaced with state institutions under democratic, public control.

An ill-fated turn in Palestinian history, however, has placed this goal further from reach than it might otherwise have been. The first intifada (1987–93) held out the promise of state development among Palestinians in a host of ways. Most important, it gave rise to a new generation of leaders known as the intifada elite, university-educated activists committed not to the interests of their kin groups but to principles of nationalism. The intifada elite sought to advance the cause of Palestinian independence by developing the institutional structures of government and civil society. Their deep, grassroots connections gave them the authority and legitimacy to construct a modern, albeit revolutionary, state.

But after Yasir Arafat returned from exile in Tunisia in 1994, in the wake of the Oslo Accords, Palestinian clan politics took a turn for the worse. To bolster his own power, Arafat undermined the institutions forged by the intifada elite and strengthened the power of clans, which he could control directly through patronage.[11]

Among the clan-friendly policies Arafat set in motion was the Palestinian election law of 1996. The law declared that representatives to the new Palestinian parliament would be selected not at the national level, which would have brought to power leaders with national prestige and accountability, but rather at the district level, which encouraged clan block voting. As one scholar writes, this policy "produced what it was designed to produce: a parliament of clan leaders, largely pliant to the wishes of Arafat and his cabinet."[12]

In addition, Arafat established a Department of Tribal Affairs, which formally endorsed the resolution of civil disputes and traditional criminal matters in clan courts.[13] Finally, and ominously, the security services also began to recruit along clan lines, funneling weapons to major family groups.

In sum, after Arafat's return, Palestinians saw what one Palestinian legislator called the "consolidat[ion of] the concept of tribalism" into their emerging state.[14]

The second intifada, beginning in 2000, was an even greater boon for Palestinian clans. With their power already fortified by Arafat, clan groups rushed to fill the societal vacuum created when the Israeli military destroyed the basic institutions by which the nascent Palestinian state maintained order, especially police stations and courts. When Arafat died in 2004, the man whose patronage kept clans in check was gone, leaving them substantially to their own devices. As a result, clans now pose a major obstacle to practical institution builders seeking to establish the rule of law in the Palestinian Authority.

This obstacle has been as vexing to the Islamists of Hamas in Gaza as it has been to the nationalists of Fatah in the West Bank. Although Islam has historically accommodated clan groups, at its heart it sets religious identity against tribal loyalty. Hamas is philosophically committed to this anticlan ideology, which regularly brings it into violent conflict with powerful Gazan families.[15] Many readers in the West were given a dramatic window onto that violence in 2007, when a BBC reporter, Alan

Johnston, was kidnapped by the powerful Daghmash clan. The clan used Johnston as a bargaining chip first against Fatah and then against Hamas, neither of which was able to penetrate the group's heavily armed al-Sabra neighborhood in Gaza City. After nearly four months, Johnston was released.

Yet as appalling as the kidnapping of any single reporter is, clans challenge Hamas in more pervasive and fundamental ways. In Gaza under the rule of the clan, incidents such as a crash between a car and a donkey cart, or an argument about whether a vendor can change the equivalent of a five-dollar bill, lead to protracted feuds in which scores of people die. In 2006 alone, human rights observers in Gaza traced 214 acts of revenge, resulting in 90 deaths and 336 injuries, to clan feuds.[16] What chance does the rule of law stand under these conditions?

The gravity of the threat posed by clans, and the frustration of those working to aid the Palestinian Authority, was recently explained to me by an American who has advised Palestinian leaders on how to develop an effective police force. John Farmer, Jr., is a towering, burly redhead with the classic chevron moustache of a police detective. He is quick to flash a warm smile despite his deep conviction that ours is a fallen world, and his fortitude in the face of human limitations, and his acceptance of them, earns him the instinctive trust of almost everyone he meets. Among his varied positions, he has served as senior counsel for the 9/11 Commission and he has been attorney general of New Jersey. (He also is the dean at the law school where I teach.)

I once asked John about his time in the West Bank and Gaza. He related the following anecdote, his experience of the Palestinian Authority in a nutshell. One afternoon, while he was following a police officer on his rounds, a loud dispute arose between some men on the street. The officer approached to investigate and quickly found himself surrounded by an angry crowd taking sides. In reaction, the officer drew his gun and waved it at the crowd. John flashed me a smile. "That's not an effective response," he said. Fortunately, the incident was diffused, and the officer was taught a more professional style of reaction, but his initial reaction was typical.

And John's experience with clans?

He grew solemn, and turned for an example to the subject of bail. One of the pillars of modern criminal justice, bail allows a prisoner to be released from custody pending trial in exchange for a monetary pledge. But in the Palestinian Authority, John explained, bail sometimes serves a different function. Occasionally, after police apprehend someone suspected of a crime of violence, bail is in effect paid not by his own family or friends but rather by the family of the victim he has allegedly injured or killed. After bail is posted, the state releases the accused, as it is required to do by law—into the hands of the victim's family, which exacts its own justice.

In this way, clan groups have used the fledgling institutions of the Palestinian Authority to undercut the rule of law it is seeking to establish.

By posing their power against the state, Palestinian clans have also diminished the personal freedom and individual rights of all Palestinians. They have undermined not only the rule of law but also the status of the individual in society—and thus, ultimately, the possibility of modern liberal citizenship. The rule of the clan undercuts personal freedom because in the absence of a robust state persons must submit to the authority of their family patriarch and the norms of traditional, honor-based society in exchange for patronage and security. As the *Arab Human Development Report 2004* argues, in words written by Arabs, "Clannism implants submission, parasitic dependence and compliance in return for protection and benefits," and it thereby becomes "the enemy of personal independence, intellectual daring, and the flowering of a unique and authentic human entity."[17]

The cost clans exact on personal self-development under principles of Status parallels the toll they take on the legal concept of individual rights. Under the rule of the clan, persons are protected less as individuals than as members of the families to which they belong, making the liberal understanding of rights, which protects persons regardless of their place within a kin group, both impracticable and inconceivable. As Hisham Sharabi writes, clannism "displaces legality and renders public institutions superfluous, tak[ing] away the individual's claim to autonomous right."[18] A state protects its citizens; clan members protect their cousins.

I will argue in chapter 10 that clans can often be important instruments of state modernization and that it is a mistake to view them as irreconcilably opposed to state development. But for there to be hope for a viable Palestinian state the rule of the clan must be fully supplanted by the rule of law—whether through the Islamist opposition of Hamas, the nationalism of Fatah, or some other democratic means. This will be a difficult task, but it is one for which, as we will see, there is much historical precedent.

To appreciate how societies governed by the rule of the clan can develop more modern constitutional arrangements, however, one first must appreciate how their decentralized constitutionalism is inextricable from their culture of group honor, customary law, and feud. It is to this subject I now turn.

PART THREE

THE CULTURAL ORDER OF THE CLAN

Let me tell you a love story. It's a story you already know, or think you know, Shakespeare's tale of two star-crossed lovers. It's also a story about the rule of the clan.

It begins with a fight. Long ago, in a small town in southern Europe, four men from two warring clans—Shakespeare calls them houses—face each other, two against two, swords drawn. Their families are locked in an "ancient" feud which, though its original cause has been lost in time, has recently erupted in two brawls on the city streets. And now here is a third fight, sparked when a foot soldier of one house provocatively bites his thumb at his counterparts from the other. Blades clash, and soon powerful men from both families are drawn into the fray, even the clan elders, followed by ordinary citizens with clubs and pikes.

Before anyone is killed, the chief executive of the town, a prince—for our purposes, the most interesting character in the story—arrives with his retinue of officers and staff. He parts the two groups, calling them "enemies to peace." Though his authority over the warring clans is tenuous, the prince is determined to establish order and impose his power, and he declares that any future fighting will be punished with death.[1]

Meanwhile, a young man and a young woman from the two houses fall in love. They first meet at a festive dinner hosted by her family, which the young man impulsively attends in disguise. When his ruse is discovered by her ill-tempered cousin, the trick is considered an affront to family "honor" and the cousin challenges him to a duel. Though the young man refuses to fight, his best friend rises to his defense and is killed, a death the young man must avenge. He kills the young woman's cousin and brings down upon his own head punishment by the prince—banishment from the town. Why the prince imposes banishment rather than death is unclear. Is it weakness? Pity? A desire to make peace with the clans through accommodation?

Whatever the reason, it doesn't work. The cycle of escalating violence ends only when the two lovers lay dead in each other's arms and, surveying the scene, the prince once again demands a peace he cannot compel. Blaming himself for allowing the feud to fester for so long, he vows to secure justice for the young couple. "Some shall be pardoned," he proclaims, "and some punished." And he asks those around him to depart and "have more talk" of the events they have just witnessed—which, naturally, are those of Shakespeare's tale of woe, of Juliet and her Romeo.[2]

Romeo and Juliet tells a story of love set within a particular cultural and legal environment. The fate of Shakespeare's protagonists is bound to a logic in which affronts to family honor unleash violent retribution and destabilize public order, a logic the weak chief executive laments but can do little to stop. As we will see, this logic has long undermined the development of personal freedom and individual rights and the strong state necessary to protect them, and it continues to do so today.

The constitutional structure for which Shakespeare's Verona stands as an archetype poses a challenge to personal liberty in nations as diverse as Afghanistan and Iraq, Kenya and Nigeria, China and the Philippines, India and Albania, and many other countries. It once was an essential fact of life on the European continent, where its lingering presence can still be felt, especially in the Mediterranean. Shakespeare's prince and his struggle lie at the very heart of who we are—as nations, as an international community, and as small creatures in a large and difficult world. I considered the nature of that constitutional structure in part II.

In the following two chapters, I turn to the culture on which that structure is predicated. I examine how the rule of the clan's essential formal feature, its decentralized constitutional organization, is based on a distinctive array of substantive values, especially the principle of group honor. Group honor is the cultural foundation on which the decentralized structure of the rule of the clan is built. Under the rule of the clan, culture and constitutionalism work in tandem.

In chapter 7 I consider the many profound benefits that flow from group honor to members of clans, especially social solidarity and what in the West would be termed social justice. I also consider how group honor, along with a customary understanding of law, provides the mechanism by which clan societies foster high levels of internal social surveillance and control over personal behavior.

Honor not only enables social control within clan groups. It also establishes the terms for relationships between them. In chapter 8 I examine how the honor principle supplies the force behind the legal mechanism regulating those relationships, especially in the event of interclan conflict: the blood feud. Just as group honor facilitates solidarity among kin, so through the ingenious institution of feud it creates the conditions for a rough peace between kin groups.

That Shakespeare's story about the rule of the clan is a story about love—that Romeo and Juliet's fates, their stars, are "crossed" by a conflict between two family groups—is no accident. Just as the houses of Montague and Capulet are symbols of clans unchecked by state power, so love is the emblem of freedom. Of this, we, too, will "have more talk."

SEVEN

SOLIDARITY, GROUP HONOR, AND SHAME

MODERN INDIA, PAKISTAN, AND AFGHANISTAN

Critics of the West sometimes denounce its culture—and often its governments—as "shameless." In Pakistan, for instance, as the linguist Tariq Rahman notes, "the idea that the West is 'shameless' and our own culture is 'pure'" is an important part of the ideology of the ruling elite. Likewise, "the kind of ideas and images which *madrassa* students encounter most" includes the view that "Western people are . . . promiscuous, profligate, shameless, greedy, selfish and cruel."[1]

Although it is unjust and unfair, such criticism is fully understandable. In socially conservative Pakistan, dominant views about sexual morality contrast sharply with those on endless-loop display in Western film and television. The West, in particular the United States, is also profoundly implicated in the violence tearing the country apart.

More important than simply being understandable, however, the charge that Western cultures are "shameless" is also substantially true—but it is true in anthropological rather than moral terms. In traditional societies, especially those governed by the rule of the clan or in the grip of clannism, shame holds a very different place than it does in industrialized liberal democracies. Salman Rushdie's third book, a political novel about Pakistan, is called *Shame* (1983)—not a title that would readily apply to a novel of national self-reflection set in France or Canada.

The fundamental difference between the way liberal societies and clan societies approach shame was brought home to me recently in a conversation with a human-rights activist and political analyst from Turkey. Ziya Meral is an urbane young intellectual with a Vandyke beard whose quick wit and uplifting sense of humor belies the fact that he regularly inserts himself into situations of substantial personal risk in countries with overeager security services. He lives in London, has written a book about Friedrich Nietzsche and Fyodor Dostoyevsky, and is passionate about single malt whiskey.

"My value in London is what I make it," he told me one afternoon, his voice crackling over our Skype connection, "whereas there [in Turkey] it's how and where I fit in, how I am seen by the collective."

Meral often travels to places beset by various forms of clannism—Egypt and Nigeria were recent destinations—where he investigates human-rights abuses, especially restrictions on religious liberty. But I was interested in learning more about his emigration to England and how it has affected him personally. To illustrate the cultural change, he told me a story about language.

Meral finds it easy to swear in English, he said. I can attest: his rhetorical gifts make his curses a floral supplement to his eloquence. But he finds it impossible to swear in his mother tongue.

"I feel horrible," he confessed, chuckling softly. "The language provides a totally different psychological context in which certain words can be used."

One Turkish word in particular he characterized as "extremely intense"—*şerefsiz*. To hurl this epithet is to call someone "shameless" or, literally, "without honor." In Turkish it is not a word one can possibly use lightly. Meral certainly wouldn't use it without a profound awareness of its consequences. The words *utanmaz*, *yüzsüz*, and *arsız* express the same idea and are similarly wounding.

By contrast, to call someone "shameless" in English isn't a major insult. He marveled: "It can even be a form of endearment!"

The ease with which English speakers use the word "shameless" is indeed striking. Advertisers promote "shameless sales" and "shameless giveaways," while recipes promise "shamelessly rich chocolate cake." In her bestselling memoir *Eat, Pray, Love* (2006), Elizabeth Gilbert describes herself as a "shameless student" and as "the most shameless of flirts," someone who makes "shameless" introductions of herself to strangers. (Roger Ebert in turn called the film based on the book "shameless wish-fulfillment.")[2]

"Let me put in a shameless plug for my new business"—words one might hear on any American street. "You said *that* to your boss? I love you! You're absolutely shameless!"—words one might overhear in any American coffee shop.

In traditional societies, however, to be called "shameless" is no light matter—a cultural fact that explains how the constitutional decentralization of the rule of the clan works.

People in Western societies are of course capable of feeling shame. But the far more common and powerful equivalent of that emotion in the West is guilt. The difference between the two emotions, and between "shame cultures" and "guilt cultures," parallels the basic difference between Status and Contract.

In shame cultures it is not a person's behavior that creates shame. It is instead the fact that the person's community has witnessed or learned of the behavior. Shame is a response to harsh external judgment. It requires at least two people. As a consequence, as the anthropologist Ruth Benedict explained in a book about Japan, "in any tribe or nation where shame is deeply felt . . . [a man] orients himself toward the verdict of others."[3]

Guilt, on the other hand, is solitary. It stems not from a disapproving community but from a bad conscience, and it can be suffered entirely in secret. In fact, guilt can be relieved by openly admitting to the transgression that prompted it, even by confessing in public, sometimes especially then—just watch any daytime television talk show, where people regularly confess before millions of viewers to behaviors that would earn them widespread censure in any shame culture, after which they admit to feeling much better about themselves. Although it can serve as a potent form of social control, guilt is essentially an individualist's emotion.

Just as societies of Status and Contract approach shame differently, giving it dissimilar weight in their hierarchy of values, they also have deeply contrasting views of honor.

In the United States, for example, honor is highly valued as a personal quality. Countless classic western films starring John Wayne and Clint Eastwood testify to the purchase honor has in the national psyche. But honor, like shame, is usually understood through an individualist lens. A typical western follows a hero who begins in a circumstance of personal degradation but achieves a newfound pride by meeting a personal test of character. The hero's honor comes from his well-earned self-respect.

In Ruth Benedict's terms, honor derives from "living up to one's own picture of oneself."[4]

Only rarely in Western societies is honor understood in collective rather than in individual terms, as deriving not solely from personal achievement but from belonging to a group from which no exit is possible. The most prominent example in the United States is the military and, at least in popular lore, the Marines. To become a Marine, in the words of its recruitment website, is to undergo a moral transformation "that cannot be undone."[5] Each Marine is bound to other Marines by unbreakable bonds of loyalty—their honor comes from the group. A disgraceful act committed by one Marine is said to bring discredit upon the Corps and every one of its members.

It is this collective understanding of honor, not of the military unit but of the extended kin group, and the correspondingly collective view of shame, that provides the cultural architecture of the rule of the clan.[6]

•

During my conversation with Meral, our talk turned to modern literature, and he mentioned that he deeply admires the work of the great postwar Japanese novelist Shusaku Endo. The affinity was telling.

In *The Samurai* (1980), Endo tells the true story of a seventeenth-century Japanese diplomatic mission to Mexico. To gain favor with their Spanish hosts, the diplomats reluctantly convert to Christianity. Their mission fails. Even worse, when they return home, the emissaries, especially a humble warrior called Rokuemon Hasekura, face persecution and disgrace for their conversion. They are condemned to live and die as outcasts in their own country.

The story appeals to Meral for reasons beyond religious faith (he himself is a Christian convert, hailing from a land where national identity and Islam are widely viewed as inseparable). More fundamentally, the story is about the grief of exile. For all his cosmopolitanism, Meral has spent his adult life bearing a loss that comes from having left the communal warmth of his native country.

The pain of leaving a country in which kin networks are culturally important—be it Turkey, Nigeria, or India—derives particularly from losing one of the greatest psychological benefits the rule of the clan provides: solidarity. Clan societies are communities in which the collective takes precedence over the individual. While this balance may strike citizens of liberal nations as oppressive, it is an oppression that comes with significant human advantages.

In clan societies, social bonds are "thick and intense," in Meral's words, beginning with relationships within the extended family. The community standing of a person's clan shapes every opportunity he or she has, from employment prospects to marital options. Independence from extended family is not an option. The only way to escape one's cousins is to move far away. But in exchange for this dependence, the clan network is devoted to providing its members with mutual aid throughout their lives. If a cousin comes to a man's door asking for assistance, the more fortunate person may feel put upon and believe that the cousin is undeserving, but he will rarely deny him the aid.

The sense of personal security kin members receive from this arrangement is profound.

So is the sense of identity it produces. In order for a kin group to function as a network of mutual support, its members must have an intimate knowledge of their lineage. Ancestral consciousness is vital to the ability to quickly forge deep alliances with people one may have never met, based on a distantly shared bloodline. In turn, lineage knowledge provides clan members with a sense of their place in the world, not only in contemporary time but across many generations in the past and, implicitly, into the future.

Many Westerners find it hard to appreciate how deep this knowledge can run.

An occasion from my own life illustrates the point. One hot summer afternoon my wife and I were spending some time in a local park with a friend from Taiwan, a professor of English, and her two young girls. I hail from three ethnic backgrounds generally known for their high degree of social solidarity and ancestral consciousness: Russian Jewish, Croatian, and Serbian. I gain real pleasure from knowing the history of my paternal grandparents, who emigrated to the United States soon after the Russian revolution of October 1917, and as I maintain relations with relatives in Croatia, I know something about my maternal great-grandfather (a weathered photograph shows a dashing man in a long, fur-lined coat). My cousins and I even jokingly refer to a small Croatian village, Oprisavci, as our clan seat.

As our Chinese friend tossed a ball back and forth with her children, I asked her about her own family history. How many generations back could she trace her own paternal line? "Not too many," she told me, throwing the ball in a slow arc to her eldest daughter. "Twenty-four."[7] Her sense of lineage belonging was as casual as a reflex.

The depth of vertical lineage consciousness in clan societies is matched by the strength of their horizontal bonds. In liberal societies, relationships established beyond the nuclear family are based primarily on choice, and they can be severed by choice as well. Such relationships are contractual. As a result, to outsiders they can seem relatively shallow. In a society of Status, relationships outside the extended family often overlap with its networks. This freights those relationships with the weight of community surveillance and lends them depth.

Leaving such a society and settling elsewhere—forsaking the security of economic interdependence and mutual aid, the unshakeable sense of personal belonging provided by lineage, and the communal warmth of a traditional culture—is thus to experience in one's own life a loss that liberal societies have undergone over the course of many generations. Few people do so without great emotional cost. I was not surprised when Meral once told me that for him one of the most moving features of Christianity is the figure of a god who suffers.

The collectivism of societies of Status is a response to practical necessity. In the face of a challenging world, kin networks allow people to pool risk. When no person can make it alone, lineage provides a natural basis for relationships of mutual dependence—with the significant advantage that this trustworthiness grows with each successive generation. Clans are like insurance companies into which one is enrolled at birth and from which one cannot unsubscribe.

Notably, in corners of modern nations where the writ of the state is weak, groups spring up to provide security and gain advantage for their members as a unit. For instance, gangs seek to provide many of the same material and psychological benefits as clans, except they are dedicated to unlawful activity. They even attempt to re-create the permanent bonds of blood relationships through mechanisms such as gang tattoos. When criminal gangs are based on actual blood ties, as in the Mafia, their resemblance to clan groups is even closer, especially in their strict internal rules and their feuding patterns.

In clan societies, the dispersal of risk in practical terms is enabled by the values of group honor and shame.

The principle of group honor ties each person's social value and moral worth to the reputation of his or her kin group. The corresponding principle of collective shame in turn means that the moral misconduct of any member of the group dishonors the group as a whole, just as the misconduct of one Marine disgraces the entire Corps. In terms of social prestige or capital, therefore, the bank accounts of individual members of a kin group within a clan society are linked. One member's overdraft, or shameful action, is charged against all the other accounts.

This creates a strong incentive for the group to ensure that its members do well according to community norms. It causes people to look out for one another in both senses of the phrase: at once assisting their fellow group members and subjecting them to constant scrutiny.

•

For all the benefits it provides—security, identity, robust interpersonal relationships—the solidarity of clan societies also imposes substantial costs. These costs are both individual and social, and they diminish the central state authority necessary to make an individualist way of life possible. Ironically, they also stem from the very principles of group honor and collective responsibility that underwrite the most positive features of the rule of the clan.

Many of these costs were eloquently diagnosed by the jurist, intellectual, and founding father of the Indian constitution, B. R. Ambedkar, in his writings about the Hindu caste system. Though the caste system is, like so many aspects of life in India, quite distinctive, it nevertheless provides a vivid illustration of the shortcomings of societies composed of a multiplicity of tightly knit kin groups. Indeed, India was one of Henry Maine's archetypical societies of Status.

The Hindu caste system grew out of the encounter between Indo-European Aryans and the indigenous people of the Indus Valley beginning in about 1500 BCE. Details of the process are necessarily obscure. Was the system imposed by a light-skinned people on those of darker coloration? Were Indo-European social categories assimilated into an already highly segmented community? Only the most painstaking historical and linguistic scholarship will ever answer such questions. But whatever the pathway, in time Indian society came to be divided into four great hereditary divisions, or *varnas*.

Three of these groups, the so-called twice born, are entitled to study the sacred Hindu texts known as the Vedas. They include Brahmans (priests and teachers), Kshatriyas (warriors), and, beneath them in social status, Vaishyas (farmers and merchants).[8] Together they comprise about 10 percent of the national population. Their second birth is said to occur during a rite-of-passage ceremony that initiates young men into full membership in their religious communities.

In addition, the *chaturvarna* system includes a fourth caste, Shudras (laborers), who are barred from Vedic study and who are regarded as inferiors by the twice-born groups, though they are still viewed as "pure." Counts vary and are extremely controversial, but a commission in the late 1970s estimated that Shudras comprise about 50 percent of the Indian population. Today their members are included in the legal designation Other Backward Classes (OBC)—groups that are entitled to a range of social benefits under the Indian constitution.[9]

More inferior still are the Dalits, once known as "untouchables," who stand outside the *varna* system altogether. Traditionally the Dalits held occupations that brought them into contact with dead animals or human bodily fluids. They are the lowest of the low, and today they are included among the Scheduled Castes that receive even greater government assistance than OBCs, including preferential treatment in higher education admissions and civil-service hiring.

Ambedkar, the foremost modern critic of the caste system, was born in 1891 into a collection of "untouchable" castes known as the Mahar, who comprise about 9 percent of the population of the large western state of Maharashtra. The state includes the city of Mumbai (Bombay), one of the most populous cities in the world. Like other Dalits, the Mahar have traditionally been regarded in the Hindu caste system as ritually impure. For orthodox Hindus of a high caste to be touched by a Dalit, or to accept food a Dalit has cooked, or to drink water from a shared well, is said to be polluting. Such defilement can only be washed away by complex religious rites.

As a child in school, Ambedkar was once called to the chalkboard by his teacher to demonstrate the solution to a problem. The high-caste Hindu children broke into an uproar because they stored their lunch boxes behind the slate. Fearing Ambedkar might ritually contaminate their food, they rushed forward and threw their lunchboxes aside before he could reach the front of the class.[10] Such experiences naturally left him bitter, and they ultimately led him to convert to Buddhism in the final year of his life. They also led him to become a tireless and effective advocate for Dalit interests and for the "annihilation of caste."[11]

They also made him a determined student. His labors would earn him a PhD from Columbia University, as well as a masters's degree from the London School of Economics, a doctoral degree from the University of London, and admission to the bar at Gray's Inn, London.

The Hindu caste system against which Ambedkar fought consists not only of the great fourfold division of society into *varnas*. The Western term *caste* in fact more precisely refers to the Indian terms *jati* and *gotra*, which supplement the *varna* system with extraordinary social complexity. While there are four *varnas*, plus the Dalits, there are some three thousand *jatis*—as their boundaries can change over time, there is no precise figure—and scores of *gotras*, rendering India a jigsaw puzzle of hereditary factions.[12]

Put succinctly, a *jati* is a local kinship group composed of multiple lineages whose members are associated with a common occupation. There are *jatis* whose members have long been potters, blacksmiths, weavers, and so forth, though a *jati* member need not follow the customary occupation of his or her group. *Jatis* are rooted in the small rural communities in which 75 percent of Indians live—those ancient villages that Gandhi and his followers unsuccessfully sought to elevate into the chief constitutional institutions of the new nation. An Indian's full name often provides a clue to his or her *jati* and to the village from which his or her lineage hails.

Jatis are governed by strict principles of purity and pollution. For instance, it is generally improper, indeed offensive, for a member of one *jati* to share a meal containing boiled rice with the member of another *jati*—doing so would be polluting. Likewise, *jatis* practice marital endogamy. Unlike members of clans in segmentary lineage societies, which are exogamous, members of a *jati* are required to marry within their group—marriage between members of different *jatis* is thought to be unclean (at the same time they are required to marry outside of their *gotra*, the lineage segment of their *jati*). The punishment for violating such purity rules, meted out by councils of caste elders, can include social ostracism and, in the case of violation of the rules of endogamy or exogamy, even death.

Jati members absorb the values of their group through the primary institution of Indian social life, the extended or joint patriarchal family. The extended family is the exacting school of the caste system and its principles. In extended Indian families, multiple generations share the same roof, enjoy an exceptionally high degree of social cohesion, and in the case of the joint family hold property in common—that is, they form a corporate body whose identity and property persists across generations. Indians in modern industrialized nations regularly refer to all Indian women of a certain age as "aunty." The practice is in part a cultural legacy of the ancient family institution at the heart of *jati* and *gotra*.[13]

From the perspective of a developed liberal society this cultural legacy can be charming. Yet the *jati* system and the extended family in which its values are imbued poses a deep challenge to Indian democracy, a challenge that is characteristic of all societies under the sway of the rule of the clan or of clannism.

At its core, the *jati* system is marked by what Ambedkar called an "anti-social spirit"—it lacks a sense of shared, common life. It lacks a belief in the public. Each *jati*, like each *varna*, is confined within itself, its horizon of concern ending at the boundaries of its membership. Caste and family are more important than the nation.

"Hindu society as such does not exist," asserted Ambedkar in stark terms:

> It is only a collection of castes. Each caste is conscious of its existence. Its survival is the be-all and end-all of its existence. Castes do not even form a federation. A caste has no feeling that it is affiliated to other castes except when there is a Hindu-Muslim riot. On all other occasions each caste endeavours to segregate itself and to distinguish itself from other castes. Each caste not

only dines among itself and marries among itself, but each caste prescribes its own distinctive dress . . . Men constitute a society because they have things which they possess in common.

This limited social perspective, Ambedkar lamented, "has prevented the Hindus from becoming a society with a unified life and consciousness of its own being." It prevented India from achieving common ends.[14]

The past fifty years suggest that the existence of caste is, in fact, not entirely inconsistent with economic and political development. The Indian program of affirmative action, which Ambedkar advocated as a remedy for centuries of discrimination against Dalits and OBCs—and which dwarfs by comparison similar programs in the United States— has actually helped perpetuate caste in the midst of India's extraordinary recent modernization.

But the essential insight that the Indian caste system is driven by an "antisocial" spirit holds true, and it illuminates not only India but also other nations governed by the rule of the clan. Societies founded on kin solidarity lack the common consciousness necessary to pursue truly public ends. They lack this essential tool for forging a state dedicated to the public interest.

Ambedkar sought to overcome this deficiency through his design for the postindependence constitution, which he hoped would reorient Indian values in two fundamental ways. By creating a strong central state—and opposing Gandhi's decentralized vision—he sought to give government the power to eradicate caste hierarchy. Only a powerful national authority, he believed, was capable of transcending local prejudices—a lesson the United States learned, on a smaller scale, during its civil rights movement.[15]

In addition, he believed that only a strong central state could vindicate the values of modern individualism. For Ambedkar, the lack of a public spirit in Hindu society was inextricably linked to its lack of individualism. By dividing itself into four great *varnas* and thousands of separate *jatis* and *gotras*, Hindu society subordinated the individual to the overarching demands of the group. "The Hindu social order does not recognise the individual as a centre of social purpose," Ambedkar wrote, in words that echo the criticisms of the *Arab Human Development Report 2004*. "In the Hindu social order there is no room for individual merit and no consideration of individual justice."[16]

This neglect of the individual is a direct consequence of how clan societies view the nature of law—a view we can appreciate by turning our attention to contemporary Afghanistan and Pakistan.

•

In the wake of the terrorist attacks of September 11, 2001, many citizens of liberal democratic states were outraged by the refusal of the Taliban regime to surrender Osama bin Laden to the United States or to international authorities. Indeed, Taliban spokesmen refused even to acknowledge that the world's most wanted terrorist was in Afghanistan, a patent deceit. The refusal seemed all the more mendacious because the same spokesmen also claimed that bin Laden was their country's "guest."

After the American-led invasion of Afghanistan, many people were likewise confounded by bin Laden's ability to elude capture. How could a man with a twenty-five-million-dollar bounty on his head vanish with scarcely a trace when trailed by the strongest and most sophisticated military organization on the planet? The answer lay partly in the rugged geography of eastern Afghanistan, which offers excellent places to hide, but clearly something more was at work.

That something more was a distinctive set of legal and cultural norms known as *pashtunwali*—norms that also help explain the Taliban's obstinate response to international pressure to hand bin Laden over. *Pashtunwali* is the ancient code of personal behavior of all Pashtuns, the tribal people that forms the majority of the population of Afghanistan and that is the principal source of the Taliban's membership. "Only the man who follows *pashtunwali*," states a traditional proverb, "can be called a Pashtun." The Pashtun are a people defined by their commitment to a particular body of law.

The values of *pashtunwali* cut across all aspects of a person's life. They include interpersonal loyalty, Islamic religious faith, female sexual purity (which demands rigorous sexual segregation), respect for elders, and unselfish behavior toward friends. They also include personal equality between men—the Pashtun are deeply egalitarian, and a de-meanor of personal servility is as unthinkable for them as it is for the Nuer tribesmen considered in chapter 4 ("What Nuer ever came when one sent for him or paid any one a cow?").

Among the many principles of *pashtunwali*, however, three are es-sential, so much so that they form the basic pillars of Pashtun society. The first principle is *badal*, the requirement to take physical retribution against a transgressor, to meet a wrong with violence in kind. The sec-ond principle is *melmastia*, the obligation to provide hospitality to guests, which mandates a level of generosity, even to strangers, indeed espe-cially to them, quite beyond anything seen in industrialized liberal soci-eties. Guests in a Pashtun home are literally given the best food, sleeping quarters, and entertainment the host can offer. The third principle is *nanawatia*, the duty to provide physical refuge to anyone who seeks it, at any time, and to guard them from harm.

Pashtuns violate these tenets at the expense of their familial and tribal honor and, thus, their ability to work their will within the world. To fail to live up to them would erode their ability to undertake essential tasks, from engaging in trade to forming favorable marriage alliances for their children.

Among the three essential principles of *pashtunwali*, the provision of refuge is especially imperative—yet from a liberal perspective it may seem the most unusual. It must be heeded even when doing so violates other principles and elemental personal feelings. According to anthro-pologist Charles Lindholm, author of a classic 1982 field study under-taken in the Swat Valley, the principle of refuge extends "to its fullest logical limit"—to the point that a man must give asylum to the mur-derer of his own son if the killer requests it.

"Cases are cited in local history," writes Lindholm, "of just such situations occurring, and of the bereaved father offering shelter and hospitality as required by custom." The requirement to provide refuge transcends even the obligation to exact retribution—*nanawatia* over-rides *badal*, at least temporarily.[17]

As Pakistani spymaster Colonel Mohammad Yahya Effendi once told a reporter for *National Geographic*, to the Pashtun providing sanc-tuary is "like a sacred mission."[18]

This mission is all the more vital, it bears emphasizing, because it is also pursued as a matter of personal and collective interest within the Pashtun cultural economy. The Pashtuns, who are renowned tellers of jokes, capture the idea through a story that, from a liberal perspective, is not especially comic. A Hindu is a guest in a Pashtun's home. The villagers gather to kill the infidel in their midst. The Hindu, terrified, asks his host what he intends to do. "Do not fear," the host replies. "Your death shall be revenged."[19]

It was this demand of the Pashtun code—at once personally exacting and self-interested—to which the Taliban referred in seeking to justify the protection they provided bin Laden in the face of predictable retaliation from the United States. It also underlay the al-Qaeda leader's own probable expectation that he would receive shelter throughout Afghanistan and Pakistan as he fled Tora Bora.

Any Pashtun who surrendered bin Laden to American forces might be twenty-five million dollars richer. But by flouting the Pashtun's "sacred mission," he would thereby disgrace himself, his family, his clan, and his tribe for generations.

While *pashtunwali* is often called the "law" of the Pashtun people, it is not the kind of law with which citizens of modern states are familiar. In this respect, Pashtun Afghanistan is characteristic of societies governed by the rule of the clan, for such societies understand law in distinctly premodern terms. Clan societies and modern liberal societies have a fundamentally different understanding of what law is.[20]

Most important, in modern states the thing we call law is distinct from many of the other rules and standards by which people live. Law is formally and conceptually separate from codes of morality and religion. The law of Germany delimits the acceptable range of financial dealings in a business transaction, and it proscribes theft and murder, but it says nothing about which months of the year are best for a man and a woman to have sexual relations or about the proper time to light a set of ritual candles. Sociologists speak of law as functionally differentiated from other spheres of life—as specialized and autonomous.

By contrast, *pashtunwali* not only governs cases in which one person causes physical harm to another—a situation that may call for *badal*, or retribution—but also dictates the proper standards of deportment between older and younger men. It reaches into areas of human experience that in modern societies would be regarded as the proper domain of normative rules other than "law."

The so-called Laws of Manu, part of the Indian body of legal obligations known as *dharmasastra*, have a similarly wide scope. The *Manusmriti* contains provisions that resemble the legal codes of any modern liberal state, such as, "At a ferry, an empty cart should be charged one penny, a man's load half a penny, a livestock animal or a woman a quarter of a penny, and a man with no load half a quarter" (a rule regulating the price of a service) and "If a man destroys a pond he should be physically punished by drowning or by simple killing; but even if the criminal repairs it, he should pay the highest level of fine" (sanctions for the destruction of an essential economic resource). Yet the same code also contains tenets such as, "If a son born to a woman who has had a Brahmā marriage does good deeds, he frees from guilt ten of the ancestors who came before him, ten later descendants, and himself as the twenty-first" and "The natural fertile season of women is traditionally said to last for sixteen nights, though these include four special days that good people despise. Among these nights, the first four, the eleventh and the thirteenth are disapproved; the other ten nights are approved."[21]

Likewise, in the traditional Confucian understanding, the customary norms known as *li* stipulate rules of proper behavior not only within the family—including at its core the relationship of the living and the dead—but also for all the hierarchical relations of social and political authority outside it. In this respect *li* was viewed as the "cement of the entire normative sociopolitical order."[22] (The Confucian approach to law stands in marked contrast to the state-centered school of Chinese Legalism.) In a similarly encompassing fashion, the specific rules governing traditional Chinese clans (*tsu*) concern subjects as various as inheritance, the remarriage of a widow, the behavior of children toward parents, the management of common clan property, ancestral rites, proper relations with nonclan relatives, proper relations with teachers, and the importance of courtesy. The *tsu* codes also prohibit gambling, opium smoking, and various sexual transgressions.[23]

Modern law and the law of clan societies differ in other respects as well. For example, in modern societies, law is preserved in written form, and legal rules are drafted, debated, and passed by the legislative bodies of the state. When asked what "the law" on a particular subject is, a lawyer in a liberal society will refer to a set of books containing the relevant statutes.

By contrast, in premodern societies much law is oral. It is held not in books but rather in the memory of the society's respected elder members. Moreover, it is customary. Developed organically over centuries, customary law seems to those who observe it simply to exist. It expresses the collective conscience and wisdom of the community. In this respect, the law is inseparable from the group and its identity. To be a Pashtun is to follow the code of *pashtunwali*.

Indeed, in traditional societies the overriding purpose of law is to maintain the group's unity and solidarity (and, in some cases, as in ancient China, its hierarchy). Rather than striving to give each person his or her due, law seeks to preserve the coherence of the community. It establishes a powerful set of internal norms, and it creates a strong sense of differentiation between the group and outsiders.[24]

As societies modernize, the nature of their law changes—in the substance of its rules, and even more crucially in its form. Law becomes more highly differentiated from other social fields. Custom gives way to legislation. A body of full-time professionals emerges to administer its provisions. Solidarity typically diminishes as a value. The importance of group honor and its affiliated principles, such as purity and pollution, diminishes as well.

The conflict in India between Ambedkar and Gandhi over the nature of the postcolonial constitution was a clash between these competing ideas of law. Gandhi envisioned a future India as a stateless society in which authority was devolved to traditional village councils and in which legal principles were grounded in Hindu scriptures. Although he embraced many modern social and political ideals, such as women's rights, his legal vision was essentially of a premodern character.

Ambedkar advocated a sharply divergent vision. Rather than radically decentralizing government and closing the gap between spiritual and secular law, he strove to create a modern state based on liberal jurisprudential principles. His constitution fostered the modernization of the very concept of law in India, enabling Jawaharlal Nehru and his successors to implement basic social and economic reforms, and furthering the nation's steady movement from Status to Contract.

As we will see, it is a transformation that is still ongoing.

•

Justice Kanwaljit Singh Ahluwalia of the Punjab and Haryana High Court was nearing the end of his patience. "Out of twenty-six matters listed before me, ten matters pertain to marriage of young people aged between eighteen and twenty-one," he complained in June 2008. "In summer vacations, I am holding the court to decide anticipatory bail applications and habeas corpus petitions." It was creating a serious problem.

The courthouse in Chandigarh is a concrete linear block designed by the modernist master Le Corbusier. Its beautiful rhythmic arcade overlooks a tranquil pool and is painted in the architect's distinctive palette of bright colors. The justices enter the building through a multistory arched portico that rests on three grand pylons tinted in a sequence of green, yellow, and orange. The design is meant to express not only the "Majesty of the Law" but also the hope that the law will provide "an 'umbrella of shelter' . . . to the ordinary citizen."[25]

Shelter is certainly what the young couples need. They come to him, Justice Ahluwalia explained, on the run from disapproving elders, "hiding themselves in the corridors of the court, chased by the parents accompanied by musclemen armed with weapons." Their offense? Falling in love and intending to marry inside their clan—breaking the rules of their *gotra*. They petition Justice Ahluwalia for "solace and balm."

While the judge had long tried to help—for intercaste marriages are perfectly legal under the Hindu Marriage Act of 1955 and intra-*gotra* marriages are legitimate under the Hindu Marriage Disabilities Removal Act of 1946—the problem had grown too large for him and his colleagues to handle. "The scene is no different on other days when the court is functioning and deciding the cases regularly," he stated. "When the arrears of cases are mounting, the High Court is flooded with petitions." The backlog was overwhelming. Greater legislative and executive action was needed.

"The state is a mute spectator," the judge lamented, in words that would be taken up by lawyers and activists. "When shall the state awake from its slumber?"[26]

Justice Ahluwalia's plea highlights the complex, transitional state of legal development in India, which rests on a thoroughly progressive, liberal vision of law it has yet to fully realize. As Markandey Katju, former justice of the Indian Supreme Court and now chairman of the Press Council of India, once put the issue, referencing a couplet by the modern Urdu poet Firaq Gorakhpuri, in Indian legal and social affairs "everything is in flux, neither night nor day, neither the old order nor the new."[27] Like many developing nations around the world, India is still struggling to overcome the rule of the clan.

In India that struggle takes many forms, but one that has attracted special attention in recent years is the conflict between the national rule of law and the customary local clan councils known as *khap panchayats*. A sort of shadow town council composed not of elected representatives but rather of ten to fifteen senior community figures who share a common race, religion, and ethnicity—and whose decisions affect only citizens with the same characteristics—a *khap panchayat* is a political and judicial body of clan elders.

Where they exist, especially in the northwest, *khap panchayats* exercise as much force over clan members as does the state. "We do not know what the law is," one villager not far from Delhi explained to a reporter from *The New York Times* in 2011. "We only know what is decided by the khap panchayat. Here it is not the Supreme Court that decides. It is the khap panchayat that decides."[28]

While *khap panchayats* are formally distinct from the lawfully elected village councils known as *gram panchayats*, which are part of the Indian political structure, their power is frequently underwritten by members of local government. Just as in the West an elected town council might hesitate before challenging the views of community leaders, so *gram panchayats* rarely contest the authority of local clans. As scholar Prem Chowdhry notes, elected village leaders in fact often "seek to emerge as supporters" of *khap panchayat* decisions.[29]

Clan members often ask *khap panchayats* to settle disputes because they deliberate swiftly. Not being bound by requirements to provide due process, they are typically more efficient than formal Indian courts—which, like Justice Ahluwalia's chambers, are backlogged with work. Their rulings are also enforced through the especially powerful mechanism of social sanctions, from ostracism to economic marginalization.

And they are unencumbered by the strictures of modern liberal individualism.

The anti-individualism of *khap panchayats*—and the struggle of Indian liberals against the rule of the clan—is embodied most vividly in the young couples seeking protection beneath the arches of Le Corbusier's court building in Chandigarh.[30] The reasonable fear that drives them is that they will be victims of the ultimate punishment sanctioned by clan elders for violating the complex marital rules of Indian clans: murder, killing in the name of clan honor.

The available statistics are untrustworthy, for "honor killings" are clandestine affairs, but it is clear that they occur regularly across India.[31] Honor killings are typically brutal and frequently savage. In a recent widely reported case from Karoda, two lovers, Manoj and Babli, eloped and married in Chandigarh. Soon after, they were chased down by the bride's family and dragged from a bus on the highway to Delhi. Manoj was strangled with a noose, and the bride's brother forced Babli to drink pesticide. Their two bodies were then dumped into a canal.

The killing was undertaken on orders of a *khap panchayat*.

Such murders are hardly limited to India. It is likely that many thousands of honor killings take place each year around the world.[32]

Not all societies governed by the rule of the clan practice killing in the name of group honor. Moreover, societies that do engage in it vary widely. Yet wherever it exists honor killing is essential to the clan's system of kin solidarity and governance.

The work of feminist social and political activists, such as the Jordanian journalist Rana Husseini, has allowed liberals to begin to grasp not only the problem posed by honor killings but also the logic that produces them. In societies based on the solidarity of the extended kin group, maintained through the cultural circuitry of honor and shame, the murder of one's own family member may at times make perfect sense. It can be understood to be as just and right according to the duties of customary law as it is wrong within the ideals of liberal individualism.

In clan societies, the social value of a kin group is based on its collective honor. A clan's honor derives from various sources, including the prestige and renown of past lineage members, but it depends at each moment on the individual members of the clan abiding by the strict behavioral obligations of community norms. The demands tend to fall especially heavily on women, whose honor is maintained above all through sexual modesty, though men possess substantial duties as well—witness the code of *pashtunwali*.

If one member of the group behaves contrary to the demands of honor, the entire group is diminished in social standing. A forbidden marriage or sexual union can cost a family its social and cultural solvency. The only way for a family to regain its lost honor is to restore its fidelity to community norms, which often requires killing the transgressor, for sexual honor is an all-or-nothing virtue. It can never be recovered through compensatory behaviors after it is lost.

Honor killing is not an act of individual vengeance or enraged punishment. The perpetrators of honor killings consider themselves to be upholding the most deeply held values of their families and communities. In journalistic reports, uncles calmly explain why they killed their nieces, brothers contemptuously call for their sisters to die, and fathers proudly describe how they maintained their family honor by killing their own daughters.[33]

It is powerful logic—so strong that it can override even the strongest liberal legal norms. Honor killings take place today in the most advanced liberal democracies of Europe and North America, perpetrated by immigrants from societies in which group honor runs deeper into private affairs than the state's writ.[34]

•

Honor killing is but an extreme instance of the core cultural values of societies of Status. It lays bare the mechanisms by which clan societies confer supreme value on group solidarity at the expense of individual freedom.

The stubborn persistence of honor killing also suggests why the rule of the clan continues to shape the lives of people wherever the state is absent or weak. Honor killing illustrates not only the diminished place of the individual in societies organized on the basis of kin solidarity. It also illustrates the depth of solidaristic feeling the rule of the clan provides, a feeling so deep it can lead parents to murder their own children.

In India, the central government is struggling to short-circuit the logic of honor killing by quashing *khap panchayats*. "There is nothing honourable in such killings," declared Justice Katju in *Arumugam Servai v. State of Tamil Nadu* (2011). "They are nothing but barbaric and shameful acts of murder." Interference with personal marital choice "is wholly illegal and has to be ruthlessly stamped out."[35]

In an important step toward this goal, the Law Commission of India recently introduced a proposal to criminalize meeting "to deliberate on, or condemn any marriage . . . on the basis that such marriage has dishonoured the caste or community tradition or brought disrepute to all or any of the persons forming part of the assembly or the family or the people of the locality concerned." Violating the law would bring a three-year prison sentence and a fine of up to thirty thousand rupees.[36]

In his opinion calling for the ruthless stamping out of *khap panchayats*, Justice Katju begins with two revealing epigrams. The first diagnoses the obstacles faced by liberals seeking to reform societies in the grip of clannism. It is the couplet from poet Firaq Gorakhpuri's figurative invocation in Urdu of life in a transitional age: "Har zarre par ek qaifiyat-e-neemshabi hai—Ai saaqi-e-dauraan yeh gunahon ki ghadi hai." Everything is in flux, neither night nor day, neither the old order nor the new.

The second articulates liberal reformers' unyielding aspirations. It is the second sentence of the American Declaration of Independence: "We hold these truths to be self-evident, that all men are created equal, that they are endowed by their Creator with certain inalienable Rights, that among these are Life, Liberty, and the pursuit of Happiness."

EIGHT

FEUD AS AN INSTRUMENT OF HARMONY
THE PHILIPPINES

Neighbors said that Khalil's voice could "quench the thirst of the farmers." His father must have been proud of him. The Maranao people of the Philippines are renowned for their arts and crafts: traditional costumes in a peacock's array of colors, fine ornamented brass, beautiful wood carving, and dances rooted deep in their pre-Islamic past. Khalil sang regularly at weddings, wakes, and harvest festivals. Sometimes he would even sing for an audience from afar through a two-way radio.

Tragically, it was Khalil's voice that set in motion the events leading to his father's death in January 2004.

Khalil's story is a tale about a place often described as "a land of promise": Mindanao, an ethnically diverse and fertile island at the southern end of the Philippine archipelago. Geography, climate, natural resources, and native talent all suggest it should enjoy peace and prosperity. Yet Mindanao is poor, violent, and unstable, a place where elections invariably bring killing.

Many factors prevent Mindanao from thriving. They include a Spanish colonial past, the mixed blessing of the Philippines' "special relationship" with the United States, the vexed relations between Muslim Moros and Christian leaders on the main island of Luzon, and a violent separatist and independence movement fought by the Moro Islamic Liberation Front (MILF).

In addition, as Khalil's father well knew—for he had come to the village of Ranon to escape it—the factors include the interclan violence that Filipinos call *rido*.

This is how *rido* worked against Khalil's family. It is a modern-day story of *Romeo and Juliet,* except that it's horribly real. My account is taken from a study by the Asia Foundation on what can be done to manage *rido* and break its cycle of killing. The names of the participants have been changed.[1]

Khalil's father, a farmer, had moved to Ranon from Sabarang in flight from the violence that "his cousins [had] brought to [his] clan." He hadn't studied beyond the second grade, but he was astute enough to hate conflict. He and his wife raised seven children, until Khalil was born, soon after which his wife passed away.

Khalil didn't like farming, or fishing, and he avoided spending time at home. Instead, he spent most of his days with his paternal aunt in Kamala, a village a few miles away. She was the mother he had lost. He would do household chores for her and village farmers would ask him to sing to them with his beautiful voice. Radio operators introduced him to Jalila and the two fell in love.

Jalila was part of a respected Moro family, one said to possess the "three Gs" of Filipino political life: gold, goons, and guns.

When Jalila was married off to another man, Khalil became disconsolate, until he learned that she had rebuffed her intended husband and refused to consummate the marriage. The couple lived and slept apart, and Jalila still had her heart set on Khalil. Indeed, her male relatives suspected that her relationship with Khalil had already become physical. After all, Khalil was once found holding Jalila's cell phone, and they were known to send letters and text messages to each other.

Khalil was warned. He prudently stopped visiting his aunt.

Then someone started a rumor. Khalil's family, it was claimed, was "mocking Jalila's kin" by claiming that their clan leader, or *datu,* a local warlord, was weak. Gossip was that the *datu* had allowed Khalil to continue his liaison with Jalila by "distancing himself from the problem."

The moon was full on January 8 when sixteen armed men arrived in a van and waited for dawn. After morning prayers, while Khalil's family was bathing in a nearby river, four of the men entered his house. Jalila's family later claimed that the four were "novices with firearms."

Khalil hid beneath his bed mat and pillows. Then, when he had the chance, he leapt from the window in his underwear and a wrap and bolted toward the river, fleeing a hail of bullets.

As he swam to safety, a stray bullet wounded a nine-year-old girl.

Shockingly—or, under the logic of the clan, just as one might expect—the bloody accident only spurred the attackers on to more violence. They had hoped simply to injure Khalil in their raid, but now they felt bound to "kill a kin of Khalil as well." The implication is that they wanted to avoid seeming bumbling and ineffective.

So they returned to Khalil's home and shot his father eight times with an M16 rifle.

Khalil's family informed the police, but they refused to pursue the matter. Even if they had thought it proper to become embroiled in a case of *rido*, there were only five police officers in the area: the rest of the force "had transferred elsewhere to avoid involvement in clan feuds."

Blood began to boil. Some of Khalil's cousins were members of the nearby unit of the MILF, and they vowed revenge. After one of Jalila's uncles expressed a desire for conciliation, the clan *datu* responded: "What has happened to him . . . ? Is he turning into a woman? They started this conflict! For mocking me I shall send four Datus . . . as angels of death against them."

Fortunately, cooler heads ultimately prevailed—a wise local woman interceded. Women often have a hand in settling feuds in the Philippines. In this respect they play a role similar to that of the leopard-skin chiefs among the Nuer. Associated with a principle of "general fertility," they symbolize "the communal need for peace and the recognition of moral rights in the community of men."[2]

The female mediator and other community leaders were able in time to bring the families together for a settlement. Jalila's family admitted to violating the honor of Khalil's family, and presented them with 100,000 Philippine pesos (about two thousand dollars) and the M16 rifle that had killed Khalil's father—blood money.

Four months after the killing, a ceremony was held inside a mosque in Mangawan. The parties "swore upon the Holy Qur'an that they forgave one another; that from now on, they were brothers; and no *rido* shall happen between their families out of the *rido* that was settled. They pledged obedience to Allah."

Needless to say, for Khalil's father it was too late. But all things considered, for the community as a whole, events could have been worse— indeed, ironically, as is often the case in a feud, the customary legal principles of *rido* brought various factions of the community together: Khalil's immediate family and his vengeance-seeking cousins, for instance, and ultimately Khalil's and Jalila's family in the communal meal at their settlement. Social conflict and cohesion went hand in glove.

•

Feuds are a special form of violence. As anthropologist Christopher Boehm notes, they differ from wars because of their scale—wars often involve great battles, whereas feuds generally proceed on the basis of targeted killing. Likewise, they differ from raids because of their purpose—the goal of a raid is to acquire goods, whereas feuds redress lost honor. And they differ from duels because of their focus—duels involve individuals, whereas feuds involve groups.[3]

But above all, as we have seen, what makes feuds special is that they are governed by a unique set of rules, which have long made feuding an instrument of rough social harmony. A kin group is dishonored through the actions of another kin group. The dishonored group retrieves its honor by killing a member of the offending family, in the process coming into an alliance with other close kin ("when Z^1 fights Y^1, Z^1 and Z^2 unite as Y^2 . . ."). Then the killing of a family member of equivalent value takes place, some offer for compensation and reconciliation is made, perhaps through a mediator—and social equilibrium is restored, at least temporarily.

Feud may seem patently irrational. That's why so many authors, since well before Shakespeare's day, have used it as a symbol of a world gone mad. It is, however, quite reasonable, if not inevitable, under the circumstances in which it occurs. To see why, it's helpful to think about feud as a tool in a legal toolbox.

Every community has goals that it deems fundamentally important, that express its basic needs or values. In liberal societies these goals include democratic accountability, individual freedom, and economic prosperity. The basic goals of some nonliberal societies include the leveling of class distinctions, as was the case in the Soviet Union, or upholding religious unity, as in contemporary Saudi Arabia.

A society's constitution is a collection of legal tools designed to achieve its basic goals. The United States achieves democratic account-ability through the schedule of regular congressional and presidential elections; it preserves political freedom by placing some matters, such as speech, outside the power of lawmakers (as demanded by the legal tool known as the First Amendment); it fosters economic prosperity by giving Congress the right to regulate commerce and to grant patents (through Article I, Section 8 of the Constitution).

All constitutional tools come with costs, no matter how well they achieve the goals for which they are designed. The American Constitu-tion, for instance, seeks to prevent the federal government from acting tyrannically. One way it does so is by creating a moderately strong firewall between the legislative, executive, and judicial branches. This firewall, known as the separation of powers, generally works well at pre-venting the undue concentration of authority in a single government branch, but under certain conditions it can also cause political gridlock. This cost is significant, but it is one the Constitution contemplates as an acceptable price for maintaining liberty.

Just as with any box of hammers, wrenches, and pliers you might have in your own basement, different constitutional tools can be used to achieve the same goal. A culture of group honor and feud is a tool used to achieve the goal of community order and harmony in the face of in-evitable human conflict. It is used in societies in which the constitu-tional tool employed to achieve that end in modern liberal states—a robust executive authority—isn't on hand.

When modern legal tools aren't available, the most effective legal mechanism for maintaining order is a tool that was invented millennia ago: a culture of group honor, collective kin responsibility, and feud.

The structure of feud is identical in all the societies that practice it. While there are, of course, local variations, feud's basic form is the same in stateless societies, societies with an incomplete state, and societies where the state is weak. Look to biblical Israel, medieval Iceland, Nuer-land, contemporary Albania, Baluchistan, the Swat Valley, or advanced but rickety constitutional democracies like the Philippines, and you will find substantially the same story told over and again: lost honor, targeted killing, the formation of kin alliance, reciprocal killing, peacemakers, blood money, harmony.[4]

•

Feud is the reason why human societies rarely break down into a war of all against all. But it comes with many costs—costs that, from a liberal perspective, are unacceptably high. Moreover, the costs reveal exactly why the rule of the clan is philosophically contrary to the most essential liberal ideals.

The costs all arise from the same factors that prompt societies to use feud as a legal tool in the first place: the lack of an effective state dedicated to public purposes and grounded in a common public identity.

One cost is that, especially in more developed, complex societies, kin-based feuds can become entangled with more general social and political conflicts. When they do so, ever-larger segments of a society can be pulled into their vortex.

In the central Mindanao province of North Cotabato, for example, a fierce battle took place in 1989 between soldiers and paramilitaries in the enclave of San Roque and members of the MILF from the village of Gligli. The battle involved tanks, artillery, and aerial bombs; it lasted for three days; it displaced thousands of people; and it left Gligli a burnt shambles.[5]

The incident did not begin with a firefight between pro-government paramilitaries and MILF rebels. Nor did it start with an outrage between Christians and Muslims. Instead, it began with a game of basketball.

Two groups of youngsters from the villages were playing against each other, and there was a fight. The boys complained to their families. The families in each village were bound together by thick webs of kinship. Each village and its families were associated with either pro- or anti-government forces. And from there, with seemingly inexorable logic, the courtside fight developed into a family feud that developed into a major battle between rival armies.

In the case of Jalila and Khalil, the female community leader who brought the two families together managed to avoid such a cataclysmic outcome. As soon as she learned that some of Khalil's cousins were members of the local MILF, she went directly to the municipal battalion commander. He then "wired all his men in Ranon, including the cousins of Khalil," and ordered them to keep the MILF out of the family dispute.

Without an effective state, feuds also can continue for many years, indeed for decades, even coming to define the community itself. In one Albanian village north of Shkodra in 2005, two families were involved in a feud, sanctioned by the customary Albanian law known as *kanun*, that began more than sixty years before.[6]

"Five years ago," one refugee from the fight told the BBC, "the family of a man who was killed came out of the blue—they said to me that my father was involved in the killing of [their] uncle, so they'd come to seek blood." The most prized target was the man's son.

"I asked the elders of the village that I used to live in if they knew anything about it," the man explained. "As far as they were concerned, my father wasn't involved."

From a liberal perspective, feuding societies possess a dreadful persistence of memory.

•

In addition, as indicated earlier, feuds can escalate, and potentially spin out of control, when its participants fail to abide by its rules of equivalence. Sometimes this failure can take place by accident or recklessness, as in the case of Jalila's "novice" kin.

But it can take place by design as well. One of the greatest of the Icelandic saga tales, *Njal's Saga*, which is set around the time of the conversion of the island to Christianity, describes a steadily escalating feud between the families of Gunnar and Njal. Gunnar is a tall, blond, blue-eyed Norseman renowned for both his strength and his reluctance to fight. He's a gentle giant. We met him in chapter 5 as he looked back upon the "pale fields and mown meadows" of his homestead while contemplating his possible exile.[7] Njal is a wise, clear-sighted farmer known for his knowledge of law and for one physical peculiarity: he is unable to grow a beard.

The two are close, if unlikely, friends. But their friendship is strained over and again by the actions of their kin.

One evening Njal's wife, Bergthora, tells Gunnar's wife, Hallgerd, to move and give up her place at a feast table—she tells her, essentially, to give way to someone more important. Both Bergthora and Hallgerd are proud women, and touchy about their honor, perhaps even more than Jalila's *datu*. Hallgerd is deeply insulted.[8]

"There's not much to choose between you and Njal," she announces to the table. "You have gnarled nails on every finger"—a sign, it was thought, of nymphomania—"and he's beardless."

"That's true," replies Bergthora, "and yet we don't hold it against each other. But your [former] husband Thorvald was not beardless, and yet you had him killed."

Hallgerd turns to her husband. "There's little use to me in being married to the most manly man in Iceland," she asserts, "if you don't avenge this, Gunnar."

Gunnar sensibly goes home, refusing "to be a cat's-paw" for his hot-headed wife.

Later, while Gunnar is at an assembly meeting, Hallgerd orders her slave Kol to kill Bergthora's slave Svart. Kol complies by sinking an axe into Svart's head.

After the murder is discovered, Gunnar and Njal meet to decide what to do.

"You must not let her have her way in everything," says Njal.[9]

Gunnar tells his friend to set the blood-money price himself. He then pays Njal the twelve ounces of silver he requests. Khalil's family and Jalila's family, meeting together in the mosque of Mangawan, came to precisely this type of agreement. Rather than a bag of silver, the blood-money price was 100,000 pesos and a valuable and symbolic weapon.

The two heroes depart as friends. Unlike the agreement between Khalil's and Jalila's families, however, this settlement doesn't last. Bergthora breaks the settlement by ordering another killing, which is then settled—after which Hallgerd breaks the settlement by ordering an even more significant killing—and so on. Eventually the feud draws in the heroes' own sons.

Without a larger force to intervene to bring feud to a close, the exchange of reciprocal violence can be ratcheted up until a community implodes in bloodshed. This outcome is especially likely when the ancient legal tool of feud is conducted with weaponry built for warfare by modern nation states.

•

But the most significant cost of feud—and the reason this ancient institution sets into clear relief the ideals of modern liberal society—is the toll it takes on the individual.

Feud puts individuals in fear. Feuding societies abound with stories like that of Khalil's father, who left his home village to escape vendetta.

In Albania, so many families live in fear of feud that the ministry of education has established a special program to ensure that children from feuding families receive proper schooling. Local authorities are forced to seek out truants who are in hiding.[10]

"The police is not involved here, because this has to do with Kanun," explains the daughter-in-law of an Albanian man in hiding because of an event that took place in 1945. "It's between the families. If we go and ask for the police to help this thing will get even worse."

Some Albanian families build walls around their gardens to protect themselves from revenge attacks.

In addition to putting people in fear, feud diminishes the very concept of the individual because as a legal tool it was designed by the course of human evolution with groups rather than individuals in mind.

In liberal societies, the goal of the legal system is to assign responsibility to particular people and to pursue justice on behalf of individuals as members of a larger public—to give each person his or her due. The goal of feud, indeed the goal of all the traditional mechanisms of customary dispute resolution in clan society, is to reestablish interfamilial harmony and community solidarity.

When Khalil's family and Jalila's family settled their *rido*, the men who shot Khalil's father eight times with an M16 were not put in prison. Instead, they are likely to have been present at the communal feast, or *kanduri*, that marked the final stage in the mediation process. Nor was the goal of Khalil's family to seek justice on behalf of Khalil's father. Rather, it was to retrieve the lost honor of the kin group as a whole.

The heart of the feuding process beats with the principle that individuals have no legal identity independent of their kin. Harms they suffer are recognized as injuries to the group. Actions taken in response to those harms are pursued by the group on its own behalf. Solutions are defined in collective terms.

In this, feud is but a particular instance of a more general dynamic of the rule of the clan. In societies with limited or weak states, the lack of a robust government whose power is exercised in the name of the public means that the individual lacks Hisham Sharabi's "claim to autonomous right."

The individual is submerged within the corporate groups that step into the breach of state power. When the state is absent, when the notion of a common public life is lacking, so is the most cherished principle of liberal society: the autonomy and freedom of the person.

But societies governed by the rule of the clan can develop and maintain legal and political structures that treat individuals as worthy in themselves. Numerous societies across the globe and throughout history have done so. By considering the processes by which the rule of the clan grows into the rule of law, citizens of modern liberal nations can appreciate what we might do to facilitate this transformation today in nations like the Philippines, Albania, and Pakistan. These are issues I consider in the following two chapters.

PART FOUR

THE TRANSFORMATION
OF THE CLAN

How do societies move from Status to Contract? How do peoples governed by the rule of the clan transform into nations guided by the liberal rule of law? How can reformers within clan societies build states that treat individuals as worthy in themselves, as citizens, rather than as members of their kin groups? And how can liberals facilitate this transformation in ways that are both effective and ethical?

These are vital questions for liberals across the globe. Both citizens of liberal nations and liberal reformers within clan societies need to understand how societies can best develop state institutions that are dedicated to the public interest and capable of fostering modern individualism. Doing so will create an enduring link between the long-term security of liberal states and the growth of personal freedom as a lived reality for people across the world.

Unfortunately, for many people these questions—to say nothing of their answers—are profoundly suspect. Posed in a public forum almost anywhere in the world today, they would quickly elicit pointed, often strident, criticism. Skeptics would claim that seeking to advance liberal values in traditional societies is an act of Western cultural arrogance. They might also charge proponents of those values with hypocrisy or, perhaps worse, with naïveté, declaring that Western powers use the language of liberal rights to conceal their true goal of extracting the world's economic resources for themselves.

Such criticism is tragically mistaken. It saps political support for indigenous liberal reformers and puts the security of liberal nations at risk. Yet it is wholly understandable. Western cultural arrogance can be breathtaking and pretense has been a recurrent fact of the exercise of Western power.

In particular, even for many people who themselves enjoy the personal freedom guaranteed by a liberal state, the question of how other societies move from Status to Contract seems irredeemably tainted by its association with the history of European colonialism. European efforts to modernize or, in the idiom of the day, "civilize" native populations brutally tore the customary social and political fabric of the Middle East, sub-Saharan Africa, the Americas, and large parts of Asia. As a result, many Europeans became rich, and many colonized societies are still mending the damage.

Colonial efforts to foster changes in societies of Status came in many forms. Most notably, some Western states simply supplanted native legal systems with their own. The approach taken by France in West Africa was especially comprehensive. Under the French policy of direct rule, local village councils, tribal chiefs, and kinship groups were all replaced by the French colonial administrator. He was, as one administrator wrote, "responsible for order, head of the militia, judge, census taker, tax collector, bookkeeper, supervisor of labor, constructor of roads and buildings, organizer of markets, urban planner, nurseryman, in charge of the progress of the economy and of public health, protector of the forests, inspector of education, [and] chief of the Europeans."[1]

In the early years of its colonial project, France had hoped to extend the ideals and practices of Napoleonic law to the new potential citizens of the countries whose raw material wealth it was seeking to appropriate. Its efforts at legal reform were accompanied by programs of cultural reeducation intended to mold native peoples into modern Western individuals. The United States, Australia, and, in the twentieth century, the Soviet Union and Japan all undertook similar colonial cultural reeducation programs in the name of their own political ideals.

But in time the French accepted a two-tiered system in which a precious few Africans were deemed *citoyens* while the vast majority were considered simply "subjects." The latter were required to abide by French administrative directives even as they possessed a limited array of French rights. Disputes among them could be resolved in the first instance according to native law, but only as applied by French administrators or subject to their full appellate review.

These policies were not without benefits from a liberal perspective. French colonialists limited slavery, polygamy, and other social evils, and they curtailed many clan and intertribal feuds. But the impact on native legal institutions was disastrous, and the human costs were incalculable. French policy undermined indigenous, local legal forms while bequeathing to Africa a fully centralized state that could be used for the worst purposes by postindependence rulers.

British policy in Africa followed a somewhat different course, but that course brought its own ill consequences. Rather than govern colonial possessions directly through a central bureaucracy, the British pursued a policy of indirect rule. Under the British model, customary law and legal practices such as communal land ownership were held to be legitimate, at least within limits. While many colonialists expected that traditional legal forms and the modes of life they supported would diminish in the course of social and economic development, they argued that in the immediate term most customary practices of subject peoples should be given government sanction. To do so, they gave their support to the institutional actors who seemed the most proper administrators of customary law—tribal chiefs.

Before colonialism, tribal chiefs had been subject to a variety of local political controls. They existed within a network of popular obligations. When the British treated chiefs as determiners of the meaning of customary law, they put the massive power of the empire behind the institution of the chieftaincy itself, amplifying its potential for corruption and despotism. As the chiefs of sub-Saharan Africa lost the income and power they had once derived through war, raiding, the slave trade, and the sale of ivory (practices the British sought to prohibit), they compensated by seeking other sources of wealth—in particular, they "claimed as customary every right that would enhance their control over others, particularly those [who were] socially weak."[2]

In recognizing customary law, in other words, the British transformed it. They upset the political equilibrium that had enabled customary law to operate effectively. The roots of postcolonial African despotism are partly African, but they are also substantially European.

Given the devastation wrought by colonialism, it is understandable that many people are critical of liberals today who seek to foster cultural and political change in traditional societies. A well-justified reputation for hypocrisy doesn't wash off easily. Indeed, liberals must not dismiss the criticism. They must welcome it as an aid to preventing future errors that would tarnish liberalism itself.

But the hypocrisy of the past is in the end no argument against the legitimacy or wisdom of policies in the present. The goal of encouraging clan societies to develop the cultural values and legal and political institutions that underpin the rule of law is both crucial in pragmatic terms and right in moral ones. These values and institutions are not identical to those of the West but rather consistent with universal liberal ideals and with the personal freedom of the individual. Moreover, liberals can claim some significant success in their democratic state-building efforts, from which policy makers still have much to learn. For example, the modern United States was built on such a state-building program in the former Confederacy.[3]

The question liberals face is thus not *whether* to encourage societies to move from Status to Contract, but *how*. Scholars from a variety of disciplines are working to answer this question, as are activists and traditional political leaders on the ground. The chapters that follow offer a perspective on the issue by looking to the past—to Anglo-Saxon England and early Islamic Arabia. These two medieval societies, in many ways profoundly different from one another, lie at the symbolic heart of two of the most influential traditions of contemporary political thought: Anglo-American liberalism and political Islam. Considering their stories of state development side by side—considering how both Germanic kingship and the early Islamic state emerged out of clan societies— sheds a powerful light on what it takes to overcome the rule of the clan today. It also can point to a shared set of aspirations and a common political self-definition uniting liberals from radically distinct cultural traditions, Christian and Islamic, West and East.

The histories of Anglo-Saxon England and early Islamic Arabia dramatically illustrate how the rule of law was built, brick by brick, from efforts to counter the drawbacks of the rule of the clan. They show as well that *persons* began to be treated as *individuals*, rather than as members of status-based groups, within the context of a robust state dedicated to public ideals. And they suggest that the kind of state capable of guaranteeing modern individual freedom developed on the basis of a common identity that transcends extended family membership—a common identity that was itself founded on a new understanding of law.

Both Christianity and Islam played an essential role in these parallel histories. Seeking modern equivalents to the role religion played in overcoming the rule of the clan, I suggest that today liberals can help diminish the political significance of kinship by encouraging the spread of new social media and the growth of the middle-class professions. The twin stories of Germanic and Arabian constitutional development also indicate that state formation in clan societies is most effective when state builders work not against clans but rather with and through them. Overcoming the rule of the clan must be a local, quintessentially political process. It must involve difficult, messy compromises and make use of traditional institutions for modern ends if it is to be both legitimate and enduring.

Together the histories of Anglo-Saxon England and early Islamic Arabia offer a common cultural resource with which to imagine the future beyond the rule of the clan. They offer a story liberals can tell ourselves about who we are and about the shared future we are building, wherever we may live.[4]

NINE

FROM KIN TO KING
STATE DEVELOPMENT IN
ANGLO-SAXON ENGLAND

In 973, in an abbey in Bath, a great Anglo-Saxon king lay prostrate before an altar while the archbishop of Canterbury wept with joy.

The king was Edgar I, known as Edgar the Peaceful, and at age thirty, he was in the fourteenth year of an exceedingly successful reign. Under his rule, England revamped its currency, streamlined its central administration, sustained its military authority over a once-restive island, and recognized its counties along lines that would remain essentially unchanged until 1974. The archbishop was Dunstan, a determined reformer of the English church and advocate for its monastic interests. Overcome by the king's humility, he sang the hymn *Te Deum* through his tears—"We praise thee O God: we acknowledge thee to be the Lord." A half century later, he would be canonized as a saint.

The occasion for Edgar's pious self-effacement and Dunstan's joy was the king's coronation. Tellingly, the ceremony was held on Pentecost, when Christians celebrate the descent of the Holy Spirit on the apostles. The age of the king, too, was significant: the same at which Jesus began his ministry.

The ritual began when Edgar, wearing a crown and holding a scepter, was led into the abbey by a parade of white-robed clerics: "a crowd of priests," in the words of the *Anglo-Saxon Chronicle*, "a throng of monks . . . in counsel sage."[1] The ensuing ceremony was filled with all the pageantry of great royal events in England today. The king would be anointed with holy oil from an animal's horn. He would be given a ring, a sword, a crown, a scepter, and a staff as symbols of his rule.

And the abbey would resound with the joyous antiphon from 1 Kings, "Zadok the Priest and Nathan the Prophet."

But in constitutional terms the most important part of the ritual came when Edgar spoke, shortly after clerics raised him from his position of humility before the altar. For it was then that he swore his coronation oath, making a public promise to rule according to certain principles. His words have echoed as loudly across constitutional history as the anthem "Zadok the Priest" echoed in the abbey at Bath that day. "In the name of the Holy Trinity I promise three things to the Christian people my subjects," he declared. "First, that God's Church and all Christian people of my realm shall enjoy true peace; second, that I forbid to all ranks of men robbery and all wrongful deeds; third, that I urge and command justice and mercy in all judgments, so that the gracious and compassionate God who lives and reigns may grant us all His everlasting mercy."[2]

In modern terms, the king had pledged to protect the church; to safeguard public order by applying the law to all persons regardless of rank; and to govern according to an abstract, Christian ideal of justice.

Edgar's pledge is the first coronation oath in the Anglo-Saxon historical record. And though it may not have been the earliest ever taken by an English king, it clearly marked Anglo-Saxon government as having come a long way from its roots in a very different way of life.

What are the preconditions for modern clan societies to develop the rule of law? What are the fruits of that transformation? The English Middle Ages—the story leading to Edgar's coronation oath and beyond—offers important clues.

•

To tell that story, we need to turn back the clock to the first century of the Common Era. There we find an archaic people living on the edges of the Roman Empire in northern Europe, a people known collectively as the Germanic tribes. They are the ancestors of the Anglo-Saxons, who share their blood and bone.

Who were these forebears of the English? "The various peoples of Germany are separated from the Gauls by the Rhine, from the Raetians and Pannonians by the Danube, and from the Sarmatians and Dacians by mountains—or, where there are no mountains, by mutual fear."[3] So begins the *Germania*, a celebrated account of the tribes written in about the year 98 by the Roman orator, public official, and historian Tacitus. Scholars know little about Tacitus's life, but he had likely served as an administrator or legion commander for the Empire and may have seen the tribes up close. His sharp observations depict the tribes with an ethnographic richness that can still transport modern readers back to the ancient world.

The Germans live in rude wooden dwellings, writes Tacitus, in communities scattered across meadows. They dress plainly, in cloaks fastened with a simple clasp or thorn. In religion, they worship their deities in sacred groves and forests. In battle, they are courageous and steadfast, fighting with spears and shields while women shout encouragement from the sidelines. When men are not fighting, they pass their days sitting by their hearth fires in their homes, where they receive guests with elaborate meals. "No nation indulges more profusely in entertainments and hospitality," Tacitus observes. "To exclude any human being from their roof is thought impious; every German, according to his means, receives his guest with a well-furnished table."[4]

Tacitus found much to admire in this hardy tribal society. In particular, he thought the Germans possessed a tough-minded, republican simplicity his own countrymen lacked. He might not have been surprised to learn that centuries later they would fan out across Europe and help bring the civilization of Rome to an end. Many modern readers of varying political persuasions have been equally admiring.[5] The tribal commitment to communitarian hospitality, the directness of their spirituality and access to the divine in nature, and their rugged independence are all appealing. Ancient Germanic life as Tacitus described it seems vital and free.

But Tacitus's account also reveals what from a liberal perspective is a grave shortcoming at the heart of Germanic government—a critical constitutional flaw: its radical decentralization. While chiefs and other important men nominally lead the tribes, major decisions are made in common by all male members gathered together under a new or full moon. At these warrior assemblies, when a tribal chief speaks he does so "more because he has influence to persuade than because he has power to command." If his counsel displeases the group, the men "reject [it] with murmurs," and if they approve, they "brandish their spears." Even the tribes' military generals, writes Tacitus, lead "more by example than by authority."[6]

This lack of hierarchy has often struck modern readers as commendable. It would even cause some scholars in the late nineteenth and early twentieth centuries to mistake the Germanic tribes for an archaic protodemocracy, a collection of local communities built on consensus. The influential historian Herbert Baxter Adams, of Johns Hopkins University, titled one of his essays "The Germanic Origin of New England Towns." "The town and village life of New England," he asserted, "is as truly the reproduction of Old English types as those again are reproductions of the village community system of the ancient Germans."[7]

But in fact such radical localism meant that Germanic central government was weak. And this weakness—as in medieval Scotland or in Somalia today—meant that the clans composing the tribes were powerful. They filled the role that is now the province of the state. Most of the seemingly admirable features of Germanic society Tacitus described were built on the foundation of a community of Status.

The sparsely populated settlements he admires were owned not by individuals but rather by extended families. Indeed, land ownership was legally inseparable from clan identity because the tribes lacked the Roman legal concept of the testamentary will, which enabled land to be transferred outside a kin group. The warriors Tacitus praises for their steadfastness fought in wedges "composed of families and clans," with relatives battling side by side.[8] The families he lauds for their hospitality held other families collectively responsible for the wrongs of their members, and they redressed their grievances through the reciprocal violence of the feud. Such feuds threatened public order, Tacitus explains, because "feuds are dangerous in proportion to a people's freedom," growing more volatile the weaker the state.[9]

In short, the ancient Germanic tribes were governed by the rule of the clan.

But not forever. If we follow the descendants of the tribes across hundreds of years of history, as they migrated over the Continent, giving rise in time not only to the Anglo-Saxons but also to many of the major national groups of modern Europe, we can watch their kin-based social organization decline as the authority exercised by their leaders grows.

We can witness the birth of the Germanic state as it wrested power away from family groups.

•

Consider the Salian Franks, a Germanic people living in an area that today includes Belgium and the Netherlands. About four hundred years after Tacitus wrote the *Germania*, the Franks translated their unwritten customary law into a written code, a major step on the path to state development.

The leader who achieved this immense task was King Clovis I, the founder of the Merovingian dynasty. Clovis's second wife, Clotilda, had been a princess of the Burgundian court and she had been raised a Catholic. For many years the queen had sought to turn her pagan husband toward Christianity. She had no success until 496, when Clovis saw his forces foundering under the assault of another Germanic people, the Alamanni, at the battle of Tolbiac. His looming defeat caused him to reconsider his spiritual commitments. According to one account, with "remorse in his heart he burst into tears and cried: 'Jesus Christ, whom Clotilda asserts to be the son of the living God, who art said to give aid to those in distress, and to bestow victory on those who hope in thee, I beseech the glory of thy aid, with the vow that if thou wilt grant me victory over these enemies, and I shall know that power which she says that people dedicated in thy name have had from thee, I will believe in thee and be baptized in thy name.'

"And when he said this," the account continues, "the Alamanni turned their backs, and began to disperse in flight."[10]

The story is too myth-making to be true—it sounds suspiciously like Emperor Constantine's conversion in 312 after the battle of Milvian Bridge—but for whatever reason Clotilda would soon have *her* victory. Whether in genuine thanks for his military success or for some more immediate political reason, Clovis was baptized by the archbishop of Reims in the late fifth or early sixth century.

By this time, many Germanic people had become Christians. But Clovis was noteworthy among Germanic kings of his day for becoming not simply Christian but Catholic. Many of the Germans who converted to Christianity, particularly the Goths, became Arians, a branch of Christianity that rejected the trinitarianism of the Nicene Creed. Arians believed that Christ is not coeternal with God the Father but instead was created by him. Trinitarians believe that God is "three in one."

By affiliating himself with the Catholic Church, Clovis gained an extraordinary institutional advantage as a ruler. In exercising power, Clovis could now draw on the talents of the Catholic hierarchy, the most learned and proficient men of the era. These men included scholars, in particular, who had been trained in Roman jurisprudence. And at Clovis's direction, they brought their technical expertise to bear on the difficult task of codifying Frankish law, completing their work between 507 and 511, more than twenty years before the Roman jurist Tribonian and his colleagues completed the *Corpus Juris Civilis* or Code of Justinian.

The Salic law reveals substantial progress in Germanic state development. For instance, it contains rigorous procedures for the conduct of litigation, a sign that courts had grown in strength and legitimacy. It imposes stern fines on litigants who fail to appear before judicial tribunals, an indication that rulers had bolstered their ability to command rather than merely persuade. The very existence of the code itself, written in Latin, is evidence that Clovis and his staff were looking to the Roman Empire for a stronger, more hierarchical model of law and government than the one offered by the ancient Germanic legal heritage.

At the same time, Tacitus would have easily recognized the society the code depicts. Most of its rules are those of an agricultural people: it contains complex provisions for the theft of pigs, goats, cattle, and other farm animals, each carefully differentiated by type and age. The code also penalizes a host of violent deeds suggestive of a warrior ethos, as when a man "tries to shoot another man with a poisoned arrow" (and misses) or when a man "strikes another man on the head so that the brain shows."[11] Though courts certainly exist, they are not so much independent adjudicative bodies as mere places where disputes are resolved.

And, most important, family groups remain essential units of the social order. Land is still owned jointly by clans. The law still lacks the concept of a testamentary will. Kin groups continue to be held collectively accountable for the crimes of their individual members—evidence of a culture of feud.

A dramatic indicator of the legal importance of kinship is evident in the procedures the *Lex Salica* lays down for a man who wishes to remove himself from his kin group and its liabilities. He is instructed to go to court and in the presence of the community "break four sticks of alderwood over his head"—no easy task. Then he is required to "throw them in four bundles into the four corners of the court" and renounce all relations with his family, including any claims to inheritance and collective compensation for the death or injury of its members.[12]

From the standpoint of the consolidation of state authority, the Salic law is a way station in the process of Germanic constitutional development. On the Continent, that process came to a head centuries later with the ascendancy of the Frankish king Charlemagne in the late eighth century. Among the Anglo-Saxons in England, it took place in the ninth century, beginning with the reign of the greatest of the Anglo-Saxon kings, Alfred.

•

The Anglo-Saxon story begins with the fall of Rome.

"Look to your own defense"—that was the pointed advice offered in 410 by the Roman Emperor Honorius to the urban authorities of Britain once the last of Rome's legions had departed for Gaul. After ruling the island for more than 350 years, Rome was leaving Britannia. The western empire was crumbling.

Bereft of Rome's protection, the Britons needed help to resist their enemies the Picts, the "painted" people from modern-day Scotland. They found ready aid across the North Sea from a diverse group of tribes now known collectively as the Anglo-Saxons, the descendants of the warriors Tacitus had portrayed three centuries earlier. According to the *Anglo-Saxon Chronicle*, the first fighters to arrive in Britain were Saxons in 449 under the leadership of two brothers named Hengest and Horsa (the names mean "stallion" and "horse"). In exchange for land and other valuables, they helped the Romano-British warlord Vortigern triumph over his intractable northern neighbors.

In accepting Germanic assistance, however, the Britons were playing with fire. Hengest and Horsa soon sent word home of "the cowardice of the Britons and the excellence of the land," and before long, the Germanic tribes turned on their paymasters.[13] The native British fight against the Anglo-Saxons would later be imaginatively remembered through the legend of Arthur, the heroic king who united the Britons against foreign invasion. The legend is an inspiring one, but in reality the Britons were no match for their enemies. The Germanic tribes relentlessly pushed them westward into Wales and across the channel to Brittany.

The ethnic cleansing was so complete that the modern English language derives extremely few Celtic loanwords from the period (a recent scholar set the "generally accepted" number of loanwords at four, whittled down from an originally proposed list of only fifteen). The language even lacks Celtic loanwords related to farm labor, which one would expect to find had the Britons been enslaved or had children from mixed marriages been raised by Celtic mothers. Recent genetic studies suggest that the Germans killed between 50 and 100 percent of the native population.[14]

With the Britons gone, England was transformed from a Celtic and Roman society into a Germanic one. Most prominently, a centuries-old Christian culture was replaced by animal sacrifice and the worship of Woden. The country reverted to paganism. Language, art, weaponry, housing, and farming techniques all assumed a Germanic form. Even the name *England* means "land of the Angles," one of the Germanic tribes.

The culture of kinship assumed a Teutonic cast as well. The earliest English literary works portray the world beyond a man's kin group as a place of cruel exile. In "The Wanderer," "sorrow upon sorrow attend / the man who must send time and again / his weary heart over the frozen waves" as "the memory of kinsmen sweeps through his mind."[15] Kinship likewise lay at the heart of early Anglo-Saxon law and governance. Most notably, like their ancestors on the Continent, and like most societies without a strong state, the Anglo-Saxons relied on the blood feud as a mechanism for maintaining order and resolving intergroup disputes.

Over time, however, the legal significance of kinship in England began to diminish. The Anglo-Saxons transformed their Germanic constitutional heritage. They overcame the rule of the clan. The precise details of this centuries-long evolution are unknown, and it resulted from numerous intersecting social and economic forces. But the historical record provides clues about the general pathway of change.

Many readers may remember having become surprisingly absorbed during a college literature class in the great Anglo-Saxon epic *Beowulf.* The story of Anglo-Saxon leadership begins with the type of ruler represented by Hrothgar, whom Beowulf helps fight the monster Grendel. In poetry of the time leaders like Hrothgar are often described as "ring-givers" and "gold-friends," because they give their retainers gifts of wealth and weapons and hold lavish feasts in dark mead halls. Their followers know them as flesh-and-blood men, and they are bound to them by ties of personal loyalty. The English word *king* reflects both this early form of Anglo-Saxon leadership and its ancient tribal roots. The king is the son of the kin—a *cyning*.

Recall that among the Germanic tribes described by Tacitus, military "generals" led not so much by authority as through example. This egalitarianism is characteristic of tribal societies around the world. Their social and political organization is based on a fairly even distribution of wealth and a lack of role specialization. By the time in which *Beowulf* is set, however, military conflict, population growth, and increasingly sedentary ways had already begun to accentuate the differences between ranks of men. Germanic society had grown more stratified and hierarchical.

As the Anglo-Saxon tribes spread out across England in the fifth and sixth centuries, the nature of Germanic leadership began to change. Through conquest and alliance, smaller Germanic groups consolidated and merged. Leaders still ruled mainly over peoples related to each other by blood, but the blood tie stretched farther than ever before. Gradually, this difference in degree became a difference in kind. No mere family patriarch or powerful warlord-chieftain, a Germanic ruler became the king of the East Angles or the king of the West Saxons.

This expansion of royal power depended above all on the growing strength of English Christianity. In 596 Pope Gregory I dispatched a group of some forty missionaries, led by the monk Augustine of Canterbury, to convert the Anglo-Saxons to the faith. For the missionaries the prospect of Christianizing the heathen Germanic tribes seemed to grow increasingly intimidating the farther Rome lay behind them, and they soon sent their leader back to the pope with a request to abandon the undertaking. The pope refused, sending back only letters of encouragement. And in fact they soon found success, first with the conversion in 597 of King Ethelbert of Kent.

In time England would possess one of the richest Christian cultures of Europe.

Both king and priest stood to gain much from each other. By converting to Christianity, Anglo-Saxon rulers buttressed their moral legitimacy and accessed the institutional support of the church. Only a few years after King Ethelbert joined the Catholic Church, he issued a code of laws, the first in Old English. In turn, by enabling the growth of royal power, the church secured increasingly effective protection of its interests, especially its ownership of land.

Christianization gradually transformed not only the religious life of Anglo-Saxon rulers and their people but also the very meaning of kingship. It also altered the concept of law to which rulers were responsible. Among the pagan Anglo-Saxons, as among all stateless peoples, law was inseparable from the customs and the interests of the extended family group of the tribe. Christianity introduced a universal set of norms by which rulers were meant to abide, what we know today as the rule of law.[16]

As Germanic society grew increasingly hierarchical, the personal identity of Anglo-Saxon rulers also gradually peeled away from the social core of extended kinship, a process facilitated by the noteworthy role the nuclear family held in European and Germanic society.[17] The growth of a distinct ruling class fostered a role identity even more powerful than collective tribal identity. The stratification of Germanic society made it possible to imagine a collective social identity beyond that of clan or tribe. It made it possible to imagine a common public.

This process was likely fostered when renowned Germanic leaders became responsible for persons who left their birth clans because they had been exiled as punishment for crimes, so-called "broken men." These were men who fled or were exiled from their communities and sought shelter with a different people, under a foreign ruler. As Rudyard Kipling put it in a poem about broken men fleeing to South America: "From ancient tales' renewing, / From clouds we would not clear— / Beyond the Law's pursuing / We fled, and settled here."[18]

Life for these men in their new home was hardly easy. Often, they became the equivalent of slaves. But when substantial numbers of broken men and their descendants were incorporated into an existing lineage group, a critical change began to occur not only in the men themselves but in the leaders of the new society they joined. The leaders developed power outside their own kin group and in time they developed responsibilities and loyalties beyond it as well. The kernel of a public identity, that is, grew from the consciousness of ruling elites whose job responsibilities transcended family ties.

Then, in a pivotal transformation, the power of Anglo-Saxon leaders came to be understood in territorial terms. Their authority extended not so much over a discrete if extended kin group as over a defined geographic area. The king of the *East Angles* became the king of *East Anglia*. The relationship between a ruler and his subjects was no longer exclusively a bond of family or personal loyalty. It was an abstract tie to a figure many persons might never have seen.

These territorial kings ruled over seven major kingdoms—Northumbria, Mercia, East Anglia, Essex, Kent, Sussex, and Wessex. Known as the Heptarchy, they continually struggled against each other for dominance.

The kings of the Heptarchy have a long list of achievements to their credit. Some changed the landscape of their country by constructing grand earthworks such as Offa's Dyke, which extends for scores of miles and even today marks the border between England and Wales. Others fundamentally transformed their economies and enabled economic growth by minting coins. Still others supported the expanding church and spurred innovation in literature and the arts.

Most essential for the future of England, some kings undertook legal reforms that strengthened the power of the state relative to clan groups, particularly by regulating and, in due course, abolishing the kin-based blood feud. Evidence of this process begins to appear especially under King Alfred of Wessex (849–99), commonly known as Alfred the Great. In one of Alfred's *dooms*, or laws, men who come across their enemies are required first to seek royal justice to redress their grievances rather than immediately attacking them at home, unawares:

> We also command that any one knowing his enemy to be at home shall not fight him before demanding justice of him in court. If the accuser has strength to surround and besiege his enemy inside the latter's house, let him be held there seven nights and not attacked so long as he will remain inside . . . If, however, the accuser lacks the strength to besiege his enemy, he shall ride to the alderman and ask him for aid; if the latter refuses him aid, he shall ride to the king before beginning a fight.[19]

As small a matter as it may seem today, the law represented a groundbreaking advance in the power of government—an indication that Anglo-Saxon kings would try to break the cycle of feud and short-circuit the process about which Tacitus had warned seven centuries earlier, in which a weak state enabled clans to undermine public order.

Similar dooms were proclaimed under succeeding Anglo-Saxon and English kings such as Edward (r. 899–924), Aethelstan of Mercia (r. 924–39), and Edgar (r. 959–75).

The curtailment of the feud by the Anglo-Saxon kings had far-reaching implications well beyond the immediate prevention of violence between families. For one, the royal effort to regulate the blood feud went hand in hand with the development of the concept of public order. The same law of Alfred that slowed the cycle of clan retribution, for example, also prohibited fighting in the king's hall. The requirement that peace be kept in the king's personal residence eventually grew into the principle that there ought to be peace over the king's entire realm—the king's peace, which the king had the responsibility to maintain.

Moreover, the effort to limit the feud was linked historically to the emergence of the idea that persons were entitled to protection as individuals per se rather than as members of families. The law that sought to regulate the feud and prevented fighting in the king's hall also included a promise of royal protection for persons without kin. The kinless notably included traveling merchants, selling their wares far from home—demands for individual freedom were made especially by those engaged in commercial exchange. And whereas clannism, to recall Hisham Sharabi's view, "takes away the individual's claim to autonomous right," Anglo-Saxon royal power made such a claim possible.[20]

The regulation of the blood feud, the growth of the notion of public order, and the protection of individuals as such, that is, were all of a historical piece—and all part of the practical expansion of the power of the Anglo-Saxon state.

When Edgar swore his coronation oath in 973 and promised to protect the church, apply the law to all persons regardless of rank, and govern according to a Christian ideal of justice, he thus signaled that his branch of the Germanic family had overcome the weaknesses of its ancient legal heritage, certainly in theory and substantially in fact. With a strong, central royal authority dedicated to the ideal of public order, Anglo-Saxon England laid the constitutional foundation for the liberation of the individual from the rule of the clan and made it possible to conceive of and to vindicate the principle of individual freedom.[21]

TEN

"WE HAVE MADE YOU INTO NATIONS AND TRIBES"

THE VISION OF EARLY ISLAM

When the missionaries sent by Pope Gregory to convert the Anglo-Saxons landed in Kent in 597, the young merchant who would become the prophet of Islam was a recently married man.

Born around 570, Muhammad had spent his early years as a shepherd and occasional trader, gaining a reputation for honesty that earned him the nickname al-Amin, the trustworthy. In 595 he wedded a prosperous businesswoman named Khadija who had hired him to lead trade caravans to Syria and Yemen. When Muhammad began to receive revelations from the Archangel Gabriel around 610, revelations later collected as the Qur'an, Khadija became the first person other than Muhammad himself to accept the new faith of Islam.

At that point Anglo-Saxon Christianity, too, was in its relative infancy. Following the death in 616 of the first Christian Anglo-Saxon ruler, King Ethelbert of Kent, many of his subjects quickly reverted to paganism.

Thereafter, signposts of religious development in England and Arabia appear on the timeline of history in striking parallel.

In 622 Muhammad settled in Medina, migrating from Mecca to escape persecution by tribal elites (the momentous *hijra* marks the first year of the Islamic calendar). In 625 the pagan King Raedwald of East Anglia was buried at Sutton Hoo with two silver spoons bearing the inscriptions "Saul" and "Paul," an indication of the growing influence of Christianity. In 627 the powerful Northumbrian king Edwin was baptized. In 630 Muhammad returned to Mecca in triumph. In 632 Abu Bakr succeeded Muhammad as the first caliph. In 635 the Irish monk

Aidan founded the famed monastery at Lindisfarne. The last pagan Germanic king in England, Arwald of the Isle of Wight, died in 686. By then Islamic forces had broken out of Arabia, set siege to Constantinople, and reached the Indus River.

Although they seem worlds apart, Anglo-Saxon Christianity and early Islam developed simultaneously—two peoples converted to monotheistic faiths at the same time.

Anglo-Saxon England and seventh-century Arabia possess another important similarity as well. Just as the Germanic peoples were once governed by the rule of the clan, so the rule of the clan is inextricable from the early history of Islam—indeed, from its history as a whole. Islam was born within a tribal society; it has been adopted by societies across the globe that have strong, preexisting tribal belief systems; and Muslim thinkers have contemplated the dynamics of group solidarity (*'asabiyya*) for hundreds of years. The medieval scholar Ibn Khaldun even made it central to his theory of history.[1]

Yet Muhammad and the early caliphs, not as outside powers but as indigenous reformers, forged a collective identity, based on a new concept of law, that sought to ameliorate many of the flaws of tribal custom. The story of early Islam is a story of a religious vision that transcended the spiritual particularism and constitutional factionalism of the rule of the clan.

Today many states with majority Muslim populations are engaged in a charged political struggle with powerful clans, including those nations emerging from the spring revolutions in the Middle East and North Africa. This struggle exists not simply in highly tribal societies like Libya and Yemen, but also in worldly, cosmopolitan ones such as Lebanon.[2]

The future of individual freedom for many Muslims will depend to a large degree on the role that clans and, more broadly, clannism, plays in the new social and political order they are building.

There will be many different models for this new order, some of them purely secular and contemporary. But one especially important model, whose meaning will itself be the subject of continuing debate, is provided by Islam's early history and ethical vision.

It is a vision that might also usefully influence liberal reformers in societies well beyond the Middle East and North Africa. For like the history of Anglo-Saxon England, the story of early Islam offers substantial resources for thinking about a common world challenge.

•

In Muhammad's day, much of the Arabian Peninsula was an island of statelessness in a sea of more developed, centralized governments. To the northeast was the Sassanid Empire of the Persians. To the northwest was the Byzantine Empire, the descendant of the empire of Rome. To the south were the kingdoms of northern Yemen. But between these polities was a vast stateless zone.

The constitutional order of the peninsula was based primarily on kinship. A decentralized legal system preserved the power of patrilineal tribes and their clans and subclans, each rooted in its own particular region of the country.[3]

The Quraysh, for instance—Muhammad's tribe—lived around the vital trading center of Mecca and was spread along the Hejaz region bordering the Red Sea. The tribe was divided into a number of distinct units. Among them were the Banu Hashim (the clan of Muhammad and Ali), the Banu Taym, the Banu Adi, and the Banu Umayya. The Arabic term *banu* is the equivalent of the Scottish term *Mac*—thus the clans of the Quraysh were the "descendants" or "children" of Hashim, Taym, and so on. Many Arabs today proudly trace their descent to clans such as these, just as many Scots are proud to be called Macpherson. The modern descendants of the ancient Banu Hashim, for instance, include the current king of Jordan.

Other tribes in seventh-century Arabia included the Banu Bakr, based near the Persian Gulf. The Banu Bakr was composed, among others, of the Banu Shayban, Banu Hanifa, and Banu Yashkur clans. Likewise, there were the Ghatafan, the Asad, the Kinana, the Harith, the Tamim, the Kalb—and a host of other tribes, each with its own array of subgroups, and subsubgroups. The Asad alone included the al-Khayun (which in turn included the al-Hassan, the al-Jayyid, the al-Janaah, and the al-Sheikh); the Bani Askari (which included the al-Abdul Amr, the al-Abeed, the al-Sheikh Ali, and the al-Shaab); the al-Wanis (which included the al-Freeh, al-Khaytan, al-Badir, al-Ghaythan, al-Jasim, al-Shaaf, al-Tarshan, al-Hamad, and al-Khamis)—and more than sixty other separate clans.

In short, the Arabian Peninsula was a segmentary lineage society, governed by the rule of the clan. Indeed, a classic nineteenth-century study of kinship and marriage in early Arabia, written by the Scottish scholar William Robertson Smith, provided an influential model for E. E. Evans-Pritchard as he constructed his anthropological theories about the Nuer.[4]

The tribal organization of Arab society both in the past and, in some parts of the Middle East and North Africa, in the present is one practical reason why many Arabs have prized and cultivated a deep knowledge of patrilineal ancestry. When law and government are structured according to the principles of segmentary lineage, not knowing the details of one's descent is comparable to an American not knowing the name of his or her senators or being unaware that the federal government is divided into three branches. The Arab Bedouin characteristically view people who are ignorant of their lineage "with suspicion" and regard them, in the pointed expression of Jibrail Jabbur, "as deficient in ambition and culture."[5]

As in other segmentary lineage societies, the decentralized constitutional order of Arabia fostered many benefits for its members. These included a host of cultural values that, from a modern liberal perspective, can seem notably superior to our own. For one, Arabian tribal life was deeply egalitarian. Material goods were often held in common and overall differences in wealth were slight (though such differences were becoming greater as Mecca prospered). Tribal life also fostered a renowned code of generosity—the same code of hospitality toward guests Tacitus found among the Germanic tribes. And it produced men celebrated for their bravery, resilience, and personal independence.

Most important of all, Arabian culture was animated by the solidarity of the tribal group, *'asabiyya*. Such cohesion benefited clan members materially, especially in times of trouble, for *'asabiyya* required "boundless and unconditional loyalty to fellow clansmen."[6] Equally significant from a liberal perspective, it provided clan members with a powerful feeling of personal belonging. "I am but the clan of Ghazīya," wrote the ninth-century Syrian poet Abu Tammam, "going astray / If it errs, and led right if it keeps to the way."[7]

These ancient tribal values—egalitarianism, hospitality, bravery, and solidarity—continue to echo powerfully in modern Arab ideals of proper personal behavior. They are values worth affirming.

Yet for all the social and cultural benefits of the tribal order, its drawbacks were profound.

The most prominent deficiency was political. Like all tribal societies, seventh-century Arabia maintained intergroup harmony through the constant threat of blood feud. The peninsula was thus beset by ancient rivalries and these rivalries, naturally, had the potential to escalate. Likewise, when Arabian tribes came together for common defense, their alliances were fleeting confederations, ever shifting in time. No central authority existed to unite the tribes for great common ends, just as no authority existed to prevent intergroup violence from spinning out of control. Nor could that authority be imposed from without by more developed states, such as the Byzantines or Sassanids: the tribes mounted ferocious resistance to any incursions into the arid interior, where lines of supply were difficult to maintain.

In the eyes of later Muslims, the tribal order contained not only a political deficit but also a corresponding spiritual deficit. Just as each Arabian clan possessed its own political identity, so tribal groups paid tribute to a variety of pagan deities, each of which had its own special power and personality. Often the deities were associated with animals—a common practice in tribal societies, where clans are often identified with totemic creatures (the phenomenon inspired Sigmund Freud's theory of human development in his 1913 work *Totem and Taboo*).[8] The North American Ojibwa, for example, are divided into six animal clans, named after the turtle, loon, crane, deer, marten, and bear. Statues of the Arabian deities were kept in and around an ancient black building in Mecca known as the Kaaba—in Muhammad's day, there were said to be 360 stone idols there.

The spiritual life of Arab peoples, in other words, was as segmented and particularized as their constitutional organization. It was also as unstable: ancient paganism posited a world of gods whose desires were capricious and who needed to be collectively appeased, rather than a knowable moral universe in which each person was held individually to account.

Muslims call this era the age of *jahiliyya*—the age of ignorance— and it was Islam's goal to transcend both its spiritual and constitutional deficiencies. The religion developed as an immediate response to the pressures an increasingly mercantile society exerted against traditional tribal values, a breakdown of 'asabiyya under the strain of commerce. Its answer to this moral disintegration was not a reinvigoration of tribalism per se but rather a faith, and a political organization, that would transcend a world divided first and foremost by lineage.

Islam's vision in this respect is embodied in the fate of the Kaaba, the black building that was the center of Arabian idol worship. During his lifetime, Muhammad destroyed the idols there (reprising the Jewish story of the Golden Calf in Exodus 32), establishing the powerful Muslim norm against idolatry that grounds contemporary Islamic prohibitions against pictorial representations of God.

In its place, Muhammad established the Kaaba as the geographic epicenter of Islamic worship. It is specifically toward this building—long since purged of the totemic idols characteristic of a clan society—that Muslims turn when they pray, symbolizing their solidarity not as members of particular clans or tribes but rather as a community bound together by shared monotheistic belief.

•

The name of this community is the *umma*, the worldwide community of believers. To join it, to become a Muslim, one need only make a sincere public declaration of the following words: "There is no god but God, and Muhammad is the prophet of God." The words are known as the *shahada*. The *shahada* encapsulates the essence of the Islamic faith, and it also contains the essence of the new collective identity Islam would construct out of the age of ignorance.

Most immediately, its words proclaim a creed of uncompromising monotheism. There is "no other god"—note the lower case—but God. All the individual tribal gods and clan totems with their individual whims and wills are rejected. God alone is the unique and supreme force of the universe. God is One, a principle known as *tawhid*. The monotheism of Islam is so categorical that it regards as anathema the concept that lies at the center of Christianity, familiar today through the Nicene Creed, that the divine contains three attributes in one being: the Father, the Son (begotten by God and made incarnate), and the Holy Spirit. Muslims believe not that Muhammad was divine but rather that he was a "messenger" of the divine. Indeed, he is said to have received revelations not from God directly but instead at one remove, through the Archangel Gabriel.

Critically, in contrast to traditional pagan practices, the one God proclaimed in the *shahada* makes demands on believers not as members of particular groups but rather as individuals. Like other monotheistic religions, Islam obliges its adherents to ask primarily, "What does God want from *me* as an *individual*?"—not, "What does *our* particular god demand from *us* as members of a specific corporate group or from me given my *station* in society?" The community Islam creates, that is, is a collection of individuals unified by a common set of principles.

Many of the basic practices of Islam, for both Sunnis and Shiites, are rituals designed to reinforce this sense of individual responsibility to monotheistic principles. These practices include the rigorous five daily prayers (*salat*), performed from dawn until evening, accompanied by ritual washing and proscribed movements of prostration. The rituals were developed especially under the spiritual leadership of Ali, Muhammad's cousin and son-in-law and the first male convert to Islam, whom Sunnis regard as the fourth caliph and whom Shiites view as Muhammad's first rightful successor. They are spiritual instruments that affirm and strengthen the relationship between an individual believer and the God to which he or she is accountable. They are religious devices for creating an Islamic sense of self. In the particular historical context of early Arabia, they were tools for internalizing the rejection of the clan-based religious identity of the age of ignorance.

But it is not only in spiritual terms that the *shahada* imagines transcending the rule of the clan. The *shahada* also envisions an *umma* bound together by common principles of law and justice despite its diversity, much the way the diverse peoples of the United States are bound together under the common legal identity of the Constitution.

Legal identity lies at the center of Islam—one scholar has called it the "epitome of Islamic thought"—and the *shahada* contains an implicit vision of law and the state that Islamic jurists would develop over centuries.[9] For in the monotheism Muhammad advanced, the ultimate source of legal rules was not the particular, worldly rules of clan or tribe but rather God, as revealed in the Qur'an. God, not the tribe, was the ultimate lawgiver.

In addition, the Muslim tradition holds that as the messenger of God, Muhammad exemplified right and proper behavior during his life. His behavioral examples are known collectively as the Sunna, which is drawn largely from a multitude of discrete stories about Muhammad known as hadith, which resemble the stories of Jesus told in the Gospels. The Sunna provides another source of the law in Islamic jurisprudence, and it, too, transcends the legal principles of the clan.

This transcendence is reflected in the history of the term *Sunna* itself. Today, the word refers to Muhammad's "way" or path: his words, deeds, habits, and views. But prior to the advent of Islam, the term referred primarily to the "ways" or customs of tribal groups—their customary law. The new public identity the *shahada* imagines rests on the transformation from a legal system of unwritten customary rules to one based on *kitab allah wa sunna nabiyihi*: the book of God, the Qur'an, and the example of the Prophet's life. The Islamic concept of law supplanted the tribal concept of Sunna in much the same way that Muhammad physically transformed the Kaaba by casting out its idols.

This new conception of community and new concept of law had practical consequences in diminishing the rule of the clan. For example, when Muhammad migrated from Mecca, where he had first proclaimed the new faith, and settled in Medina, he hoped to enable early Muslims to escape persecution at the hands of the Meccan Quraysh. He also had been invited to the city to serve as an intermediary between warring clans—Jewish, Christian, pagan, and Muslim—and to settle their longstanding grievances.

After he arrived in Medina, Muhammad brought the clans together for a historic agreement known as the Constitution of Medina, which united fractured elements of the political community under a common set of principles. In this respect, the *shahada* also contains an ideal of political organization that transcends tribalism. It imagines the early Islamic state that Muhammad and the first caliphs would forge amid the Arabian tribes and that would enforce the new principles of Islamic law.

Likewise, bringing the fractured tribes of the Arabian interior together under a single identity and command enabled Islamic forces to storm northward after Muhammad's death, into Persia and beyond, especially under the first caliph, Abu Bakr.

During Muhammad's lifetime, numerous Arabian tribes formally pledged their loyalty to Islam. But upon his death, a number of them balked and refused to pay taxes to the new Islamic state (*sadaqa*). These tribes included especially the Ghatafan, Tayyi', and Tamim. In their refusal, the tribes seemed to understand their original pledge of loyalty not in religious terms but rather in tribal ones. Their promise had been to Muhammad as the leader of a political group and not to the permanent religious and political community he had forged.

The resulting military conflict, known as the *Ridda* Wars, or wars of apostasy, were a resounding defeat for the rebellious tribes. The Muslim victory in turn bound the tribes of the peninsula so tightly together into a new cohesive state that they shortly conquered the Near East and beyond. The war against the tribal upstarts set the stage for the expansion of Islam beyond the peninsula. A common cause and religious identity channeled the power that the tribes of Arabia had previously used to fight amongst themselves.

More directly, legal principles of early Islamic law often worked to soften or diminish the most dangerous substantive legal principles of tribal life. Consider the case of murder. To work against the escalating dynamic of feud, Islamic law urges families to accept monetary compensation for the death of one of their members rather than to exact physical retribution. In addition, the Islamic legal principle of *qisas*, or retribution, sanctions the execution of the murderer and has been elaborated into a more general principle of an eye for an eye.[10]

"O you who believe," the Qur'an announces, "*equivalence* is the law decreed for you when dealing with murder."

While to modern ears this principle may itself seem tribal, it was in fact an effort to curb abuses within a tribal culture. When applied, the principle of an "eye for an eye" short-circuits the tendency of feuds to escalate when an aggrieved group responds to an offense in a disproportionate way—when someone takes "two eyes for an eye."

Thus after announcing that "equivalence is the law decreed for you when dealing with murder," the Qur'an continues: "Anyone who transgresses beyond this incurs a painful retribution."[11]

The significance of Muhammad's vision for Arabian tribal society and its values was not lost on Muhammad's early opponents.

One of his most prominent enemies was Abu Jahl, an elder of the Banu Makhzum clan of the Quraysh tribe. In the battle of Badr of 624, a critical early victory for Islamic forces, the clan elder echoed the views of many of Muhammad's rivals in crying out: "O God, destroy this morning him that more than any of us hath *cut the ties of kinship* and wrought that which is not approved!"[12]

Abu Jahl was killed in the battle.

•

A story was told long ago about Muhammad that, if true—its authenticity is hotly disputed—suggests that in his efforts to overcome the rule of the clan he once made a brief concession to clan-based polytheism. The story goes that in the early years of Islam, when Muhammad was seeking the friendship of various tribal groups around Mecca, he suggested that the Archangel Gabriel had permitted them to continue to worship three female bird deities that were part of the pantheon of Arab gods.

"Have ye considered al-Lat and al-Uzza and Manat?" Muhammad is said to have announced before the Kaaba while reciting one of the Archangel's revelations. "These are the swans exalted, Whose intercession is hoped for."

In one ancient account, "on hearing this the Meccans were delighted, and at the end when Muhammad prostrated himself, they all did likewise."[13]

But the words Muhammad apparently spoke do not in fact appear in the Qur'an. Instead, in chapter 53 of the Qur'an (The Unfolding), the same crane gods are ridiculed. "These are nothing but empty names which you have invented—you and your forefathers—and for which God has bestowed no warrant from on high," reads the relevant passage. "They who worship them follow nothing but surmise and their own wishful thinking—although right guidance has now indeed come unto them from their Sustainer."[14]

What happened to Muhammad's first proclamation? According to the story conveyed by Ibn Ishaq, he later repealed it, indicating that Satan had influenced him to briefly sanction polytheistic worship. The proclamation is thus sometimes known as the "Satanic verses"—it is from them that the writer Salman Rushdie drew the title for his controversial fourth novel.

If Muhammad did make a temporary concession to Arab polytheism, it would not have been the first time in world history that a monotheist made an expedient calculation to temporarily forsake principle in the name of long-term practical success. We have seen that in Iceland after the conversion, pagans were for some years allowed to continue idol worship, animal sacrifice, and infanticide, as long as they did so in secret.

If true, the story would also vividly dramatize a process evident throughout the history of early Islam. The method by which Muhammad and his successors sought to overcome the spiritual and constitutional features of the rule of the clan was always a political one—it involved strategic give-and-take with tribal groups with diverse interests—and it was undertaken entirely from within.

As the scholar Fred M. Donner reveals, the earliest Muslim sources show Muhammad advancing the Islamic cause in a variety of eminently practical ways. He established important tribal alliances through marriage. He shored up the power of potentially sympathetic tribal leaders by honoring them with gifts, including the prestigious gift of associating with Muhammad himself. He eased tribal opposition to Islam through calculated financial payments. He played tribal groups against each other for his own advantage. He knew which tribal leaders were unbending foes and, when necessary, he and his successors fought and killed them.

In making these strategic calculations, Muhammad relied on the detailed, ground-level knowledge of Arabian clans he had gained through his experience as a merchant and a mediator of tribal disputes. The construction of Islam's universalist vision depended entirely on local, ground-level knowledge—and it was a process that today would be called messy.

Indeed, in constructing the new Islamic state, Muhammad and his successors did more than simply honor particular tribal leaders whose alliances they sought. They coopted the tribal form itself for Islamic purposes. Lineage heads were actively incorporated into the apparatus of the new state. Military payroll was not distributed centrally but instead through clan elders, thus making duty to the Islamic state and duty to the clan one and the same. Tax agents were drawn from tribal ranks.[15]

Rather than reject tribal identity and the tribal tie outright, they harnessed it to advance the interests of the new government in Medina. They worked not directly against but rather through clan structures to bring Arabian tribal groups into a new, nontribal political entity. Muhammad used the tribal tie for a larger purpose, and he gave clans a "substantial incentive to invest in the state" (the words are those of a scholar writing of modern Central Asia).[16]

This path to state development is a frequent one. Ireland, India, Mexico, along with many other societies once governed by the rule of the clan, have made "effective use of kin machinery . . . within centralized political domains."[17] Likewise, in neo-Confucian China and other East Asian nations, the principle of patriarchal family authority is central to the very ideology of government and the well-ordered family is understood to be critical to the authority and effectiveness of the state itself.

One can witness a similar recognition of the importance of clans today in the construction of the state in Afghanistan, which has utilized the Pashtun tribal institution of the *loya jirga*.[18] Oman likewise distinguished itself from Yemen in its more successful modernization by attaching tribal sheiks to the state, notably the Ministry of Interior, over time binding the tribal tie to a centralized government structure.[19] Similarly in contemporary South Sudan, the land of the Nuer, the nascent path to state development entails not the rejection but rather the revival of certain principles of customary tribal law.[20]

Making use of the tribal tie eases the transition to legal modernization, and it can secure long-term acceptance of the developing state from clan leaders. It thereby decreases the likelihood that clan institutions will resurface in instances when the state weakens. Moreover, it binds the state to institutions of local governance, which are essential for any healthy democratic society.

Muhammad's seemingly contradictory effort to turn Arabian society away from the age of ignorance by recognizing the importance of clan loyalty is encapsulated in an ethical injunction of the Qur'an itself.

There in chapter 49, known as the Private Apartments, one finds a moving set of verses requiring believers to respect individual human dignity. "O you who have attained to faith!" begins the passage. "No men shall deride other men: it may well be that those whom they deride are better than themselves; and no women shall deride other women: it may well be that those whom they deride are better than themselves." The chapter then explains that God has made humanity in many different images. "We have created you all out of a male and a female," it indicates, "and have made you into nations and tribes."

At this point the passage would seem to affirm the very spiritual and constitutional fragmentation characteristic of *jahiliyya*.

But the passage then reveals the *reason* God divided humanity into tribal groups—"so that you might come to know one another."[21]

For Muhammad, clan identity was not an end in itself but rather a path to universal brotherhood.

•

Anglo-Saxon England and early Islamic Arabia—the medieval societies that laid the foundations for two of the most important social and political traditions of the modern world—were different in obvious ways. But with respect to the history of the rule of the clan, they shared telling similarities. Both developed states that sought to address the shortcomings of kin-based constitutionalism. In both cases the primary motive force of their development came from within, rather than being imposed from without. And in both cases the growth of a public identity transcending clan loyalty, an identity based on a new concept of law, was a precondition of state development.

Reformers seeking to surmount the rule of the clan in their own societies today can learn from both cases. Equally important, liberals can learn from them as well.

For a society to overcome the rule of the clan, it must forge, and it must maintain, a common identity that rises above the particular clan groups of which it is composed. Affiliations with craft and professional guilds, religious organizations, and all the varied voluntary institutions of civil society can contribute to a sense of belonging to a larger community. A robust public identity draws upon these affiliations to construct a sense of citizenship. Patriotic nationalism provides the widest cultural framework through which radically different people can understand themselves as part of an integrated public.

The existence of a public identity, in turn, enables the state to protect its citizens not as members of corporate groups but rather as individuals. To create that identity, it is necessary to do precisely what Abu Jahl criticized Muhammad for doing. It is necessary to "cut the ties of kinship"—to create a cultural identity that, while not replacing family bonds, trumps their significance, and that displaces the authority of the extended family with the revolutionary, individuating power of the nuclear family.

In addition, a society must develop, and it must maintain, state institutions that are able to enforce the legal rules that are enacted in the name of its common identity. It must create institutions that provide the benefits that clan-based constitutionalism provides, but more effectively. Its courts must be efficient and legitimate arbiters of disputes; its police must become professional and neutral enforcers of the law and guarantors of safety; and its agencies must deliver services through fair processes that are free of corruption. To accomplish these aims, ironically, it is often necessary to work not against kin groups, but rather with and through them.

The motivation for these developments must arise from within clan societies themselves. The process must be internal because its legitimacy and staying power depend upon political compromises between competing interest groups. An effective state cannot be imposed from above; it can only grow from a collection of countless negotiations and agreements in which groups are given national incentives to cede local power. Liberals should avoid the fantasy that the rule of the clan can be overcome without give-and-take between competing interests as decisively as we should reject the dangerous fantasy within our own societies of a government that transcends politics and compromise (a fantasy that besets the Right and Left in equal measure).

While the transformation of the rule of the clan must ultimately occur from within, however, there are also ethical means, consistent with liberal principles, to encourage the process from without. In addition to wielding hard international power when advisable and morally and legally justified, liberal states can use economic and soft institutional influence to encourage societies to move from Status to Contract. The broad framework for such influence, as well as some of the specific means by which it can be furthered, can be found in modern parallels to the process of state development in Anglo-Saxon England and early Islamic Arabia.

Consider the issue of religion. Religion continues to provide a powerful basis for conceiving of a polity in common terms, just as it provides a space for competing interest groups to reconcile their differences for a common cause. Thus during the Egyptian election of 2011, the first since the overturning of the Mubarak government, the success of Islamist political groups derived in part from their ability to appeal beyond clan loyalties. But for religion to play this role most effectively over the long term and to avoid becoming its own form of sectarian clan, it is essential that liberal governments support robust policies of international religious freedom. The lack of religious and political freedom allows religion to be used for factional ends, a phenomenon apparent especially in many Muslim-majority societies, where charges of blasphemy or apostasy are often used as weapons to squelch liberal political and cultural dissent.[22]

At the same time, liberal societies must maintain robust religious freedom themselves, and they must welcome religious commitment on the part of their citizens. Religious communities not only confer many of the same benefits of solidarity provided by the rule of the clan but also provide an important symbolic resource for people to conceive of individuals in universal terms and in turn to imagine the state as serving public interests.

With respect to the rule of the clan, however, religion is an old cultural technology. Today there exists another powerful tool to break the bonds of extended kinship, and it doubtless will have consequences for social and political development in the future similar to the influence of monotheistic religion in the Middle Ages: social media. Web-based tools such as Facebook and Google decrease the costs of establishing social ties across kin lines, and they increase the potential benefits of doing so, especially in a free-market economy. By reducing the cost of establishing relationships of all kinds beyond one's kin group, they substantially increase the likelihood that people will construct their essential relationships based not on lineage but rather on personal choice. They facilitate the development of a public identity "from below."

The role of social media in diminishing the rule of the clan was encapsulated for me recently over breakfast in Menlo Park, California. I was meeting in a local coffee shop with Reid Hoffman, the founder and chairman of the professional networking site LinkedIn. Hoffman has always had a knack for looking into the future (we have known each other since college) and he has been thinking for a long time about how the Internet will restructure the global social environment.

From his perspective, I asked, what did he think about countries in which lineage was a core social and political institution?

"In the future," he said, without missing a beat, "everyone will choose their own family." He smiled as he said the words, indicating that it is the core idea within the exaggeration that will eventually become true.

For societies governed by the rule of the clan, the proliferation of personal communications technology, from smart phones and tablets to whatever new device lies just around the corner, will in time knit people together across kin lines much as the ethical technology of religion has done. By reducing the cost of establishing connections between tribes, it will create, in the words of the anthropologist Lionel Tiger, a "new tribe."[23] As B. R. Ambedkar wrote, "The only way by which men can come to possess things in common with one another is by being in communication with one another."[24] Liberals can encourage the transformation of the constitutional structure of clan societies by helping the people of those societies gain access to the global information system, thus fostering a transformation from kinship to social networks. We can do so at the state level through assertive free-trade and antitrust policies. Within civil society, we can encourage technology-based entrepreneurship through organizations that provide funding and mentorship to start-up companies in developing nations.

Liberals can also help societies overcome the rule of the clan by looking to the lessons of England and harnessing the cultural power of elites—not only tapping power from below through social media, but rather leveraging it from above. Among the Anglo-Saxons a common public identity developed first within a distinct ruling class that was responsible to groups beyond their extended kin and guided by universalistic ideals. Today a parallel class exists at the very foundation of modern liberal society: members of the professions.

Professionals are responsible above all not to the claim of kinship but to the public-spirited ideals of their learned guilds. Lawyers, doctors, accountants, scientists, teachers, and other professionals draw their identity from the neutral standards of expertise they uphold in the name of the general good. By serving those high ideals, moreover, they help bring them to life among the people they serve, spreading them well beyond their occupational groups.

Modern liberal states can thus support the constitutional development of clan societies by supporting the professions and the power of
the professional class, thereby fostering public identity "from above."
On the level of national policy, the professions can be strengthened
through international educational development and exchange programs
and by pursuing free-trade policies that enable the middle class to grow.
Individual citizens in liberal societies can likewise facilitate links between their own professional associations and equivalent professional
groups abroad, seeking to deepen their independence—thereby providing them with an external base of political support—and they can offer
professional organizations abroad aid, counsel, and expertise. The American Bar Association's Rule of Law Initiative, which provides assistance
to reformers abroad in a variety of justice-related fields, is an example of
such a program in the realm of law. Another prominent example, again
in the field of law, is the backing many American lawyers gave in 2007
to the Pakistani attorneys who were standing up to President Pervez
Musharraf.

The same support of the professions, and of professional identity
distinct from business and marketplace identity, is necessary to sustain
liberal societies themselves. The existence of public life in liberal societies is predicated on the vitality of truly independent professions, which
guarantee that authority of various kinds is exercised in the name of the
public interest.

To help societies overcome the rule of the clan, liberals can also
encourage the development of the distinctive imaginative sensibility that
lies at the core of the liberal rule of law. It is to that sensibility, which
provides citizens with the fundamental symbolic tools to imagine themselves as individual members of a common public, that I now turn.

PART FIVE

THE PERSISTENCE
OF THE CLAN

It would be comforting to view the relation between the rule of the clan and liberal modernity as one of binary opposition, as an either-or. Either kinship or the state, custom or law, collectivism or individualism, Status or Contract. In this view, after a society develops liberal legal institutions, an evolutionary switch is flipped and the rule of the clan fades into the darkness of the historical past, like other outmoded social and political ideas. It becomes something that no longer has the power to touch us.

But this view is not only mistaken, it also poses a direct threat to liberal modernity itself. The relation between the rule of the clan and modern liberalism is not binary, it is dialectical. The clan persists even within the most advanced liberal societies, and understanding how and why is vital for protecting those societies and the individualist way of life they support.

The following chapters consider two reasons why the clan will always be with us. Ironically, both stem from the success of liberalism itself.

The first reason is that the historical movement from Status to Contract has come with a steep price. All the precious advances in personal freedom that liberalism has achieved have been accompanied by the loss of important benefits that are provided by the rule of the clan.

Societies of Contract enable citizens to forge their own professional lives and personal identities, but societies of Status provide their members with deep social and psychological security. Societies of Contract foster the economic growth that comes from individual competition, but societies of Status advance the principle of social justice. Societies of Contract liberate citizens from the dead hand of tradition, while societies of Status initiate kinsmen into a profound communion across generations. At bottom, liberal societies offer citizens personal freedom, whereas the rule of the clan provides its members with a powerful feeling of community and solidarity.

Although liberalism's trade-off of solidarity for personal freedom is morally right, societies of Contract are threatened by the forces of psychological isolation and social instability that are unleashed when traditional norms break down. In the classic formulation of the sociologist Émile Durkheim, liberal societies are threatened by anomie. The term is a telling one. It literally means a loss of normative coherence, especially the kind provided by customary law.

It is this loss that generates the romanticized, idealized portrait of the rule of the clan in modern liberal culture. The valorization of the clan, whether in pubs like Molly MacPherson's or in films like *Avatar*, is an inevitable expression of individual and social yearning. The cultural presence of the clan within liberal societies is therefore unlikely to fade. It soothes an ache for everything that is lost in the movement from Status to Contract.

Addressing that ache is an essential challenge for liberal society. In chapter 11 I consider some of the ways in which modern intellectuals and artists have sought to meet that challenge, sometimes to liberalism's detriment, but sometimes by reimagining the clan in ways that advance and sustain the culture of the liberal rule of law.

The second reason why the clan will always be with us is that it reasserts itself wherever the state is weak or absent.

Many liberals understandably forget that only a robust state working in the public interest can provide the conditions for individual freedom.

For most citizens of liberal democracies, individual liberty may seem like the default impulse of human communities, an instinct the state does little more than suppress. But this assumption is the product of the liberal state's success, which has skewed our understanding of human nature. By looking to communities "beyond the writ of civilized governments," we can see that in the absence of state power, humans seek "to maintain and restore justice by defining the legal personality as a collective."[1] This is as much the case in districts within industrialized democracies where state power is weak, such as inner cities, as it is in North Africa or South Asia.[2]

The natural drive of human beings is to create legal structures in which individual freedom is diminished.

From a legal perspective, societies of Status are not a distant Other. Instead, they are what liberal societies would quickly become, in a process of evolutionary reversion, if we lost our political will to maintain an effective state dedicated to public purposes.

The clan will never leave us because it is an expression of a basic human drive. The question liberals face is not how to eliminate it entirely, but rather how to manage the impulses underlying it.

In chapter 12 I imagine what might happen if we fail in that effort.

ELEVEN

THE ROMANCE OF THE CLAN

I said that I would like to march with the free people"—so the beguiling Ellen Jaspar explains her decision to join a clan of Pashtun nomads and disappear into the wilds of Afghanistan in James Michener's best-selling novel *Caravans* (1963).[1] The novel follows the exploits of Mark Miller, an upstanding graduate of Groton and Yale, as he tracks the peripatetic Jaspar on behalf of the American embassy in Kabul. His mission: find the missing young woman, report her whereabouts, and ease the minds of her frightened parents in suburban Dorset, Pennsylvania.

Jaspar is not a typical heroine. Although she is smart, vibrant, and bold, she isn't easy to love. Despite a comfortable middle-class upbringing by devoted Presbyterian parents—indeed, precisely because of it—during her junior year at Bryn Mawr, in the mid-1940s, she seeks to "outrage" her father's "whole petty scale of judgment" (he is in insurance by trade, and during the war was chair of the local draft board) by doing "the most ridiculous thing I could do."

The "most ridiculous thing," she decides, is to "run off with an Afghan who had a turban and another wife" and move to Kabul. But in the end even this act isn't enough to satisfy her desire to upend the values of the American bourgeoisie. She soon grows disillusioned with her educated Afghan husband, Nazrullah, an engineer in charge of an irrigation project, concluding that he is "one of the most boring men on earth." "That turban," she complains. "He wore it in Philadelphia for show. He'd never think of wearing it in Kabul."

She absconds to the country's hinterlands in the arms of a nomadic chief, Zulfiqar, who is leading his caravan on its annual two-thousand-mile migration from Afghanistan to India.[2]

Despite her lack of filial loyalty and marital fidelity, however, Jaspar is also a deeply compelling person. She may not be easy to love, but there is something about her sincerity that's admirable—and something, too, about the depth of her commitment to Afghanistan. "Just think!" she cries excitedly to an incredulous Miller one afternoon as they observe an Afghan village from horseback. "In a few years Afghanistan will destroy prisons like this . . . and the country will go back to the ancient freedom of the caravan." She embraces the beauties of nomadic Pashtun life body and soul. Indeed, she may believe in it more than Zulfiqar.

"You're right about the past," the chief tells her, while Miller listens from atop his horse. "He's right about the future. Some day all of us will live in villages like this. But they will be better villages."[3]

I once asked a high-level corporate consultant whose clients have included the likes of IBM and Eastman Kodak if she had read Michener's novel. I knew she had spent many years in the 1970s traveling alone in Afghanistan and Pakistan. The sophisticated Ivy League law school graduate looked at me over the dinner table and smiled wistfully. "Did I read it?" she replied, her eyes turning inward to memories of her youth. "*Of course* I read it! Every Western woman traveling in South Asia back then did!"

Like Ellen Jaspar, a great many citizens of industrialized liberal societies have embraced Afghanistan and its people. U.S. Supreme Court Justice William O. Douglas, a renowned and observant traveler, called Afghans "the most friendly and hospitable people I have met." "One could go to any Afghan home and be warmly received," he enthused in 1952 in *Beyond the High Himalayas*. "He would get the best food the family had to offer. The house would be his home, though he were a total stranger. If there were only one room, it would be turned over to him."[4]

The caravan Jaspar joins is one branch of a larger caste of herdsmen known as the Kuchis. Hailing from east and southwest Afghanistan, they include Pashtuns from a number of separate tribes or tribal confederacies. They know no national boundaries, dividing their time between winters in present-day Pakistan and summers in Afghanistan, forever on the move with their camels, goats, and sheep. As Khaled Hosseini writes in his novel *The Kite Runner* (2003), "Afghans like to say: Life goes on, unmindful of beginning, end . . . crisis or catharsis, moving forward like a slow, dusty caravan of *kochis*."[5] Estimates of their numbers vary, but in Afghanistan there are now about three million, most of whom maintain their nomadic ways.[6]

Occasionally they make headlines. They are engaged in a centuries-old conflict over pasture land with the Shiite Hazara and in part for this reason they have been strong supporters of the Taliban.

What captures Ellen Jaspar's imagination about these people and their difficult life? Most of all, she is attracted to those features of Kuchi society that fly in the face of liberal modernity, most notably its statelessness. "A million of us pass back and forth each year and no one knows where we go or how we feed ourselves," she boasts to Miller after he confesses that the embassy was utterly bewildered about her location. "We're the wanderers who make fools of petty nations."[7] In the absence of a state, the Kuchis possess the deep solidarity of their wandering caravans. They possess the normative and cultural principle of group honor, and all the social and psychological benefits of the rule of the clan.[8]

They also possess its drawbacks, which Michener highlights dramatically in the novel's moral climax. Jaspar and Miller travel with the clan to "Qabir," an encampment where tens of thousands of tribesmen gather annually to select their leaders, to engage in commerce, and to play rough sports. After some days there, Zulfiqar brings Miller to Qabir's headquarters, "a large Russian-style yurt, whose primitive sides were made of skins and whose spacious interior was decorated with guns, daggers, sabers and three handsome red-and-blue Persian rugs"—the "center from which the encampment [is] governed." The leaders of the camp are two *sharifs*, a Kirghiz gunrunner and a Hazara trader, serious men who are weighed down by the difficulty of their task.

In the fourth week of the assembly, a Tajik is caught stealing from an Uzbek, and he is dragged into the yurt. The *sharifs* deliberate as to how to respond.

At this point Miller, whose unprecedented access to tribal society has also put him under its spell, has a revelation. "I realized that no nation exercised any sovereignty over this congregation of seventy or eighty thousand people. By consent these two sharifs . . . enjoyed absolute control. If they now decided to execute the trembling Tajik, they could."

The *sharifs* decide on a lesser punishment—they cut off the Tajik's right hand—but the point is sufficiently established. "In this camp two sharifs hold absolute power," Miller says to Jaspar. "Half an hour ago this Tajik was caught stealing; his trial took about four minutes. This is the clean-cut primitive life you wanted, Ellen." Jaspar faints at the sight of the Tajik's bloody stump.[9]

The entire episode—one that, as we will see, recalls a classic scene in Walter Scott's novel *Waverley*—underscores the fact that for all its romance the clan offers a legal order in which "the people" might be free, but individuals are not. Even more, in the chasm between her life in Pennsylvania and the normative order Jaspar confronts in Qabir, the incident throws into relief a curious paradox of modern and, especially, liberal society.

Despite the clan's profoundly antiliberal character, in the midst of modernity, or when a society is undergoing a notable liberalizing transition—as the United States was in the 1960s, when Michener wrote his novel—the clan is frequently an object of romantic yearning. Many of us are, in greater or lesser ways, Ellen Jaspar.

Why should this be so?

•

One of the myriad reasons—a sense of loss—can be glimpsed in the recent history of Korea, a region that, despite the rapid and comprehensive modernization of the south, remains closely tied to its clan history and continues to cherish lineage as a central cultural value.

The Korean people are among the most genetically homogenous in the world. But even more striking than the fact of their uniformity is the way Koreans talk about it.

Koreans traditionally view themselves as common descendants of a single apical ancestor, Dangun Wanggeom (Tan'gun). He is said to have reigned more than four thousand years ago, beginning in 2333 BCE.[10] His origins are semidivine, for he is the grandson of the Emperor of Heaven. His father was called Hwanung, and his mother was a bear whom Hwanung transformed into a woman after she won a contest of patience with a tiger. In their national mythology all Koreans trace their ancestry back to the son produced by this union, which may itself be a cultural memory of a long-forgotten conflict between two totemic-animal clans.

The story of Dangun is the foundation of Korean identity, and it naturally came to assume special importance in the aftermath of outside occupation in the twentieth century, especially at the hands of the Japanese. From 1945 to 1961, the year 2333 BCE was reckoned as the first year of the Korean calendar. In 1993, the North Korean English-language *People's Daily* featured two main headlines on its front page to introduce the discovery of eighty-six bone fragments said to be those of Dangun and his queen: "5,000 Year-Long History and Homogeneity of Nation Corroborated" and "Tan'gun, Founder of Ancient Korea, Born in P'yongyang."[11]

For a Westerner, the full significance of Dangun is easy to overlook. The Dangun myth is not merely the Korean equivalent of the American adage that George Washington is the "father of his country." Dangun is understood to be the father of his country literally. As one scholar of the cultural aspects of Korean state formation, Hyung Il Pai, explains, "When Koreans refer to themselves as belonging to one 'blood lineage,'" the implication is that they are "related as members of different segmentary lineages descended from one big extended family."[12]

Within that family, consciousness of ancestry has had profound social and, for many years, legal significance. When Neo-Confucianism came to Korea during its Choson (Yi) Dynasty (1392–1910), it gradually restructured Korean principles of kinship. What began as an ancient indigenous practice of bilateral or matrilineal kinship was replaced by a strictly patrilineal system.[13]

In the clan system that developed, lineage groups traced their descent to a common male ancestor (*sijo*) and centered themselves geographically around a village clan seat (*pon'gwan*). These clans provided their members with social prestige and a range of legal entitlements, especially access to the all-important civil-service exam, based on the relative status of their patrimony. The patrilineal principle of Korean society became so marked that married women gained rights to child custody in the event of divorce only in 1991.[14]

Those familiar with Korean culture will know how many people of Korean descent seem to have one of a few family names such as Kim,

Park, Lee, and Jung. But these names tell only a small part of the story of a Korean's ancestral identity. Every Korean name is divided into many distinct and unrelated branches—clans—each identified with a separate ancestral village. Just as in England in the nineteenth century one might have asked a man whose last name was Thorne whether he belonged to the Thornes of Ullathorne or the Thornes of Thistlethwaite, so in Korea even today family names possess geographic epicenters.

The notorious leader of North Korea, Kim Jong-il, bore the family name of Kim. In Western terms Jong-il was his "first" or given name; thus his father and predecessor, Kim Il-sung, bore the given name Il-sung, and his son and successor bears the given name Jong-un. But the fact that the leader's family name was Kim does not mean that he was related to the 21 percent of the Korean people who also bear that name. Rather Kim Jong-il was a member of the Kims of Jeonju, in present-day South Korea. Jeonju was his family's clan seat, its *pon'gwan*.

Marriage between members of the same clan is prohibited under South Korean law.

In the late nineteenth century Japan turned its colonial ambitions toward Korea, beginning a period that remains enormously contentious in both popular memory and the historical literature.[15] Korea was formally annexed by Japan in 1910. The Japanese occupation of Korea, which was fully supported by the West, ended only after World War II.

During its administration of the peninsula, Japan undertook a wide variety of programs to weaken clan consciousness and modernize Korean society. Land surveys and land reform, economic development and capital programs, energy and construction projects, legal improvements, social and educational advances—the list is extensive. These modernization efforts were imposed in an authoritarian, bureaucratic manner (a pattern later followed by the government of South Korea in its own economic development program), but they produced benefits for the peninsula. Especially telling from the perspective of liberal political principles was that, as the Korean legal scholar and women's rights activist Lee Tai-Yung writes, "women's societal-legal position in the period of Japan's rule improved remarkably, compared with that of the Yi

[Choson] dynasty," which had fully absorbed the principles of female subordination embodied in the normative body of lineage rules known as "clan codes."[16]

In addition, looking to European colonial practice, including the history of Celtic peoples in the United Kingdom, Japan sought to "assimilate" Koreans into Japanese cultural identity. The nation pursued this policy by the principle known as *Naissen ittai* (roughly, "Japan and Korea unified," or "Japan and Korea as one body").[17] One aspect of this assimilation drive has been the subject of especially bitter memories.

This was the bureaucratic policy, announced in early 1940, of "encouraging" Koreans to change their names—to abandon their native surnames, with all the social and psychological weight of lineage history they carried, and adopt Japanese family names in their place. Soon more than three-quarters of the population, 3.17 million households, recorded new, Japanese designations. As one scholar of the period notes, the policy "struck at the most personal and perhaps the most cherished source of Korean identity."[18]

Some Koreans adopted names that cleverly maintained a reference to their old name or some family characteristic. Pak Sŏngp'il, a farmer and fisherman born in 1917, long resisted the name-change policy because "I had lost my grandfather and then my father, and had taken over the responsibility of eldest son." But he finally capitulated and became Otake. The name was carefully chosen: "The O in Chinese characters is Korean *Tae*, the first syllable of the place where I was born. The *take*, meaning bamboo, is for the huge bamboo grove behind our house. So my name signified that I was born in Taebyŏn township in the house with the bamboo grove in back."[19] The consolation was real but small.

Indeed, in a nation in which ancestor worship is a fundamental social and religious practice, the name-change policy undermined the symbolic tie between the generations, fraying the connection between the living and the dead. "If I change my family name," asks the Korean landowner Sŏl Chin-yŏng in Kajiyama Toshiyuki's moving story "The Clan Records," "what excuse can I offer to my ancestors?"[20] Likewise in Richard Kim's autobiographical story collection *Lost Names* (1970), the celebrated Korean American author movingly depicts a cemetery visit by three patrilineal generations of a family that, after much resistance, has changed its name to Iwamoto (Foundation of Rock—a biblical reference to Peter). Grandfather, father, and son stand before the gravestones of their ancestors, which in the winter snow are so filled with ice that one "can barely distinguish the outlines of the letters."

"The three of us are on our knees," Kim writes, "and, after a long moment of silence, my grandfather, his voice weak and choking with a sob, says, 'We are a disgrace to our family. We bring disgrace and humiliation to your name. How can you forgive us!' "[21]

The family is experiencing the psychological pain, the metaphysical grief, that attends modernization and the development of the rule of law. The intergenerational communion between the living and the dead has been severed. It is a loss that those who experience it directly, and even more potently those who inherit it when young—for they have known an intergenerational communion only in the half-understood time of childhood—regularly seek to assuage. Not only in the land of Dangun but across the world the clan may become an object of deep affection just as its practical rule diminishes. But this makes the pain of its loss no less real.

Nor does this sense of loss cease once the actual rule of the clan has passed into distant memory. Even at the height of modernity, the clan often serves as a symbol of redemption. As we will see, this was notably the case in nineteenth-century Europe, in the midst of liberal modernity's birth, where the symbol of the clan enabled artists and intellectuals to imagine at least three forms of deliverance from the deficiencies of their social order.

These three paths of redemption were economic collectivism, individual heroism, and the culture of historical romance. It is the last path, which rests on a distinctively liberal literary sensibility, that continues to provide the greatest hope of the three for the future of liberal constitutionalism and the individualism it makes possible.

•

The first path of redemption lay in concrete political alternatives to liberalism itself, particularly those that reformed its individualist property-holding regime. The most important of these alternatives was provided by the rich and complex intellectual tradition of Marxism. Although

few people are aware of the fact, the development of Marxist theory depended on an American anthropologist and his study of kinship. His
influential analysis of the clan provided a foundation for Marxism's
vision of a future world of egalitarianism and solidarity.

His name was Lewis Henry Morgan, and, like Henry Maine, he was
at once a lawyer and a scholar.

While Maine began his career in the university and later moved
into the world of administration and practical affairs, Morgan moved in
the opposite direction. His preeminence as a scholar came only after
many years as a corporate attorney.

Born in 1818 to a well-to-do family in Aurora, in Upstate New
York, he attended Union College, in Schenectady, and in 1844 moved
to the growing city of Rochester. There he practiced law for more than
twenty years, and beginning in 1861 he served for the better part of a
decade as a representative to the New York state legislature. As a lawyer, he specialized in that most fundamental of modern industries, the
railroad. His chief clients were investors in a transportation network
that over time came to link the iron ore operations across the Upper
Peninsula of Michigan. Morgan himself put money into the project,
and in 1855 he became the director of the newly established Bay de
Noquet and Marquette Railroad Company, whose successor is now a
subsidiary of the Canadian Pacific Railway. The investment made him
rich.[22]

With his new wealth, Morgan could turn his full attention to the
great intellectual passion of his life, the study of Native American
culture.

Like many Americans of his day, Morgan was fascinated by native
peoples, and he lived in a region with an especially captivating native
history. Upstate New York was the birthplace of the Iroquois League, an
alliance of six distinct tribes, the Seneca, Cayuga, Onondaga, Tusca-
rora, Oneida, and Mohawk. In the early 1840s Morgan helped establish
a group dedicated to studying the alliance and its people and to lobby-
ing for their interests. The men called themselves the Grand Order of
the Iroquois, and they fashioned their organizational structure on the
constitutional model of the Iroquois League itself. In recognition of
his work on their behalf, the Seneca adopted Morgan into their tribe in

1846, bestowing on him the name of *Da-ya-da-o-wo-ko,* or bridging-the-gap.

In 1859 Morgan began a Smithsonian-backed multiyear field trip to research the native peoples of the west, an expedition that would lead him to write one of the great scholarly works of the era, *Ancient Society* (1877). Morgan focused on the same topic that was capturing Henry Maine's interest in England—kinship—but his approach was different. Instead of directing his attention to law, Morgan investigated language. Specifically, he sought to collect all the terms with which native languages designate the range of people to whom an individual can be related within a family: mother, father, brother, sister, sister's son, sister's daughter, brother's son, brother's daughter, mother's father, mother's mother, and so on. These terms are profoundly revealing about how a society is organized.

For instance, in the Seneca language a man's brother's son and daughter are designated not by the terms for *nephew* and *niece* but rather by the terms also used for *son* and *daughter* (in Morgan's transliteration, *Ha'-ah'-wuk* and *Ka-ah'-wuk*). These children in turn refer to the man English speakers would call *uncle* as *father.* By contrast, the son and daughter of a man's *sister* are designated by the standard terms for nephew and niece (*Ha-yă'-wan-da* and *Ka-yă-wan-da*). Why the difference?

Morgan hypothesized that when the Senecan family system was formed, the wives of a man's brother were considered to be the man's wives as well, but that a man's sister could never be his wife. Under the rules of Senecan clan organization, his sister's children thus stood in a remoter relationship to him than did his brother's.

After collecting data on scores of native languages, Morgan began researching kinship terms across the globe, and in doing so he found some striking similarities to and differences from the Iroquois he had first studied. For instance, in the Tamil language of southern India, the word for a man's brother's son is the term for *son* (*măkăn,* in Morgan's transliteration), whereas for a man's sister's son it is the term for *nephew* (*mărŭmăkăn*). This replicates the pattern of usage in Seneca. In the Hawaiian language, though, the son of a man's sister and the son of a man's brother are designated by the same word, namely that for *son* (*käi'-kee kä'-na*).

Morgan grouped the classification patterns he found into six major types, publishing his results in 1871 as *Systems of Consanguinity and Affinity of the Human Family*, a book that established the central place of the concept of kinship in the field of anthropology, where it remains to this day.

Six years later, Morgan published his next book, *Ancient Society*, and it was this study that planted his ideal of kinship in the soil of left-wing revolutionary thought. Morgan had come to believe that the kinship systems he had classified provided a window not only onto social patterns, the six great systems of consanguinity and affinity of the human family, but also onto the trajectory of societal development. Here he took a cue from the discipline of philology, with its suggestive insights into how the history of a people is carried in the development of their language. We have glimpsed such insights by noting that English has very few early loanwords from Celtic, which provides evidence of sixth-century ethnic cleansing. Morgan argued that kinship systems could shed a similar light on the evolution of the people who used them.

In fact, he thought they would illuminate human evolution as a whole. Like languages, kinship patterns had shifted over time, and by understanding how, scholars could paint a more detailed portrait of the course of human history.

In surveying this history, Morgan concluded that societies tend to evolve along a single path. Through millennia and in the present moment, all societies were passing through a series of "ethnical periods," beginning in a condition of "savagery," which Morgan subdivided into three distinct stages, then passing through three stages of "barbarism," and arriving finally at "civilization." Morgan argued that each of these stages was associated with a particular type of kinship structure—Hawaiian kinship, for example, belonged to a very early stage of human development, whereas the Senecan and Tamil to a later period—as well as with a distinct form of technology, mode of food production, and conception of property. Humankind was gradually progressing through these stages toward increasingly complex, sophisticated social and cultural forms.

Within this evolutionary framework, the rule of the clan played a pivotal role.

According to Morgan, all ancient societies were characterized by a constitutional arrangement he called gentile, in which kin groups form the basic units of governance, much as in Maine's societies of Status. He took the term from the history of ancient Rome, where the *gens*, or clan, constituted a core unit of society.[23] Each *gens* was headed by a paterfamilias holding absolute authority over his kin. Morgan observed a similar social structure among the Iroquois and ultimately in all other societies in a premodern stage of development.

"The Irish *sept*, the Scottish *clan*, the *phrara* of the Albanians, and the Sanskrit *ganas*," he asserted, "are the same as the American Indian gens, which has usually been called a clan. As far as our knowledge extends, this organization runs through the entire ancient world upon all the continents . . . [and] wherever found is the same in structural organization and in principles of action."[24]

In Morgan's view, though ancient societies are always characterized by their clan-based organization, the ways clans were structured evolved over time. Most important, in their initial stages clan societies traced a person's descent through the female line, but they eventually evolved to trace kinship through the male line, or agnatically (the pattern followed by Korea, as we have seen). Similarly, whereas early in a society's evolution the property of a person who died passed to the group as a whole, later it passed only to the person's agnatic kindred, and finally it passed to their children alone. Once these changes in kinship and inheritance had taken place, the conditions were set for the emergence of modern society, in which the *gens* was discarded as the basic unit of government.

From that point onward, government "dealt with persons through their relations to territory" rather than through their clan. After this transformative moment, societies progressed still further toward the conditions present in Morgan's society, with its sophisticated technology, social stratification, and protection of individual property rights.

Unlike Maine, however, Morgan believed that the evolution of human society would not end with a society of Contract. "A mere property career," he asserted, "is not the final destiny of mankind, if progress is to be the law of the future as it has been of the past."[25] Instead, he thought society would continue to evolve toward a more advanced stage and would solve the ills of anomie and inequality that critics of liberal modernity have long noted. What would the next stage of civilization be like?

To answer that question, Morgan looked back to the very clan societies through which early social evolution had passed. The future of modern civilization, he wrote, *will be a revival, in a higher form, of the liberty, equality and fraternity of the ancient gentes.*[26]

Civilization would evolve into a more elevated version of the Iroquois community.

Karl Marx and Friedrich Engels were deeply influenced by *Ancient Society* and Morgan's earlier writings on native kinship. The italics in the passage above are not Morgan's—Engels added them for emphasis when he used the passage as the final line of *The Origin of the Family, Private Property, and the State* (1884). The book is a classic of the Marxist intellectual tradition, and in its circular view of history it exhibits the way, to quote the philosopher Ernest Gellner, that Morgan "saved" Marxism from certain theoretical inconsistencies.[27] Had those inconsistencies not been resolved, they might have led to Marxism's earlier collapse as an ideology.

Morgan's view of social evolution beginning and ending in a form of clan society played a key role in sustaining the most powerful alternative to liberalism in the twentieth century. The centralization of political authority in the Communist Party, the abolition of private property, the nightmare of Soviet state surveillance—all were part of an effort to re-create a world of clan solidarity through force of law. The effort ended in slavery, in a new, modernist society of Status that subsumed the individual into the demands of the group.

The ideal of clan society as redemptive is thus part of the intellectual DNA of the most compelling, terrifying alternative to liberal society in modern times.[28]

•

In Valencia, Spain, a woman with matted blonde hair, whose arms and torso are covered with black tribal tattoos, crouches on a stage and looks longingly at the wounded warrior before her, who returns her ardent stare. The string section of the orchestra fills the hall with a gorgeous, expansive theme.

The woman tends to the warrior's injuries and, as the two sit before an enormous tree projected onto the screen behind them, the veins of its countless interlacing branches pulsating with red, orange, yellow, and brown light, she gives him a cup of sweet mead to quench his thirst. The warrior stands up to leave, but the woman bids him stay and wait for her husband, Hunding.

What the two do not yet know, but will soon discover, is that they are twin brother and sister, Siegmund and Sieglinde. They are the children of a mortal mother and the god Wotan, and they are members of the celebrated Völsung clan of Norse mythology, a clan of heroes.

After some hesitation, the warrior agrees to stay. He tenderly caresses the woman's hair as she kneels. But soon the great tree turns color from orange to blue, a pair of green eyes emerges from beneath its branches, and the backdrop on stage transforms into a menacing face. Tubas blow a series of decisive, threatening notes, signaling Hunding's arrival.

So began a recent production of *Die Walküre* (*The Valkyrie*) by Richard Wagner, the second opera in his four-part *Ring* cycle. Directed in 2008 by Carlus Padrissa for the avant-garde theater company La Fura dels Baus, the production was exceptional not only for its fine singing and commanding orchestra, but also for its daring staging and set design. Acrobats flew through the air. Singers bedecked in futuristic costumes thundered as they were hoisted by agile cranes. Haunting three-dimensional images flickered in the shadows. Giant ravens fluttered about the tree, and when Siegmund announced his true identity to Sieglinde, the letters of his name coursed up its boughs and through its branches before fluttering to the ground like leaves.

For those who aren't familiar with Wagner's drama, it's common to picture the *Ring*, with all its ancient Germanic mythology, as an exercise in musty antiquarianism. But in fact the cycle grew from Wagner's conviction that the heroic values of this tribal mythology provided a solution to the problems that beset the modern age.

The composer was a fervent supporter of the European revolutions of 1848, which brought the middle and working classes together in an armed revolt for republican and nationalist reform. The active role he played in the 1849 May Uprising in Dresden forced him into exile in Switzerland. His friends included anarchists such as Mikhail Bakunin, and he was influenced by writings of socialist thinkers such as Pierre-Joseph Proudhon.

As George Bernard Shaw pungently explained in 1898, far from creating "'a work of art' pure and simple," when Wagner wrote he had current social and political issues firmly in mind. He was thinking of "shareholders, tall hats, whitelead factories, and industrial and political questions looked at from the socialistic and humanitarian points of view."[29] The *Ring* offers a searing social and political analysis.

In the allegory Wagner develops in the cycle, three classes of beings stand in for the "three main orders of men" in modern civilization.

First there are the dwarfs. They represent "the instinctive, predatory, lustful, greedy people." Then there are the giants. These are the "patient, toiling, stupid, respectful, money-worshipping people." And then there are the gods, especially, in *Die Walküre*, Wotan and his exacting wife, Fricka. They represent the putatively "intellectual, moral, talented people who devise and administer States and Churches." They develop and defend the legal ideologies of the established order—the "State Law"—that the revolutions of 1848 sought to overturn.

In their "lame and cramped government," the gods seek to tear apart the adulterous and incestuous union of Siegmund and Sieglinde.[30]

By pitting the gods against Siegmund and Sieglinde, *Die Walküre* thus establishes a thematic opposition, echoing the ancient Greek drama *Antigone*, between Law and Love. A 1960s radical before his time, Wagner was not far from the worldview of the Beatles, who famously encapsulated their social and artistic vision in the refrain "All you need is love," a spontaneous human community beyond the reach of government.

In Wagner's operatic vision, the order of dwarfs and giants, whose supine compromises ensured the defeat of the 1848 revolutions, is waiting to be redeemed by an order completely outside the class system, an order of heroes even more noble than the gods.

Those heroes are to be found in the clan of the Völsungs. In Wagner's artistic vision, that is, the thematic conflict between Law and Love is symbolized in the strife between the gods and an ancient Germanic clan—in the siblings Siegmund and Sieglinde and, later, in their son Siegfried. To follow Claude Lévi-Strauss's analysis of myth, one can say that the Völsung clan provides a symbolic resolution to the actual social contradictions, or conflicts, of modern industrialized society.[31] The possibility of redeeming modern industrial humanity lies with a heroic tribe whose bonds are those of prepolitical kinship.

That Wagner's work could be later embraced and appropriated by German fascists is no surprise. Wagner used an ancient Germanic clan as a symbol for a new society centered on social justice and led by a heroic class of moral geniuses. It is a fairly short, if a crosswise, leap from that idea to a philosophy that seeks to build a society whose principles of social justice pertain only to the actual descendants of Germanic tribes living under an all-powerful national state guided by heroic leaders. Nazism roundly rejected the principles of internationalism and universalism against which the clan is also pitted. Not surprisingly, recent research has demonstrated that images of another clan society, that of North American Indians, played a vital role in Nazi ideology.[32]

But to see merely latent fascism in the artistic use of the clan as a heroic symbol would be a profound mistake. For just as often it has been a device for imagining and advancing liberal political ends—most influentially in the work of the Scottish writer Walter Scott.

•

In the writings of Walter Scott, especially his beloved novel *Waverley* (1814), the clan serves an entirely better purpose—a liberal purpose. Morgan and Engels looked to the clan as a model for a new society that would displace modern liberalism by upending its property regime. Wagner used it as an artistic vehicle for imagining a world of redemptive individual heroism. Scott instead sought to use the clan to create the cultural resources with which modern liberal government could be sustained.

In doing so, he helped construct the distinctive literary sensibility of liberal constitutionalism.

Waverley was one of the essential books of nineteenth-century Europe. "The unexpected newness of the thing," explained the Scottish lawyer Henry Cockburn, "the profusion of original characters, the Scotch language, Scotch scenery, Scotch men and women, the simplicity of the writing, and the graphic force of the descriptions, all struck us with an electric shock of delight."[33] Yet the novel remains remarkably contemporary after almost two hundred years, vital for both citizens of liberal nations and liberal reformers within modern clan societies.

The book tells the story of Edward Waverley, a young English soldier who comes of age amidst the Jacobite Rising of 1745. Known widely as the Forty-Five, the rebellion was a military campaign led by Prince Charles Edward Stuart to return the house of Stuart to the British throne. The Scottish Stuarts had been cut out of the dynastic transfer of royal authority in Britain in the wake of the Glorious Revolution of 1688, when parliamentary forces overthrew the absolutist—and Catholic— James II. The deposed monarch escaped to France, spending the remainder of his days plotting to regain power.

The path of British royal succession was thereafter determined by two parliamentary acts, the Bill of Rights of 1689 and the Act of Settlement of 1701, which guaranteed that all subsequent British monarchs would be Protestants in communion with the Church of England. Following the deaths of Mary II (in 1694), William III (in 1702), and Anne (in 1714), the throne passed to the Germanic house of Hanover, beginning with George I in 1714. By then the Act of Union of 1707 had also brought England and Scotland together under a single parliament and crown. British royal authority remains to this day descended from the Hanoverian line through Queen Victoria, though under the more suitably British name of the house of Windsor.

Enter Prince Charles, affectionately dubbed Bonnie Prince Charlie. Thirty-one years after the disputed "Hanoverian succession," the twenty-five-year-old grandson of James II sought to restore the power of his house. His cause was known as Jacobitism, after the Latin name for James (a movement not to be confused with Jacobinism, the radical wing of the French Revolution). The Jacobites found especially strong support among Scotland's Highland clans, who had been favorably treated by James II and also saw Jacobitism as a means to advance their interests against rival clans.

The rebellion began with some real promise, at least in Scotland. Landing in Lochaber in July, Charles raised an army of twenty-five hundred men, and he made quick work of British forces, who were light in experience and few in number. Most of them had already been sent to the Continent to fight against France in the War of the Austrian Succession. But the prince's victories dwindled, and he found precious few volunteers in England as his forces moved south. His army grew ragged and hungry.

The rebels were utterly crushed in April 1746 in the battle of Culloden. The carnage began with a devastating British cannon barrage. The redcoats then used a novel bayonet strategy to put the Jacobites to rout. Rather than thrusting straight ahead, as was standard practice, they fought at an angle. As the rebels charged, each soldier would step back slightly and then jab into the unprotected side of the Scotsman attacking directly to the right along the British line.

The strategy required great courage and discipline. Each soldier's life depended on whether his neighbor would protect the man to his right while ignoring the Highlander running straight at him with a sword and shield.

The battle lasted forty minutes. From a force of nine thousand soldiers, the British lost fifty men. Prince Charles lost 20 percent of his army—one thousand soldiers, including many Highland clan chiefs, lay slaughtered on the field.

Charles spent the next five months fleeing British troops, disguised for a time as an Irish spinning maid, before finally escaping to France.

The rebellion not only foreclosed the dream of Stuart restoration, it also spelled the end of Scottish clans as an autonomous legal force. In the wake of the Forty-Five, Britain tightened its laws to disarm the Highlanders and prevented the wearing of kilt and tartan.

Most important of all, with the Heritable Jurisdictions Act of 1746 Parliament abolished the traditional inherited authority of Scottish lairds and clan chiefs to adjudicate disputes arising on their land, the forfeiture of which was the penalty for noncompliance. The act struck at the heart of the rule of the clan in Scotland by undermining its decentralized legal structure. Clan chiefs could no longer hold their own court, inherited from their forefathers.

It is this spectacular defeat that provides the scene for Scott's great coming-of-age story—the world's first historical novel and one of its first political novels as well.

When readers meet Edward Waverley, he is a confused and uncertain young man. In matters of the heart he is unattached. In matters of politics he is torn between two paths. On one hand he has before him the liberal model of his father, a Whig who works for the Hanoverian government in London. On the other hand he has the example of his uncle, a Scottish baron from the Lowlands, who is a cultural nationalist sympathetic to the Jacobite cause.

The genius of Scott's book is to resolve these two uncertainties, of love and politics, the individual and the public, within a single story. The technique is now familiar to modern readers, but it was one of the distinctive innovations of nineteenth-century European literature. By tracing the development of a young man into adulthood, Scott imagines the transformation of Scotland into full political maturity in the wake of the Jacobite rebellion. He dramatizes an ideological conflict through a love plot.

The story begins when Edward's regiment is sent to Scotland. There, he is introduced to Rose, the lovely and amiable daughter of one of his uncle's friends. Her virtues are those of the home. Marriage to Rose seems possible, but soon Edward is invited to visit the mountain hideaway of the Mac-Ivors, a colorful clan of Scotch Highlanders. There he comes to know their courageous leader, Chieftain Fergus.

He also meets Fergus's beautiful and fiery sister, Flora, with whom he naturally falls in love. Flora is passionately devoted to her clan, even more fervently than her brother. The "zeal of her loyalty," writes Scott, "burned pure."[34]

Rose and Flora—Edward's marital decision becomes a choice between two very different flowers.

It is a difficult decision, for the Mac-Ivors certainly cut a romantic figure. Scott meticulously depicts the life of the clan, drawing on his many years of folkloric research, and these detailed portraits comprise some of the most memorable parts of the novel. The ring of highland pipes, the lilt of Gaelic poetry, the grace of Scottish dance, the bountiful spread of a hospitable clan chief's table, the sublimity of the cragged landscape—nothing escapes Scott's loving description. Edward even meets Bonnie Prince Charlie himself.

Indeed, the Mac-Ivors are not simply cultural nationalists. When Edward first encounters them, they are actively engaged in paramilitary preparations for the Stuart rebellion. The turning point in the book comes when Edward deserts his regiment and joins them to fight for Prince Charlie's cause, drawn in by his love for Flora and the romantic life of the clan.

The rebellion fails, of course, but Edward isn't lost. Through some twists of plot, he escapes execution and he ultimately marries Rose, leaving behind the exciting life of the Highlanders and their antiliberal political commitments, all the while actively kindling his experience with them into a sustaining, romantic memory. Edward will be a man of the Lowlands and a British subject, with an eternal recollection of his grand Highland romance.

Notably, one of the special objects of Scott's anthropological eye is Highland law. Scott was a lawyer by training, reared to join the family firm, and in all his novels he approached legal issues with a special sensitivity.[35] In *Waverley*, Chieftain Fergus is the hereditary leader of a legal world unto itself. He metes out justice among its members, and he is the guardian of their interests and collective honor. He also plays a venerable role mediating between the various clans of the region. "He applied himself with great earnestness to appease all the feuds and dissensions which frequently arose among other clans in his neighborhood," writes Scott, "so that he became a frequent umpire in their quarrels."[36] Scott depicts the Mac-Ivors as an autonomous legal community within the decentralized constitutional order of the rule of the clan.

If Edward's choice between Rose and Flora is difficult, the choice posed by the two visions of law he encounters is obvious. For while the Mac-Ivors may cut a handsome figure, they represent a normative world Scott decidedly rejects in favor of the rationality and liberalism of the Hanoverian state. At the end of the novel Chieftain Fergus and his rebels stand trial in London in a model of due process. In contrast, in one of the climactic moments of the novel, Fergus deals out justice by striking one of his kinsmen on the skull, nearly splitting it open, to Edward's horror—a scene James Michener implicitly reprised with *Caravans*.[37]

For Scott, writes one critic, "final solutions are legal solutions," and he imagined the solution of the conflict between England and Scotland to be the demise of the Highland clans as autonomous legal entities.[38]

But in a seeming paradox, for Scott the end of the rule of the clan did not spell the end of the clan per se; if anything, it made the clan even more essential. As the legal force of Scottish clans declined, their cultural importance grew. For Scott, the new, superior legal order which took the place of the clan could be maintained only if the culture that sustained the clan itself—the rich folk life of tartan and ballad he so painstakingly chronicled—were given a place of honor in national memory. The paramilitary exploits of the Mac-Ivors, even their chieftain's difficult law, could no longer have an active political or legal significance, but they would have to become as culturally sustaining for a unified Britain's common liberal institutions as was Edward's memory of the Highlands.

It's this historical consciousness, with all its sociolegal implications, to which Scott gives novelistic expression. A liberal legal order would rest on the embrace in wistful memory of antiliberal kinship associations.

•

Indeed, the fact of that embrace in Scott's own work might be said to have been one of the cultural signs of modern liberalism's true legal advent. The development of romantic memories of the clan is often a sign not of an atavistic regression but rather of liberalism's birth—a phenomenon it will be essential for liberals to bear in mind as we watch political development in clan societies across the globe, including those in the Middle East, North Africa, and other Muslim-majority states. As the social and legal power of clan and clanlike networks abates, many clan identities will come to be an object of public celebration and veneration.

Recalling the Scottish experience, liberals should be prepared to embrace this cultural turn, to welcome the latest equivalent of Molly MacPherson's and its commemoration of the fearsome Macpherson cat.

Scott's own embrace of the clan went well beyond his novels. In 1822 he orchestrated one of the great ceremonial pageants of the modern British monarchy: the visit of King George IV to Scotland, the first visit of a reigning English monarch to Scotland since the 1630s. Intending to deflect attention away from the labor radicalism that had recently rocked the country and to unite Scotland under a common liberal political identity, Scott organized a two-week Celtic cultural revival, placing the Hanoverian monarch at its head.

"King George IV comes hither . . . [as] our kinsman," Scott explained revealingly to his fellow citizens in *Hints Addressed to the Inhabitants of Edinburgh, and Others, in Prospect of His Majesty's Visit.*

While our Douglases, our Stewarts, our Hamiltons, our Braces, all our high nobility, are his acknowledged relations—it is not too much to say, that there is scarcely a gentleman of any of the old Scottish families who cannot, in some way or other, "count kin" with the royal house from which our Sovereign is descended . . . In short, we are THE CLAN, and our King is THE CHIEF. Let us, on this happy occasion, remember that it is so; and not only behave toward him as a father, but to each other, as if we were, in the words of the old song, "ae man's bairns."

The king's visit culminated in a grand "Highland ball," where "no Gentleman is allowed to appear in any thing but the ancient Highland costume."[39]

The liberal political philosopher Walter Bagehot liked to speak of the "ornamental" aspects of the modern British constitution—those ritualistic, aesthetic features of British government that while slowing the efficiency of administration captured the imagination of everyday people and bound them emotionally to the state.[40] Liberal constitutionalism requires the vitality of many such "ornaments," and not because most citizens are incapable of appreciating their government without them, as Bagehot argued, but because they provide a positive human good—solidarity—without which the liberal state collapses into anomie.

Scott was a cultural activist encouraging pride in clan identity for the purpose of strengthening the liberal state.

In combining the yearning for the clan with liberal political principles, Scott was representative of a deep tradition of English writing. Throughout the Romantic and Victorian eras in Britain, a wide variety of liberal artists and intellectuals took an intense interest in the Germanic tribal past, finding there the very conceptual wellsprings of British liberty. As the historian J. W. Burrow notes, nineteenth-century British liberals yoked a pious respect for the tribal past to a belief in progressive historical development.[41]

From this perspective, the Middle Ages provided a vital cultural resource for present-day liberal institutions, which demanded continual imaginative engagement to survive.

Nor was Scott's achievement for Britain alone. In helping to transform the Scottish clan from a legal to a purely cultural form, Scott also influenced literary liberals around the world. For instance, the Bengali writer Bankim Chandra Chatterji was inspired by Scott when he composed the founding novel of Indian nationalism, *Anandamath* (1882). He imagined a future liberal, independent India by depicting a primitive, egalitarian village community of ascetics. Living in an isolated jungle retreat, Chatterji's warrior-monks describe themselves in familial terms as children of the same mother—Mother India (*Vande Mataram*). Like Scott, Chatterji found the cultural resources for a modern, forward-looking India in the communal normative order of the past.[42] As in Scotland, Indian liberalism was built on a literary foundation that valorized many aspects of its communalist tradition.

Moreover, Scott created a universal template for liberal citizenship—for the kind of persons who would form the foundation of a stable liberal society. Like Edward Waverley, they could proudly inhabit a particular cultural community yet do so on a fully voluntary basis, affirming the past not for its own sake but rather for its vitality for present life. They could look back as part of looking forward. They could affirm a strong cultural identity in the midst of the possibility of leaving it. They could live with Rose but remember the world of Flora.

This movement of the self requires persons to recognize themselves implicitly as a blank slate, and thus in abstract individual terms, as in some meaningful sense presocial and prepolitical, an understanding of the self necessary for imagining the existence of a common public interest. The very exercise of *choosing* to affirm a clan identity, and to continually reaffirm it, makes it possible to imagine a common good greater than the needs of the self.

Scott developed the symbols and the stories to enable individuals to do so in Great Britain and he advanced a view of the imagination that allowed a similar movement of the self elsewhere—a liberal view of the imagination. This view values the imagination for the service it renders to individuals making their lives in contemporary circumstances. The liberal imagination is flexible in its attitude toward interpretation, looking to history without slavishly following it.

At bottom it is this vision of the imagination, and the artistic and cultural works it produces, that is the foundation of a liberal society. The liberal imagination of artists like Scott and Chatterji provides citizens of modern states with a language, a mode of personhood, and a relation to the past that enables them to understand and navigate their world.

Intellectuals and artists in societies struggling under clannism today understand this matter well.

Many readers will recall Salman Rushdie's 1988 novel *The Satanic Verses*, which followed the publication in 1983 of *Shame*, his political novel of Pakistan. Written in the inventive style of magical realism, the book follows the story of two Indian expatriates who are miraculously saved when their hijacked plane explodes over the English Channel. The novel also includes a number of scenes that portray Muhammad and the world of early Islam with irreverent humor.

Many Muslims deemed these scenes to be blasphemous, and the book sparked strident and sometimes violent protests upon its publication, especially in nations long mired in political tyranny and unaccustomed to vigorous free expression.

Then in early 1989 Iran's Ayatollah Khomeini issued a ruling, or fatwa, enjoining the writer's murder—a duty, he proclaimed, of all Muslims.

The power of the ayatollah's edict to draw a line between people who fundamentally believe in intellectual and artistic freedom and those who do not cannot be overstated. I vividly recall a discussion I had at the time with a Muslim convert, a deeply kind and thoughtful intellectual, on the steps of a residence hall at Stanford University. Beneath the beauty of the California sun, he earnestly insisted that the writer should be killed. (Bridges ought not to be burnt, but we never spoke again.)

What is less known in the West is that the title phrase of Rushdie's book refers to the incident, discussed in chapter 10, in which Muhammad likely made a brief, politically motivated concession to clan-based polytheism. The reconstructed story is one of the subplots of the novel.

"O the sweet songs that he knew," writes Rushdie of Satan. "With his daughters as his fiendish backing group, yes, the three of them, Lat Manat Uzza, motherless girls laughing with their Abba, giggling behind their hands at Gibreel, what a trick we got in store for you, they giggle, for you and for that businessman [Muhammad] on the hill."[43]

One of the liberating goals of Rushdie's book is to imaginatively reconstruct within this central moment of Islamic history a principle of artistic play, interpretive flexibility, and individual freedom—what Hisham Sharabi calls "the overcoming of *literalness*."[44] Rushdie looks to a moment in the medieval past when Islam and the rule of the clan confronted each other and discovers precisely there the cultural resources for a liberal society.

TWELVE

THE CLAN'S RETURN

As unrest spread across Libya at the start of the North African Spring in 2011, Colonel Muammar al-Qaddafi's son and heir apparent, Seif al-Islam al-Qaddafi, pointedly warned of dire consequences if his father's government collapsed. "Unlike Egypt and Tunisia, Libya is made up of tribes and clans and alliances," he cautioned. "There will be civil war."[1]

The speech was delivered in the ineffably weird style of the colonel—rambling, incoherent, strange—and it was widely ridiculed.

But on this point the son was prescient and he had ample cause for concern.

It's common to think of Colonel Qaddafi as a mere strongman, a hulking military brute who kept the Libyan people in check with a big stick. He was that. But he was also a man guided by a coherent political vision. He spelled out that worldview in a slim volume known as *The Green Book*, Qaddafi's counterpart to Chairman Mao's "Little Red Book."

After he was brought to power in 1969 in a coup overthrowing King Idris, Qaddafi made a momentous decision about how revolutionary Libya would be ruled. The commander rejected conventional modern ideas of government and chose instead to draw his model of law and politics from the Bedouin peoples of the region. Looking to the ancient tribal traditions of the desert, he argued that the state is a tyrannical imposition of authority over natural social arrangements.

"The imminent danger threatening freedom," Qaddafi wrote in his manifesto, "lies . . . with man-made laws." His ambition in building a new

Libya was thus to apply "the ultimate solution" to the essential "problem" of government itself.[2]

According to Qaddafi, the true foundation of society, on which the Libyan revolution would stand, is the family and its clan and tribe.

As a practical matter, asserted Qaddafi, the tribe provides its members with "collective protection and security," "collective reparations," "collective compensation for bodily injury," and (presumably collective) "revenge."

Equally important, it grants individuals meaning, personhood, and morality. "The code of ethics enforced by the tribe on its members is a kind of social education better and nobler than any school education," he wrote. The tribe's power in this regard is even greater than the family's. While "an individual may sometimes behave in a dishonourable manner that a family will not condone," because "the family is relatively small in size, this individual will not be aware of its supervision. In contrast, individuals as members of a tribe cannot be free of its watchful eyes."[3]

Acknowledging this natural basis of society, Qaddafi forged a government that was highly local and decentralized. Officially, power was dispersed to people's "congresses" and "committees." In practice, it devolved to Libya's scores of tribes and smaller lineage units. Rather than overcome the rule of the clan, he made clans the core of the state.

His new Libya "denie[d] *The Leviathan* almost root and branch."[4]

During his years in power, Qaddafi exerted a great deal of his authority to ensure that Libya's tribes supported his revolutionary aims as well as his self-aggrandizing ones. He did so through a system of calibrated rewards and punishments directed at Libya's numerous independent tribal and great-family groups (there are about 140 distinct tribes, but only a few dozen are politically powerful). For tribes that helped him there was government patronage—jobs. For tribes whose members were disloyal, there was collective punishment.

Notably, as one expert observes, "this principle of obedience reproduced itself in the tribes themselves." The loyalty Qaddafi demanded of tribal elders in exchange for his largess was demanded in turn by tribal elders of lineage members.[5] In a rentier economy based on oil profits, Qaddafi's patronage reinforced the anti-individualist values of communities of Status.

When the Libyan uprising began in 2011, however, the tribes Qaddafi had sought to keep in check were cut loose from his control. The Misurata and the Abu Llail in the east supported the uprising while the al-Awaqir opposed it. In the west the Warfalla fought Qaddafi's forces, though the tribe had long been given prominence within the Libyan security apparatus, while the colonel naturally received support from his own tribe, the Qadhafah. The Magariha, also long favored in the security services (its members included the Lockerbie bomber, Abdel Baset Ali al-Megrahi), wavered.

Libya faced the possibility of explosive intertribal and interclan conflict. Tribal differences threatened to tear apart even the ranks of the rebellion itself, to fracture resistance to Qaddafi along tribal lines. When the chief rebel military commander, General Abdul Fattah Younnes, was assassinated in July 2011, his powerful eastern tribe, the Obeidi, pointed a finger at the rebel leadership.[6]

This danger has persisted long after Qaddafi's fall—if anything, it has grown more menacing.[7]

The future of Libya will thus depend on whether its new leaders can forge a government that takes the path Qaddafi rejected in *The Green Book*. It will depend, that is, on whether Libyan statesmen put the tribal cork back in the bottle by constructing a modern government or whether they surrender their country to an especially potent form of the rule of the clan. Can they build a liberal state capable of preventing Seif al-Qaddafi's warning from coming true?

As they make this effort, citizens of developed, liberal nations can learn from them, for our own challenges are not unrelated to theirs.

•

In *The World America Made*, Robert Kagan recently asked readers to imagine what the world would look like today had the United States "never been born." What would have been the character of the international order, he asks, "had the United States not been the preeminent power shaping it for the past six decades," and what might it look like "if America were to decline, as so many nowadays predict"?[8] Would the international order remain as favorable to democracy, economic growth, and national security as it has been since World War II?

Many people, Kagan asserts, are not troubled by the question.

"There is a general sense that the end of the era of American preeminence need not mean the end of the present liberal international order," he writes. "The expectation, if not assumption, is that the good qualities of that order—the democracy, the prosperity, the peace among great powers—can transcend the decline of American power and influence."[9]

Such expectations are in Kagan's view fundamentally flawed. The modern international order is an American one, he argues. It has been predicated on the projection of American power abroad.

In the absence of American national will, or in the face of American decline, the liberal institutions and norms of this order are likely to disappear. The conditions that have been so favorable to democratic development over the past sixty years will vanish.

There is nothing natural about our current liberal international climate and its values, Kagan asserts. It will survive "only as long as those who imposed it retain the capacity to defend it."

The alternative to American global power is not "peace and harmony but chaos and catastrophe."[10]

The relation between individualism and the state is similar. Just as American power guarantees a liberal order in international affairs, so a robust state is essential to true individual freedom. A decline of the state would bring chaos and catastrophe for individualism just as a decline of American power would be disastrous for the prospects of democratic development.

To be sure, the state can be an instrument of tyranny. Nobody who has lived in the twentieth century can fail to be profoundly aware of the dangers posed by state power. Overreaching states have utterly crushed individual freedom in the Soviet Union (from which my own ancestors fled), Germany, China, and a host of other nations. But this fact should not lead to radical cynicism about state power per se. Nor should it cause us to be cavalier about the consequences that would ensue if the state were to be critically weakened.

As modern nations across the world have grappled with the recent financial crisis, there has been a widespread call not merely to streamline the public sector and make it more efficient (a thoroughly positive goal), but to engage in the wholesale dismantling of public institutions. Indeed, the very concept of the public and public interest have been attacked.

If these criticisms are successful—if they sap the collective political will and lead liberals to turn away from the state as an instrument to advance common ends—it will be a catastrophe for individual freedom. Giving up on the promise of liberal modernity, we will find ourselves living under a new, postmodern form of the rule of the clan.

It is worth contemplating for a moment what such a future would look like.

Imagine that fifty years from now a confluence of antigovernment ideology and tight economic times have rendered the liberal state a mere shadow of its former self.

Public institutions no longer provide the services that modern citizens generally expect government to supply or at least to guarantee. Education, public health and welfare, market regulation, police—in the place of the state, most of the responsibility and authority that today vest in democratic government has been formally devolved to or seized by a host of institutions that lay claim to the state's past power.

These institutions include, first, traditional lineage groups. The experience of post-Soviet Central Asia, the Middle East, and North Africa illustrates how quickly lineage politics can reemerge once the lid of the state is lifted. The blood tie is a natural way of organizing relationships between people and of structuring community affairs.

And so where once the Germanic state grew by wresting power away from families, in this postmodern what-if world extended families have taken that power back. Clans have returned in their most ancient form, as kinship groups. They ensure that their members have their material needs met, and they guarantee their safety, providing security as well to their fictive kin (typically members of the same race).

More strikingly, this postmodern rule of the clan is also composed of a wide variety of other corporatist associations. Human history has created a range of powerful new institutions that now vie with lineage groups to fill the vacuum created by the decline of state power.

Religious organizations overlap with major families to provide social security in exchange for the agreement of members to live by their internal codes of law, enforced through their own courts. They not only perform marriages but also oversee divorces, arrange adoptions, structure inheritance, and regulate contract and property disputes among their adherents.

Militant trade unions and guilds have taken on similar functions, regulating themselves according to their own standards and seeking to vindicate their institutional interests rather than those of the individual people they serve.

In core urban areas and isolated rural communities, where the state's writ no longer runs, racial gangs and organized crime syndicates provide services in exchange for loyalty. In the absence of a police force, injuries are avenged through various forms of group vigilantism, from the exaction of physical violence to the expropriation of property. Individuals are required to condition the extent of their freedom on the needs and will of the organizations that provide them with jobs and economic security.

Finally, transnational corporations serve many traditional state functions. Whereas primary education is the province of family, religious, and trade groups, universities have been captured by international businesses and enterprises to train their professional workforce. Transnational corporations monitor international borders, control immigration, enforce treaties, and manage natural resources.

The only courts that arbitrate between the many diverse clan and clanlike groups that now proliferate and compete are administered by large companies. To bring suit against the errant jogger, for example, a person doesn't contact his or her own lawyer directly. Instead, he or she calls the "Justice Department" of the company for which he or she works. The lawyers there, in consultation with the chief financial officer, determine whether or not to bring suit on their employee's behalf. The suit itself is heard in one of the vestigial institutions of government, a courthouse, before a privately hired judge. In turn, the employee's suit is directed not against the jogger per se but rather against his employer.

All these new clans, from extended families and gangs to churches and corporations, offer a wide range of goods and services previously furnished by the state or dispersed under its watchful guidance. The various functions of the state continue to be discharged.

But there is a difference. Whereas the state once provided its many goods to individuals *as* individuals, these groups afford them to their members only. And they are guided not by the abstract ideals of the public good and the inherent rights of the individual but rather by the practical needs of their organizations and by the internal hierarchies within them.

No longer predominantly citizens in the eyes of the law, people base their varied legal claims on their roles within the social groups to which they belong. In this world, legal actions are not undertaken by individuals alone. They are pursued only on behalf of groups. Individuals relate to the legal order only through corporate or other postmodern clan proxies.

In Hisham Sharabi's terms, individuals lack a "claim to autonomous right."[11]

Under such circumstances, people's behavior naturally begins to change in myriad ways. Most of all, their clans become a central part of the face they present to the world. Knowing that their gang, family, or company is responsible for their physical protection, most people make sure that their clothing is always prominently emblazoned with the symbol of their group. Social interactions are mediated by a constant awareness of group affiliations and of hierarchies between and within clans and quasi clans. Choices about whom to marry, where to make a home, and how to make a living are never made by individuals alone.

Where once liberal nations existed, providing the benefits of citizenship on equal terms, there are now a host of new clans in a horrifying archipelago of Status.

The most probable outcome of a radically diminished state is thus neither a collection of empowered individuals liberated from the constraints of government nor a grand community of equality and solidarity. Rather, it is a riven, fractured, unequal world in which both individuals and the larger public are sacrificed to the needs of clans of all sorts.

The fundamental question of human political community is not *whether* an overarching political authority exists but rather what *kind* of overarching authority exists and what values it serves. If liberal society doesn't create conditions where human needs can be met, then support for liberal society itself will dwindle and those needs will be met in other ways, spelling the end of our most cherished values.

For while the rule of the clan has ancient origins, it can also be born anew in every age.

•

But liberals need not surrender to the rule of the clan, either at home or abroad, if we understand its structures and are mindful of its lessons.

By way of a final reflection on those lessons, especially the lesson of individualism's paradox, let me briefly look back at the path we have traced in this book.

We began by defining liberal societies as those that place a central value on individual freedom and self-development. They are societies oriented fundamentally toward the person.

By the rule of the clan, on the other hand, I have meant Henry Maine's societies of Status, the range of communities around the world whose legal structures and cultural values are oriented primarily toward kinship. Under the rule of the clan, people are valued less as individuals per se than as members of their extended families. Individuals are submerged within the essential social groups to which they belong and from which they cannot exit.

Both the rule of the clan in its strongest form and clannism, its historical echo, pose an urgent challenge to liberal nations and to their core value of individual freedom.

From without, the rule of the clan destabilizes regions of the world that are vital to liberal security needs and that provide hiding places for our enemies. Liberal national interests are tied directly to societies in which the clan remains a vital force. Whether or not established liberal democracies flourish in the future depends on the success or failure of today's liberal reformers abroad.

Within liberal societies, the rule of the clan haunts liberal nations as a specter of what they might become. Meeting its challenge is an essential task of national stewardship.

How, I asked, does the rule of the clan work as a form of government?

Though clan societies vary a great deal in their particulars and though the rule of the clan can exist in stronger or weaker forms, at its heart the rule of the clan links a decentralized legal and political structure with a culture of group honor and shame.

Under the rule of the clan, legal and political authority resides in the main not in a central state but rather in a host of separate and distinct extended kin groups, with the likes of the Macphersons in Scotland, the Sturlungs in Iceland, the Gaawar in Nuerland, the Daghmash in Gaza, or the Shaman Khel branch of the Mahsud in Pakistan. These groups are highly cohesive and they provide many tangible benefits to their members, including the physical and material security that comes with solidarity and the dignity that accompanies an unshakable feeling of personal belonging.

Group honor is at once the cultural expression of this cohesion and the practical mechanism for enforcing it. In a community animated by the principle of group honor, harms done *to* a group's individual members and misdeeds done *by* them affect the social worth of the group as a whole, as we saw in the case of India and the Philippines. This principle is the cultural fuel of the institution of feud even as it also enables multiple kin groups to exist in rough harmony within a single territory.

Group honor undergirds the decentralized constitutionalism of the rule of the clan and the anti-individualist values it supports.

Understanding the rule of the clan, I argued, is essential to liberals for three reasons.

First, it allows liberals to appreciate how best to assist native reformers abroad who seek to turn their societies toward more liberal legal arrangements. Looking to the cases of Anglo-Saxon England and early Islamic Arabia, I explained that state development requires the growth within clan societies of a robust public identity, based on a modern concept of law, which transcends particularistic family loyalties. A public legal identity provides the basis for the growth of more centralized state institutions that are capable of treating people as individuals, and it displaces one of the primary functions of kinship in honor cultures by insuring against collective risk.

Over time, the development of a common public identity helps transform the clan from a hard legal regime to a soft yet meaningful source of personal identity. It pushes the clan from the realm of law to that of culture—it domesticates the Macpherson cat. I observed that studying history suggests ways to nurture public identity today both "from below" and "from above," by promoting social media, thereby encouraging a transformation from kinship to social networks, and by supporting the middle-class professions.

Second, the rule of the clan reveals that, at home as much as abroad, liberals must affirm the cultural conditions that provide the foundation for the rule of law. Guided by an appreciation of the benefits clans provide their members, liberals must strengthen civil institutions that root individuals in solidaristic communities organized around shared values.

These institutions range from grassroots political organizations to religious groups—all the normative associations of civil society.

At the same time, liberals must defend each person's inherent right to intellectual, economic, religious, and personal choice. Such freedom is essential in its own right and it is the single greatest counterforce to the culture of group honor and the decentralized constitutionalism of the rule of the clan.

Personal freedom is also the cornerstone of liberal politics. As the great works of the modern literary tradition demonstrate, liberalism depends on a human person who voluntarily chooses who they would most like to be.[12] When choosing a profession, a community, a faith, or a personal identity, the liberal individual imagines himself or herself as one of many free persons within a common public.

Third, and most important, by illuminating the nature of individualism's paradox, the rule of the clan points to the need for individualists to support the state.

It highlights the need for people dedicated to individualism to foster a strong and effective government capable of vindicating the public interest. People dedicated to individual freedom must have the clarity and the courage to defend the state that makes freedom possible.

NOTES

PART I: THE CHALLENGE OF THE CLAN

1. INDIVIDUALISM'S PARADOX

1. For a classic argument in favor of the liberal, individualist mode of life, see John Stuart Mill, *On Liberty*, ed. David Bromwich and George Kateb (New Haven, Conn.: Yale University Press, 2003), especially chapter 3 ("Of Individuality, as One of the Elements of Well-being").

2. Ron Paul, "Political Power and the Rule of Law," *Texas Straight Talk*, February 5, 2007, accessed June 29, 2012, http://paul.house.gov/index.php?option=com_content&task=view&id=1106&Itemid=69.

3. M. Al. Gathafi [Muammar al-Qaddafi], *The Green Book: The Solution to the Problem of Democracy; The Solution to the Economic Problem; The Social Basis of the Third Universal Theory* (Reading, U.K.: Ithaca Press, 2005), 26. On Qaddafi's theory of the state, see generally John Davis, *Libyan Politics: Tribe and Revolution* (London: I. B. Tauris, 1987).

4. Granville Austin, *The Indian Constitution: Cornerstone of a Nation* (Oxford, U.K.: Oxford University Press, 2012), 31, and see generally 27–49. On the individualist justification for centralization, see B. R. Ambedkar, "Basic Features of the Indian Constitution," in *The Essential Writings of B. R. Ambedkar*, ed. Valerian Rodrigues (Oxford, U.K.: Oxford University Press, 2002), 473–94, 485–86.

5. On the presence of other "tribal impulses" in modern society, see Robin Fox, *The Tribal Imagination: Civilization and the Savage Mind* (Cambridge, Mass.: Harvard University Press, 2011).

6. Francis Fukuyama has recently explored a related set of issues under the terms "patrimonialism" and "repatrimonialism" in his important work *The Origins of Political Order: From Prehuman Times to the French Revolution* (New York: Farrar, Straus and Giroux, 2011), 49–94. See also the discussion of "Ancient Nepotism" in Adam Bellow, *In Praise of Nepotism: A History of Family Enterprise from King David to George W. Bush* (New York: Anchor Books, 2003), 79–112. Although the term "clan" is controversial among anthropologists, I use it here because it captures the full range of social and legal phenomena I examine and is current in everyday speech.

7. United Nations Development Programme, Regional Bureau for Arab States, *Arab Human Development Report 2004: Towards Freedom in the Arab World* (New York: United Nations Development Programme, 2005), 145–46.

8. Henry Sumner Maine, *Ancient Law: Its Connection with the Early History of Society and Its Relation to Modern Ideas* (Gloucester, Mass.: Peter Smith, 1970; originally published in 1861), 165.

9. George Feaver, *From Status to Contract: A Biography of Sir Henry Maine, 1822–1888* (London: Longmans, Green, 1969), 8. On Maine's legal theories, see R.C.J. Cocks, *Sir Henry Maine: A Study in Victorian Jurisprudence* (Cambridge, U.K.: Cambridge University Press, 1988).

10. George Feaver, "The Victorian Values of Sir Henry Maine," in *The Victorian Achievement of Sir Henry Maine: A Centennial Reappraisal*, ed. Alan Diamond (Cambridge, U.K.: Cambridge University Press, 1991), 35.

11. Karuna Mantena, *Alibis of Empire: Henry Maine and the Ends of Liberal Imperialism* (Princeton, N.J.: Princeton University Press, 2010), 6.

12. Henry Sumner Maine, *Lectures on the Early History of Institutions* (New York: Henry Holt, 1875), 11–12, 39–41. See also Henry Sumner Maine, *Village-Communities in the East and West: Six Lectures Delivered at Oxford* (London: J. Murray, 1871).

13. Maine, *Ancient Law*, 165.

14. Thomas R. Trautmann, *Lewis Henry Morgan and the Invention of Kinship* (Berkeley: University of California Press, 1987), 180.

15. Akbar S. Ahmed, *Islam Under Siege: Living Dangerously in a Post-Honor World* (Cambridge, U.K.: Polity Press, 2003), and Abdullah Saeed and Hassan Saeed, *Freedom of Religion, Apostasy, and Islam* (Aldershot, U.K.: Ashgate, 2004), 118–19.

16. Angus Maddison, *Contours of the World Economy, 1–2030 AD: Essays in Macro-Economic History* (Oxford, U.K.: Oxford University Press, 2007), 382, and *Monitoring the World Economy, 1820–1992* (Paris: Development Centre of the Organisation for Economic Co-operation and Development, 1995), 23–24.

17. The roots of this argument lie in Max Weber's analysis in *Economy and Society* of the tendency of modern law to drift into antiformalism. A related argument about corporatist trends in "postliberal" society has been advanced by Roberto Mangabeira Unger in *Law in Modern Society* (New York: Free Press, 1976). My own concerns center not on rising antiformalism and corporatism within the state, but rather on the anti-individualist consequences of an erosion of support for the state through a lack of political will, as well as on the threats clan-based societies abroad pose to the liberal state and its values.

18. Alexis de Tocqueville, *Democracy in America*, vol. 2 (New York: Vintage Books, 1990), 99 (book 2, chapter 2, "Of Individualism in Democratic Countries").

2. FROM CLAN TO CLUB

1. W. Croft Dickinson, *Scotland from the Earliest Times to 1603*, 3rd ed., rev. and ed. Archibald A. M. Duncan (Oxford, U.K.: Clarendon Press, 1977), 6.

2. For an accessible introduction to Highland culture, especially literature and song, from a Gaelic perspective, see Michael Newton, *Warriors of the Word: The World of the Scottish Highlanders* (Edinburgh: Birlinn, 2009). On clan culture, see 122–63.

3. Archibald A. M. Duncan, "Clans, Scottish," in *Dictionary of the Middle Ages*, ed. Joseph R. Strayer (New York: Charles Scribner's Sons, 1982–89), 3:407.

4. Alistair Moffat, *The Highland Clans* (New York: Thames and Hudson, 2010), 41.

5. On the relation between American values of individualism and clubs as a mechanism of social integration, see Francis L. K. Hsu, *Clan, Caste, and Club* (New York: D. Van Nostrand, 1963).

6. See, for example, William Cheyne-Macpherson, *The Chiefs of Clan Macpherson* (Edinburgh: Oliver and Boyd, 1947), 87.

7. On the modern invention of Scottish tradition, see Hugh Trevor-Roper, "The Invention of Tradition: The Highland Tradition of Scotland," in *The Invention of Tradition*, ed. Eric Hobsbawm and Terence Ranger (Cambridge, U.K.: Cambridge University Press, 1983), 15–42.

3. NATIONAL SECURITY AND CLAN HONOR

1. Sadie Bass, "How Many Different Ways Can You Spell 'Gaddafi'?" ABC News, September 22, 2009, accessed June 29, 2012, http://abcnews.go.com/blogs /headlines/2009/09/how-many-different-ways-can-you-spell-gaddafi. See also Eoin O'Carroll, "Gaddafi? Kadafi? Qaddafi? What's the Correct Spelling?" *The Christian Science Monitor*, February 22, 2011, accessed June 29, 2012, www.cs monitor.com/World/2011/0222/Gaddafi-Kadafi-Qaddafi-What-s-the-correct -spelling.

2. For an insightful discussion consistent with this perspective, see generally David Ronfeldt, *In Search of How Societies Work: Tribes—The First and Forever Form*, WR-433-RPC (Santa Monica, Calif.: RAND, December 2006), and 71–3.

3. *Iraq Tribal Study—Al-Anbar Governorate: The Albu Fahd Tribe, The Albu Mahal Tribe, and the Albu Issa Tribe* (Study Conducted Under Contract with the U.S. Department of Defense, June 18, 2006).

4. Vernon Loeb, "Clan, Family Ties Called Key to Army's Capture of Hussein: 'Link Diagrams' Showed Everyone Related by Blood or Tribe," *The Washington Post*, December 16, 2003, A27.

5. Isaiah Wilson III, "Saving Westphalia: Countering Insurgency Through Tribal Democratization," in *Countering Insurgency and Promoting Democracy*, ed. Manolis Priniotakis (New York: Council for Emerging National Security Affairs, 2007), 245–62, 250. On anthropology and counterinsurgency, see Montgomery McFate, "The Military Utility of Understanding Adversary Culture," *Joint Force Quarterly* 38 (2005): 42–48, and "Anthropology and Counterinsurgency: The Strange Story of their Curious Relationship," *Military Review* (March–April 2005): 24–38. On the importance of understanding local allegiance specifically in Afghanistan, see Seth G. Jones, "It Takes the Villages: Bringing Change from Below in Afghanistan," *Foreign Affairs* 89 (May/June 2010): 120–27.

6. For other approaches to the economics of clan behavior, see Jack L. Carr and Janet T. Landa, "The Economics of Symbols, Clan Names, and Religion," *Journal of Legal Studies* 12 (1983): 135–56; Kathleen Collins, *Clan Politics and Regime Transition in Central Asia* (Cambridge, U.K.: Cambridge University Press, 2006), 28–30; Avner Greif, "Reputation and Coalitions in Medieval Trade: Evidence on the Maghribi Traders," *Journal of Economic History* 49 (1989): 857–82; and Janet T. Landa, "A Theory of the Ethnically Homogeneous Middleman Group: An

Institutional Alternative to Contract Law," *Journal of Legal Studies* 10 (1981): 359–62, and "The Enigma of the *Kula Ring*: Gift-Exchanges and Primitive Law and Order," *International Review of Law and Economics* (1983): 137–60.

7. For an example, see Sarah Rainsford, "The Turkish Peacemaker," BBC News, November 11, 2006, accessed June 29, 2012, http://news.bbc.co.uk/2/hi/programmes /from_our_own_correspondent/6137236.stm.

8. For an anthropological discussion, see Christopher Boehm, *Blood Revenge: The Anthropology of Feuding in Montenegro and Other Tribal Societies* (Lawrence: University Press of Kansas, 1984). For a discussion by a legal scholar, see William Ian Miller, *Eye for an Eye* (Cambridge, U.K.: Cambridge University Press, 2006).

9. See the classic Marcel Mauss, *The Gift: The Form and Reason for Exchange in Archaic Societies*, trans. W. D. Halls (New York: W. W. Norton, 1990), and Lewis Hyde, *The Gift: Imagination and the Erotic Life of Property* (New York: Vintage Books, 1983).

10. For a discussion of the phenomenon in Africa, see Mahmood Mamdani, *Citizen and Subject: Contemporary Africa and the Legacy of Late Colonialism* (Princeton, N.J.: Princeton University Press, 1996). See also Martin Chanock, *Law, Custom, and Social Order: The Colonial Experience in Malawi and Zambia* (Portsmouth, N.H.: Heinemann, 1998), and Sally Falk Moore, *Social Facts and Fabrications: "Customary" Law on Kilimanjaro, 1880–1980* (Cambridge, U.K.: Cambridge University Press, 1986).

11. BBC News, "Kenyans 'Rearming for 2012 Poll,'" October 7, 2009, accessed June 29, 2012, http://news.bbc.co.uk/2/hi/africa/8293745.stm.

12. For an incisive study of Pakistani immigrants in Norway advancing this thesis, see Dagmar I. Larssen, *SüdSüdOst Mekka: Pakistanische Muslime in Norwegen* (Berlin/ Münster, Germany: LIT Verlag, 2010), 19.

13. For an academic discussion of the virtues of society outside the state, see Thomas J. Barfield, *The Nomadic Alternative* (Englewood Cliffs, N.J.: Prentice-Hall, 1993), and James C. Scott, *The Art of Not Being Governed: An Anarchist History of Upland Southeast Asia* (New Haven, Conn.: Yale University Press, 2009). On the tendency of the centralized state to disregard local culture and knowledge, see Scott's *Seeing Like a State: How Certain Schemes to Improve the Human Condition Have Failed* (New Haven, Conn.: Yale University Press, 1998). Liberals disregard such local knowledge, as well as the romance of the clan in popular culture, at our peril.

PART II: THE CONSTITUTIONAL ORDER OF THE CLAN

1. For a legal history challenging the myth of laissez-faire in the United States, see William J. Novak, *The People's Welfare: Law and Regulation in Nineteenth-Century America* (Chapel Hill: University of North Carolina Press, 1996). For a recent study that provides a symbolically important example of how the modern state often obscures the depth of its influence and promotes the idea that the social benefits it has made possible "resulted solely from impersonal market forces," see David M. P. Freund, *Colored Property: State Policy and White Racial Politics in Suburban America* (Chicago: University of Chicago Press, 2007), 9, and "Mar-

keting the Free Market: State Intervention and the Politics of Prosperity in Metropolitan America," in Kevin M. Kruse and Thomas J. Sugrue, eds., *The New Suburban History* (Chicago: University of Chicago Press, 2006), 11–32.

4. LAW WITHOUT A STATE: THE NUER OF SOUTHERN SUDAN

1. Liberator, May 11, 2011 (7:33 a.m.), and Adam, May 12, 2011 (9:20 a.m.), comments on Ngor Arol Garang, "Clashes Claim over 80 Lives in Warrap State," *Sudan Tribune*, May 10, 2011, accessed June 29, 2012, www.sudantribune.com /lashes-claims-over-80-lives-in,38850 (spelling and punctuation altered for readability).
2. James Copnall, "Can Sudan's Oil Feed North and South?" BBC News, July 4, 2011, accessed June 29, 2012, www.bbc.co.uk/news/world-africa-12128080.
3. For an introduction to the anthropology of kinship, see Robin Fox, *Kinship and Marriage: An Anthropological Perspective* (Cambridge, U.K.: Cambridge University Press, 1967). In the remainder of this chapter, when speaking of "the Nuer," I refer to the society in the period studied by Evans-Pritchard, unless otherwise indicated.
4. E. E. Evans-Pritchard, *The Nuer: A Description of the Modes of Livelihood and Political Institutions of a Nilotic People* (New York: Oxford University Press, 1940), 10.
5. Ibid., 7.
6. Ibid., 11.
7. Ibid., 10.
8. Ibid., 10.
9. Ibid., 11.
10. Ibid., 12.
11. Ibid., 12.
12. Ibid., 12–13.
13. Ibid., 13.
14. Ibid., 12.
15. Ibid., 14.
16. Ibid., 182.
17. D. M. Koch, "Sudan: Anyuak and Cholo's Kingdoms Are Our National Heritage!" Anyuak Media, August, 21, 2009, accessed June 29, 2012, www.anyuak media.com/com_temp_09_08_22.html (spelling and punctuation altered for readability).
18. Evans-Pritchard, *The Nuer*, 6; Clinton Bailey, *Bedouin Law from Sinai and the Negev: Justice Without Government* (New Haven, Conn.: Yale University Press, 2009). For some classic works of legal anthropology about social order in the absence of a state, see Roy Franklin Barton, *Ifugao Law* (Berkeley: University of California Press, 1919); Max Gluckman, *Custom and Conflict in Africa* (Oxford, U.K.: Basil Blackwell, 1970; originally published in 1956); Rafael Karsten, *Blood Revenge, War, and Victory Feasts Among the Jibaro Indians of Eastern Ecuador* (Washington, D.C.: U.S. Government Printing Office, 1923); Karl N. Llewellyn and E. Adamson Hoebel, *The Cheyenne Way: Conflict and Case Law in Primitive Jurisprudence* (Norman: University of Oklahoma Press, 1941). For a microlevel

examination of dispute resolution and social order outside the law in Shasta County, California, see Robert C. Ellickson, *Order Without Law: How Neighbors Settle Disputes* (Cambridge, Mass.: Harvard University Press, 1991).

19. Marshall D. Sahlins, "The Segmentary Lineage: An Organization of Predatory Expansion," *American Anthropologist*, n.s. 63 (1961): 322–45. See also Marshall D. Sahlins, *Tribesmen* (Englewood Cliffs, N.J.: Prentice-Hall, 1968).

20. Akbar S. Ahmed, *Resistance and Control in Pakistan*, rev. ed. (London: Routledge, 2004), 11–23, and "Mahsud," Program for Culture and Conflict Studies, U.S. Naval Postgraduate School, accessed June 29, 2012, www.nps.edu/programs/ccs /Docs/Pakistan/Tribes/Mahsud.pdf. See also "Wazír," *Glossary of the Tribes and Castes of the Punjab and North-West Frontier Province: Based on the Census Report for the Punjab, 1883* (Patiala, India: Languages Department Punjab, 1970; originally published in 1883), 3: 493–507, 502–504 (note slight difference in classification scheme for Khali Khel).

21. Ioan M. Lewis, *Blood and Bone: The Call of Kinship in Somali Society* (Lawrenceville, N.J.: Red Sea Press, 1994). See also Afyare Abdi Elmi, *Understanding the Somalia Conflagration: Identity, Political Islam, and Peacebuilding* (London: Pluto Press, 2010), 29–30 (providing slightly different classification). For sharp criticism of Somali clan culture, see Ayaan Hirsi Ali, *Infidel* (New York: Free Press, 2007), and *Nomad: From Islam to America—A Personal Journey Through the Clash of Civilizations* (New York: Free Press, 2010).

22. For a rich account from the Arabic, see Jibrail S. Jabbur, *The Bedouins and the Desert: Aspects of Nomadic Life in the Arab East*, trans. Lawrence I. Conrad, ed. Suhayl J. Jabbur and Lawrence I. Conrad (Albany: State University of New York Press, 1995), 259–326. For an introduction to kinship structures and the tribal ideal of the Arab Middle East, see Charles Lindholm, *The Islamic Middle East: Tradition and Change*, rev. ed. (Malden, Mass.: Wiley-Blackwell, 2002), 49–62, and Dale F. Eickelman, *The Middle East and Central Asia: An Anthropological Approach*, 4th ed. (Upper Saddle River, N.J.: Prentice Hall, 2002), 115–39. For a spirited critique of the political implications of the tribal ideal, see Philip Carl Salzman, *Culture and Conflict in the Middle East* (Amherst, N.Y.: Humanity Books, 2008), 175–212.

23. John Davis, *Libyan Politics: Tribe and Revolution* (London: I. B. Tauris, 1987), 257.

24. Francis Fukuyama, *The Origins of Political Order: From Prehuman Times to the French Revolution* (New York: Farrar, Straus and Giroux, 2011), 49–94. On early political evolution, see Allen W. Johnson and Timothy Earle, *The Evolution of Human Societies: From Foraging Group to Agrarian State*, 2nd ed. (Stanford, Calif.: Stanford University Press, 2000), and Timothy Earle, *How Chiefs Come to Power: The Political Economy in Prehistory* (Stanford, Calif.: Stanford University Press, 1997). See also Morton H. Fried, *The Evolution of Political Society* (New York: Random House, 1967), and Lawrence Krader, *Formation of the State* (Englewood Cliffs, N.J.: Prentice-Hall, 1968), 29–42.

25. Evans-Pritchard, *The Nuer*, 60, 141.

26. Ibid., 143–44.

27. Ibid., 160.

28. Ibid., 183.

29. Ibid., 182, 183.
30. Ibid., 182.

5. A STATE WITHOUT A KING: MEDIEVAL ICELAND

1. *Njal's Saga*, trans. and intro. Robert Cook (New York: Penguin Books, 2001), 123 (section 75).
2. On Icelandic kinship, see Kirsten Hastrup, "Kinship in Medieval Iceland," in *Island of Anthropology: Studies in Past and Present Iceland* (Odense, Denmark: Odense University Press, 1990), and *A Place Apart: An Anthropological Study of the Icelandic World* (Oxford, U.K.: Clarendon Press, 1998). See also George W. Rich, "Problems and Prospects in the Study of Icelandic Kinship," in *The Anthropology of Iceland*, ed. E. Paul Durrenberger and Gísli Pálsson (Iowa City: University of Iowa Press, 1989), 53–79.
3. *The Book of Settlements: Landnámabók*, trans. and intro. Hermann Pálsson and Paul Edwards (Winnipeg: University of Manitoba Press, 2006), 15.
4. [Ari Þorgilsson], *Íslendingabók*, in *Íslendingabók/The Book of the Icelanders; Kristni Saga/The Story of the Conversion*, trans. Siân Grønlie (London: Viking Society for Northern Research, University College London, 2006), 3, and Aelfric, "Passion of Saint Edmund," in *Old and Middle English, c. 890–c. 1400: An Anthology*, 2nd ed., ed. Elaine Treharne (Malden, Mass.: Wiley-Blackwell, 2004), 132–39, 135.
5. Snorri Sturluson, *Heimskringla: History of the Kings of Norway*, trans. and intro. Lee M. Hollander (Austin: University of Texas Press for The American-Scandinavian Foundation, 1964), 74.
6. On the legal aspects of this process, see Alan Harding, *Medieval Law and the Foundations of the State* (Oxford, U.K.: Oxford University Press, 2002).
7. For a discussion of medieval Icelandic society with a sensitive discussion of the *goði-thingman* bond, see Jesse L. Byock, *Viking Age Iceland* (New York: Penguin Books, 2001), and *Medieval Iceland: Society, Sagas, and Power* (Berkeley: University of California Press, 1988).
8. For accounts of the story, see [Ari Þorgilsson], *Kirstni Saga* in *Íslendingabók/The Book of the Icelanders; Kristni Saga/The Story of the Conversion*, 35–50, and *Njal's Saga*, 179–81 (sections 104–5).
9. *Kristni Saga*, 48–49. While there is some textual evidence of human sacrifice in Iceland, the practice does not seem to have been at all common. See *Íslendingabók/The Book of the Icelanders; Kristni Saga/The Story of the Conversion*, 69, n. 83.
10. *Njal's Saga*, 181.
11. For a concise overview, see "Social and Political Structure," in *The Sagas of Icelanders: A Selection* (New York: Penguin Books, 2000), 735–39. For more extended and scholarly treatments, see Byock, *Viking Age Iceland*, 170–184; Jón Jóhannesson, *Íslendinga Saga: A History of the Old Icelandic Commonwealth*, trans. Haraldur Bessason (Winnipeg: University of Manitoba Press, 2006), 35–93; Gunnar Karlsson, *The History of Iceland* (Minneapolis: University of Minnesota Press, 2000), 20–27; and William Ian Miller, *Bloodtaking and Peacemaking: Feud, Law, and Society in Saga Iceland* (Chicago: University of Chicago Press, 1990), 13–41.
12. *Laws of Early Iceland, Grágás: The Codex Regius of Grágás, with Material from Other Manuscripts*, trans. and ed. Andrew Dennis, Peter Foote, and Richard Perkins (Winnipeg: University of Manitoba Press, 2000), 2:84.

13. The source of the controversial remark is an interview Prime Minister Thatcher gave to *Woman's Own* magazine in September 1987. See Margaret Thatcher Foundation, "Interview for *Woman's Own*," accessed June 29, 2012, www.margaret thatcher.org/document/106689.

14. *Egil's Saga*, trans. Bernard Scudder, ed. and intro. Svanhildur Óskarsdóttir (New York: Penguin Books, 2004), 3. *The Saga of the People of Laxardal*, trans. Keneva Kunz, in *The Sagas of Icelanders*, 276–421, 276.

6. CLANNISM AND DEMOCRATIC REFORM: THE PALESTINIAN AUTHORITY

1. S. Frederick Starr, *Clans, Authoritarian Rulers, and Parliaments in Central Asia* (Washington, D.C.: Central Asia–Caucasus Institute and Silk Road Studies Program, 2006), 13–14. See also Edward Schatz, *Modern Clan Politics: The Power of "Blood" in Kazakhstan and Beyond* (Seattle: University of Washington Press, 2004).

2. Kathleen Collins, *Clan Politics and Regime Transition in Central Asia* (Cambridge, U.K.: Cambridge University Press, 2006), 21.

3. Peter P. Ekeh, "Colonialism and the Two Publics in Africa: A Theoretical Statement," *Comparative Studies in Society and History* 17 (1975): 91–112, 109.

4. On the distinctive contemporary mode of Chinese individualization, which in contrast to European individualization has emphasized the importance of family as a source of self-identity and *guanxi* for economic prospects, see Yunxiang Yan, *The Individualization of Chinese Society* (Oxford, U.K.: Berg, 2009). On Chinese lineage, see Maurice Freedman, *Chinese Lineage and Society: Fukien and Kwangtung* (Oxford, U.K.: Berg, 2007), and *Lineage Organization in Southeastern China* (London: Athlone Press, University of London, 1970). See also Hsien Chin Hu, *The Common Descent Group in China and Its Functions* (New York: Viking Fund, 1948). For a discussion of criticisms of Freedman's model, see Xin Liu, *In One's Own Shadow: An Ethnographic Account of the Condition of Post-Reform Rural China* (Berkeley: University of California Press, 2000), 31–34.

5. United Nations Development Programme, Regional Bureau for Arab States, *Arab Human Development Report 2004: Towards Freedom in the Arab World* (New York: United Nations Development Programme, 2005), 17.

6. Hisham Sharabi, *Neopatriarchy: A Theory of Distorted Change in Arab Society* (New York: Oxford University Press, 1988), 55.

7. *Arab Human Development Report 2004*, 17.

8. For an introduction to the challenge clans pose to Palestinian state development specifically in Gaza, see "Inside Gaza: The Challenge of Clans and Families," Middle East Report No. 71 (Gaza, Jerusalem, and Brussels: International Crisis Group, December 20, 2007). For an overview of clan structures in Palestinian society, see Glenn E. Robinson, "Palestinian Tribes, Clans, and Notable Families," *Strategic Insights* 7, no. 4 (September 2008): n.p. On Arab kinship structures generally, see Charles Lindholm, *The Islamic Middle East: Tradition and Change*, rev. ed. (Malden, Mass.: Wiley-Blackwell, 2002), 49–62.

9. "Informal Justice: Rule of Law and Dispute Resolution in Palestine: National Report on Field Research Results," Institute of Law, Birzeit University (2006), 139–43.

10. On traditional mechanisms of mediation in Palestinian society, see Robert Terris

and Vera Inoue-Terris, "A Case Study of Third World Jurisprudence—Palestine: Conflict Resolution and Customary Law in a Neopatrimonial Society," *Berkeley Journal of International Law* 20 (2002): 462–95.

11. On Arafat's political strategy, see Glenn E. Robinson, *Building a Palestinian State: The Incomplete Revolution* (Bloomington and Indianapolis: Indiana University Press, 1997), 174–200. See also "Inside Gaza," 2–5.

12. Robinson, "Palestinian Tribes, Clans, and Notable Families," 5. On the election law of 1996, see also "Informal Justice," 56.

13. "Informal Justice," 59–60. On the significance for state development of Arafat's stance toward informal justice, see Hillel Frisch, "Modern Absolutist or Neopatriarchal State Building? Customary Law, Extended Families, and the Palestinian Authority," *International Journal of Middle East Studies* 29 (1997): 341–58.

14. "Informal Justice," 120 (citing unnamed member of Palestinian Legislative Council, expressing consensus of all PLC interviewees).

15. For a vivid journalistic account of the conflict between Hamas and tribal principles of law, see Erin Cunningham, "Long the Glue of Gaza, Clans Say Hamas Is Undermining Tribal Justice," *The Christian Science Monitor*, January 22, 2010, accessed June 29, 2012, www.csmonitor.com/World/Middle-East/2010/0122/Long-the-glue-of-Gaza-clans-say-Hamas-is-undermining-tribal-justice.

16. "Inside Gaza," 5. On Palestinian feuds, see also Frisch, "Modern Absolutist or Neopatriarchal State Building?" and Terris and Inoue-Terris, "A Case Study of Third World Jurisprudence."

17. *Arab Human Development Report 2004*, 145.

18. Sharabi, *Neopatriarchy*, 46.

PART III: THE CULTURAL ORDER OF THE CLAN

1. William Shakespeare, *Romeo and Juliet*, act 1, scene 1, line 74, in *The Norton Shakespeare*.

2. Shakespeare, *Romeo and Juliet*, act 5, scene 3, lines 306–7.

7. SOLIDARITY, GROUP HONOR, AND SHAME: MODERN INDIA, PAKISTAN, AND AFGHANISTAN

1. Tariq Rahman, "Language-Teaching and Power in Pakistan," *Indian Social Science Review* 5, no. 1 (January–June 2003): 45–62, accessed June 29, 2012, www.tariqrahman.net/language/language-teaching%20&%20power%20in%20pakistan%20(amended).htm, and "Images of the 'Other' in Pakistani Textbooks," *Pakistan Perspectives* (July–December 2002): 33–49, accessed June 29, 2012, www.tariqrahman.net/language/images%20of%20the%20%27other%27.htm.

2. Elizabeth Gilbert, *Eat, Pray, Love: One Woman's Search for Everything Across Italy, India, and Indonesia* (New York: Penguin Books, 2006), 42, 269 (italics removed); Roger Ebert, "Eat Pray Love," rogerebert.com, August 11, 2010, accessed June 29, 2012, http://rogerebert.suntimes.com/apps/pbcs.dll/article?AID=/20100811/reviews/100819999.

3. Ruth Benedict, *The Chrysanthemum and the Sword: Patterns of Japanese Culture* (New York: Mariner Books, 2005; originally published in 1946), 224.

4. Ibid., 223.

5. "Principles & Values," U.S. Marine Corps/Marine Recruiting/Marines.com, accessed June 29, 2012, www.marines.com/history-heritage/principles-values.

6. For an influential discussion of group honor, see Ahmed Abou-Zeid, "Honour and Shame Among the Bedouins of Egypt," in *Honour and Shame: The Values of Mediterranean Society*, ed. J. G. Peristiany (Chicago: University of Chicago Press, 1966), 243–59. On collective responsibility among the same group, see Joseph Ginat, *Blood Revenge: Family Honor, Mediation, and Outcasting*, 2nd ed. (Brighton, U.K.: Sussex Academic Press, 1997). On honor and kinship, see also J. K. Campbell, *Honour, Family, and Patronage: A Study of Institutions and Moral Values in a Greek Mountain Community* (New York: Oxford University Press, 1964).

7. For a similar example, see Ayaan Hirsi Ali, *Infidel* (New York: Free Press, 2007), 3–4.

8. For two succinct introductions to Indian society and social divisions, see Stanley Wolpert, *India*, 4th ed. (Berkeley: University of California Press, 2009), 110–46, and Thomas R. Trautmann, *India: Brief History of a Civilization* (Oxford, U.K.: Oxford University Press, 2011), 85–101.

9. For a listing, see "Central List of Other Backward Classes," National Commission for Backward Classes, accessed June 29, 2012, http://ncbc.nic.in/Centrallistifobc .html.

10. Dhananjay Keer, *Dr. Ambedkar: Life and Mission* (Bombay: Popular Prakashan, 1954), 17–18.

11. B. R. Ambedkar, "Annihilation of Caste," in *The Essential Writings of B. R. Ambedkar*, ed. Valerian Rodrigues (Oxford, U.K.: Oxford University Press, 2002), 263–305. See also "Castes in India," 241–62 and "Reply to the Mahatma," 306–19.

12. David G. Mandelbaum, *Society in India*, vol. 1 (Berkeley: University of California Press, 1970).

13. For a discussion of the significance of this linguistic usage, including how it reveals a society in which "the normal patriarchal forms of hierarchy within the family are maintained as the prevalent pattern throughout institutional life," see Probal Dasgupta, *The Otherness of English: India's Auntie Tongue Syndrome* (New Delhi: Sage Publications, 1993), 201.

14. Ambedkar, *The Essential Writings of B. R. Ambedkar*, 267–68. On Ambedkar's views of the Hindu social order, see M. S. Gore, *The Social Context of an Ideology: Ambedkar's Political and Social Thought* (New Delhi: Sage Publications, 1993), 260–84.

15. On Ambedkar's conflict with Gandhi, see Christophe Jaffrelot, *Dr. Ambedkar and Untouchability: Fighting the Indian Caste System* (New York: Columbia University Press, 2005), 108–14.

16. B. R. Ambedkar, "The Hindu Social Order—Its Essential Principles," in *Dr. Babasaheb Ambedkar: Writings and Speeches*, vol. 3, comp. Vasant Moon (Bombay: Education and Employment Department, Government of Maharashtra, 1987), 95–115, 99.

17. Charles Lindholm, *Generosity and Jealousy: The Swat Pukhtun of Northern Pakistan* (New York: Columbia University Press, 1982), 234.

18. Tim McGirk, "On Bin Laden's Trail," *National Geographic*, December 2004, accessed June 29, 2012, http://ngm.nationalgeographic.com/features/world/asia/pakistan/pashtun-text.html.

19. Charles Lindholm, *Generosity and Jealousy*, 234.

20. On the characteristics of the modern legal tradition of the West, see Harold J. Berman, *Law and Revolution: The Formation of the Western Legal Tradition* (Cambridge, Mass.: Harvard University Press, 1983), 7–10.

21. *The Laws of Manu*, intro. and trans. Wendy Doniger, with Brian K. Smith (New York: Penguin Books, 1991), 195, 227, 46–48 (parentheses in original translation removed for readability).

22. Benjamin I. Schwartz, *The World of Thought in Ancient China* (Cambridge, Mass.: Belknap Press of Harvard University Press, 1985), 67. On Chinese Legalism, see 321–49, and see John King Fairbank and Merle Goldman, *China: A New History*, 2nd ed. enl. (Cambridge, Mass.: Belknap Press of Harvard University Press, 2006), 183–86.

23. Hui-Chen Wang Liu, *The Traditional Chinese Clan Rules*, Monographs of the Association for Asian Studies VII (New York: J. J. Augustin for the Association for Asian Studies, 1959), 217–21.

24. For a prominent example of the role of customary law in differentiating in-group from out-group, see Walter O. Weyrauch and Maureen Anne Bell, "Autonomous Lawmaking: The Case of the 'Gypsies,'" in *Gypsy Law: Romani Legal Traditions and Culture*, ed. Walter O. Weyrauch (Berkeley: University of California Press, 2001), 11–87.

25. "Building," High Court of Punjab and Haryana, Chandigarh, India, accessed June 29, 2012, http://highcourtchd.gov.in/index.php?trs=building.

26. Saurabh Malik, "Runaway Couples; Evolve Compassionate Mechanism: HC," *The Tribune* (Chandigarh, India), June 24, 2008, accessed June 29, 2012, www.tribuneindia.com/2008/20080625/main6.htm.

27. "Justice Katju—Media Debate: Justice Markandey Katju on the Role of Media in India," Law Resource India, accessed June 29, 2012, http://indialawyers.wordpress.com/tag/justice.

28. Jim Yardley, "Unelected Councils in India Run Villages with Stern Hand," *The New York Times*, June 4, 2011, accessed June 29, 2012, www.nytimes.com/2011/06/05/world/asia/05india.html.

29. Prem Chowdhry, *Political Economy of Production and Reproduction: Caste, Custom, and Community in North India* (Oxford, U.K.: Oxford University Press, 2011), 350.

30. For a study exploring the personal, social, and political aspects of such unions, see Perveez Mody, *The Intimate State: Love-Marriage and the Law in Delhi* (New York: Routledge, 2008).

31. In the face of estimates suggesting that as many as one thousand cases occur in India each year, primarily in Haryana, Punjab, and western Uttar Pradesh, *The New York Times* cautiously reports that "new cases of killings or harassment appear in the Indian news media almost every week," Jim Yardley, "In India, Castes, Honor and Killings Intertwine," *The New York Times*, July 9, 2010, accessed June 29, 2012, www.nytimes.com/2010/07/10/world/asia/10honor.html.

32. One United Nations report puts the number of women and girls murdered in honor killings each year as "perhaps as many as 5,000," *Lives Together, Worlds Apart: Men and Women in a Time of Change*, State of the World Population 2000 (New York: United Nations Population Fund, 2000), 29 (ch. 3), accessed June 29, 2012, www.unfpa.org/swp/2000/english/index.html.

33. For two examples, see John Leland and Namo Abdulla, "A Killing Set Honor Above Love," *The New York Times*, November 21, 2010, accessed June 29, 2012, www.nytimes.com/2010/11/21/world/middleeast/21honor.html, and Afif Sarhan and Caroline Davies, "'My Daughter Deserved to Die for Falling in Love,'" *The Observer*, May 10, 2008, accessed June 29, 2012, www.guardian.co.uk/world/2008/may/11/iraq.humanrights.

34. For a recent prominent example, see Ian Austen, "Afghan Family, Led by Father Who Called Girls a Disgrace, Is Guilty of Murder," *The New York Times*, January 29, 2012, accessed June 29, 2012, www.nytimes.com/2012/01/30/world/americas/afghan-family-members-convicted-in-honor-killings.html.

35. *Arumugam Servai v. State of Tamil Nadu*, Criminal Appeal No. 958, with Criminal Appeal No. 959 (April 19, 2011), 2011 STPL(Web) 403 SC, accessed June 29, 2012, 4 (par. 16), www.stpl-india.in/SCJFiles/2011_STPL(Web)_403_SC.pdf.

36. Prohibition of Unlawful Assembly (Interference with the Freedom of Matrimonial Alliances) Bill, 2011, accessed June 29, 2012, http://lawcommissionofindia.nic.in/reports/cp-Honour%20Killing.pdf.

8. FEUD AS AN INSTRUMENT OF HARMONY: THE PHILIPPINES

1. Monalinda Emperio Doro, "Management and Resolution of Rido Among Meranao in Baloi, Lanao del Norte: Case Studies," in *Rido: Clan Feuding and Conflict Management in Mindanao*, ed. Wilfredo Magno Torres III (Makati City, Philippines: Asia Foundation, 2007), 201–53, 221–26.

2. Max Gluckman, *Custom and Conflict in Africa* (Oxford, U.K.: Basil Blackwell, 1970; originally published, 1956), 17.

3. On feud, see Christopher Boehm, "Ambivalence and Compromise in Human Nature," *American Anthropologist* 91 (1989): 921–39, and *Blood Revenge: The Anthropology of Feuding in Montenegro and Other Tribal Societies* (Lawrence: University Press of Kansas, 1984); Margaret Hasluck, *The Unwritten Law in Albania* (Cambridge, U.K.: Cambridge University Press, 1954); Mervyn Meggit, *Blood Is Their Argument: Warfare Among Mae Enga Tribesmen of the New Guinea Highlands* (Palo Alto, Calif.: Mayfield, 1977).

4. On Israel, see Pamela Barmash, *Homicide in the Biblical World* (Cambridge, U.K.: Cambridge University Press, 2005). On the Swat valley, see Charles Lindholm, *Generosity and Jealousy: The Swat Pukhtun of Northern Pakistan* (New York: Columbia University Press, 1982).

5. Jose Jowel Canuday, "Big War, Small Wars: The Interplay of Large-scale and Community Armed Conflicts in Five Central Mindanao Communities," in *Rido*, ed. Torres, 254–89, 272–76.

6. Majlinda Mortimer and Anca Toader, "Blood Feuds Blight Albanian Lives," BBC News, September 23, 2005, accessed June 29, 2012, http://news.bbc.co.uk/2/hi/europe/4273020.stm.

7. *Njal's Saga*, trans. and intro. Robert Cook (New York: Penguin Books, 2001), 123 (section 75).

8. For the complete story, see *Njal's Saga*, 57–78 (sections 35–45). For a discussion of Icelandic feud, see William Ian Miller, *Bloodtaking and Peacemaking: Feud, Law, and Society in Saga Iceland* (Chicago: University of Chicago Press, 1990). For an approach to the Icelandic feud focusing on the role of the *goðar* as legal advocate, see Jesse L. Byock, *Feud in the Icelandic Saga* (Berkeley: University of California Press, 1982).

9. *Njal's Saga*, 57, 59.

10. Mortimer and Toader, "Blood Feuds Blight Albanian Lives."

PART IV: THE TRANSFORMATION OF THE CLAN

1. Hubert Deschamps, quoted in James S. Wunsch, "Foundations of Centralization: The Colonial Experience and the African Context," in *The Failure of the Centralized State: Institutions and Self-Governance in Africa*, eds. James S. Wunsch and Dele Olowu (Boulder, Colo.: Westview Press, 1990), 23–42, 25.

2. Mahmood Mamdani, *Citizen and Subject: Contemporary Africa and the Legacy of Late Colonialism* (Princeton, N.J.: Princeton University Press, 1996), 122.

3. Jeremi Suri, *Liberty's Surest Guardian: American Nation-Building from the Founders to Obama* (New York: Free Press, 2011). On democracy promotion, see Michael McFaul, *Advancing Democracy Abroad: Why We Should and How We Can*, Hoover Studies in Politics, Economics, and Society (Lanham, Md.: Rowman & Littlefield in cooperation with the Hoover Institution at Stanford University, 2010).

4. The literature on state formation is extensive. I have been influenced especially by Joseph R. Strayer, *On the Medieval Origins of the Modern State* (Princeton, N.J.: Princeton University Press, 1998; originally published in 1970). On European state development, see Thomas Ertman, *Birth of the Leviathan: Building States and Regimes in Medieval and Early Modern Europe* (Cambridge, U.K.: Cambridge University Press, 1997), and Charles Tilly, *Coercion, Capital, and European States, AD 990–1992* (Cambridge, Mass.: Blackwell, 1992). For intriguing alternatives to the state system in European development, see Hendrik Spruyt, *The Sovereign State and Its Competitors* (Princeton, N.J.: Princeton University Press, 1994).

9. FROM KIN TO KING: STATE DEVELOPMENT IN ANGLO-SAXON ENGLAND

1. *The Saxon Chronicle*, trans. J. Ingram (London: Longman, Hurst, Rees, Orme, and Brown, 1823), 159. For a more recent rendering, see *The Anglo-Saxon Chronicle*, trans. and ed. M. J. Swanton (New York: Routledge, 1998), 118.

2. "Coronation Oath of Edgar," in *Sources of English Constitutional History*, ed. and trans. Carl Stephenson and Frederick George Marcham (New York: Harper and Brothers, 1937), 18. On Edgar's coronation and English coronations generally, see Roy Strong, *Coronation: A History of Kingship and the British Monarchy* (New York: HarperCollins, 2005).

3. Tacitus, "Germania," trans. Harold Mattingly, in Tacitus, *The Agricola and The Germania* (New York: Penguin Books, 1970), 101.

4. Tacitus, "Germany and Its Tribes" (*Germania*), trans. Alfred John Church and William Jackson Brodribb, *The Complete Works of Tacitus*, ed. and intro. Moses Hadas (New York: Random House, 1942), 709–32, 719.

5. For a discussion of the most unsavory admirers, see Christopher B. Krebs, *A Most Dangerous Book: Tacitus's* Germania *from the Roman Empire to the Third Reich* (New York: W. W. Norton, 2011).

6. Tacitus, "Germany and Its Tribes," 714, 712.

7. Herbert Baxter Adams, "The Germanic Origin of New England Towns," *Johns Hopkins University Studies in Historical and Political Science*, ser. 1, no. 2 (Baltimore: Johns Hopkins University, 1882), 5–38, 8.

8. Tacitus, "Germany and Its Tribes," 714, 712.

9. Ibid., 719.

10. Gregory of Tours, *History of the Franks*, trans. Ernest Brehaut (New York: Norton, 1969; originally published 1916), 46.

11. "Title XVII, Concerning Wounds," *Pactus Legis Salicae*, in *The Laws of the Salian Franks*, trans. Katherine Fischer Drew (Philadelphia: University of Pennsylvania Press, 1991), 82.

12. "Title LX, Concerning Him Who Wishes to Remove Himself from His Kin Group," *The Laws of the Salian Franks*, 123.

13. *The Anglo-Saxon World: An Anthology*, trans. Kevin Crossley-Holland (Oxford, U.K.: Oxford University Press, 1999), 37 (*The Anglo-Saxon Chronicle*, 449 CE).

14. Markku Filppula, Juhani Klemola, and Heli Paulasto, *English and Celtic in Contact* (New York: Routledge, 2008), 126 (citing the work of Richard Coates, while themselves suggesting a considerably stronger influence of Celtic on English than previously acknowledged). For genetic studies, see Mark G. Thomas, Michael P. H. Stumpf, and Heinrich Härke, "Evidence for an Apartheid-like Social Structure in Early Anglo-Saxon England," *Proceedings of the Royal Society B* (2006): 2651–57, and Michael E. Weale, Deborah A. Weiss, Rolf F. Jager, Neil Bradman, and Mark G. Thomas, "Y Chromosome Evidence for Anglo-Saxon Mass Migration," *Molecular Biology and Evolution* 19 (2002): 1008–21, accessed June 29, 2012, www.ucl.ac.uk/mace-lab/publications/articles/2002/Weale-MBE-02-AS.pdf.

15. "The Wanderer," in *The Anglo-Saxon World: An Anthology*, trans. Kevin Crossley-Holland (Oxford, U.K.: Oxford University Press, 1999), 50–53.

16. On the influence of Christianity on conceptions of law in the Germanic world, and the institutionalization of Christian jurisprudence into the West's first modern legal system, see Harold J. Berman, *Law and Revolution: The Formation of the Western Legal Tradition* (Cambridge, Mass.: Harvard University Press, 1983), 62–84, 199–224.

17. On the role of the nuclear family within a wider kindred in England, see Jack Goody, *The European Family: An Historico-Anthropological Essay* (Oxford, U.K.: Blackwell, 2000), 60–61.

18. Rudyard Kipling, "The Broken Men," *Rudyard Kipling: Complete Verse* (New York: Anchor Press, 1940), 96–98, 96.

19. "Dooms of Alfred (871–901)," *Sources of English Constitutional History*, 10–12, 12 (brackets in original translation removed for readability).

20. Hisham Sharabi, *Neopatriarchy: A Theory of Distorted Change in Arab Society* (New York: Oxford University Press, 1988), 46.

21. On other ways in which modern individualism is rooted in the European Middle Ages, see Colin Morris, *The Discovery of the Individual: 1050–1220* (New York: Harper and Row, 1972).

10. "WE HAVE MADE YOU INTO NATIONS AND TRIBES": THE VISION OF EARLY ISLAM

1. Ibn Khaldūn, *The Muqaddimah: An Introduction to History*, trans. Franz Rosenthal, abr. and ed. N. J. Dawood (Princeton, N.J.: Princeton University Press, 2005).

2. On clans and state development in the Middle East, see generally, Philip S. Khoury and Joseph Kostiner, eds., *Tribes and State Formation in the Middle East* (Berkeley: University of California Press, 1990). See also *Islam in Tribal Societies: From the Atlas to the Indus*, ed. Akbar S. Ahmed and David M. Hart (London: Routledge and Kegan Paul, 1984). On Yemen, see Shelagh Weir, *A Tribal Order: Politics and Law in the Mountains of Yemen* (Austin: University of Texas Press, 2007). On Libya, see John Davis, *Libyan Politics: Tribe and Revolution* (London: I. B. Tauris, 1987).

3. On early Arabia, see Marshall G. S. Hodgson, *The Venture of Islam: Conscience and History in a World Civilization*, vol. 1 (Chicago: University of Chicago Press, 1974); W. Montgomery Watt, *Muhammad at Mecca* (Oxford, U.K.: Oxford University Press, 1953), *Muhammad at Medina* (Oxford, U.K.: Clarendon Press, 1956), and *Muhammad's Mecca: History in the Qur'an* (Edinburgh: Edinburgh University Press, 1988); Elias Shoufani, *Al-Riddah and the Muslim Conquest of Arabia* (Toronto: University of Toronto Press, 1973); and Fred McGraw Donner, *The Early Islamic Conquests* (Princeton, N.J.: Princeton University Press, 1981) and *Muhammad and the Believers: At the Origins of Islam* (Cambridge, Mass.: Belknap Press of Harvard University Press, 2010).

4. William Robertson Smith, *Kinship and Marriage in Early Arabia* (Cambridge, U.K.: University of Cambridge Press, 1885).

5. Jibrail S. Jabbur, *The Bedouins and the Desert: Aspects of Nomadic Life in the Arab East*, trans. Lawrence I. Conrad, ed. Suhayl J. Jabbur and Lawrence I. Conrad (Albany: State University of New York Press, 1995), 264.

6. Philip K. Hitti, *History of the Arabs: From the Earliest Times to the Present*, 10th ed., rev. (New York: Palgrave MacMillan, 2002; originally published in 1970; original edition published in 1937), 27.

7. Cited in Jabbur, *The Bedouins and the Desert*, 317.

8. Sigmund Freud, *Totem and Taboo: Some Points of Agreement Between the Mental Life of Savages and Neurotics*, ed. and trans. James Strachey (New York: Norton, 1950; originally published in 1913).

9. Joseph Schacht, *An Introduction to Islamic Law* (Oxford, U.K.: Clarendon Press, 1982), 1.

10. Khaled Abou El Fadl, "Retaliation," in *Encyclopaedia of the Qur'ān*, gen. ed. Jane Dammen McAuliffe (Leiden, The Netherlands: Brill, 2001–2006), 4:436–37.

11. *Quran: The Final Testament: Authorized English Version, with the Arabic Text*, trans. Rashad Khalifa, 4th rev. ed. (Capistrano Beach, Calif.: Islamic Productions, 2005), 27 (2:178 [The Cow]) (emphasis added).

12. Alfred Guillaume, *The Life of Muhammad: A Translation of Ibn Ishaq's Sirat Rasul Allah* (Oxford, U.K.: Oxford University Press, 1955), 301 (emphasis added).

13. Watt, *Muhammad at Mecca*, 102; for Watt's treatment of the "Satanic Verses," see 100–109.

14. *The Message of the Qur'ān: The Full Account of the Revealed Arabic Text Accompanied by Parallel Transliteration*, trans. Muhammad Asad (Bristol, U.K.: Book Foundation, 2003), 926–27 (53:23 [The Unfolding]) (brackets in original translation removed for readability).

15. Donner, *Early Islamic Conquests*, 255–63.

16. Kathleen Collins, *Clan Politics and Regime Transition in Central Asia* (Cambridge, U.K.: Cambridge University Press, 2006), 21.

17. Richard G. Fox, *Kin, Clan, Raja, and Rule: State-Hinterland Relations in Preindustrial India* (Berkeley: University of California Press, 1971), 150.

18. For the work of a key architect of Afghanistan's reforms, see Ashraf Ghani and Clare Lockhart, *Fixing Failed States: A Framework for Rebuilding a Fractured World* (New York: Oxford University Press, 2008).

19. Uzi Rabi, *The Emergence of States in a Tribal Society: Oman under Sa'id bin Taymur, 1932–1970* (Brighton, U.K.: Sussex Academic Press, 2006). See also Abdulrahman al-Salimi, "A Comparison of Modern Religious Education in Arabia: Oman and Yemen," *IjtihadReason* (n.d.), accessed June 29, 2012, www.ijtihad reason.org/articles/modern-religious-education.php. On Yemen, see Victoria Clark, *Yemen: Dancing on the Heads of Snakes* (New Haven, Conn.: Yale University Press, 2010), 185–90.

20. Aleu Akechak Jok, Robert A. Leitch, and Carrie Vandewint, "A Study of Customary Law in Contemporary Southern Sudan" (World Vision International, 2004).

21. *The Message of the Qur'ān*, 903–904 (49:11–13 [The Private Apartments]) (brackets in original translation removed for readability).

22. Paul Marshall and Nina Shea, *Silenced: How Apostasy and Blasphemy Codes Are Choking Freedom Worldwide* (New York: Oxford University Press, 2011).

23. Lionel Tiger, "Zuckerberg: The World's Richest Primatologist," *The Wall Street Journal*, February 6, 2012, accessed June 29, 2012, http://online.wsj.com/article/SB 10001424052748703421204576327443487322026.html.

24. B. R. Ambedkar, *The Essential Writings of B. R. Ambedkar*, ed. Valerian Rodrigues (Oxford, U.K.: Oxford University Press, 2002), 268.

PART V: THE PERSISTENCE OF THE CLAN

1. Clinton Bailey, *Bedouin Law from Sinai and the Negev: Justice Without Government* (New Haven, Conn.: Yale University Press, 2009), 1, 60.

2. On the social system of small gangs, see R. Lincoln Keiser, *Vice Lords: Warriors of the Streets* (New York: Holt, Rinehart and Winston, 1969); on the crucial role of status within the group as a determining factor in whether retaliatory violence will be pursued in the face of an injury from a member of another club, see 32–34. On the creation of *constructive* networks of fictive kin in the face of economic adversity and state failure, see Carol Stack, *All Our Kin: Strategies for Survival in a Black Community* (New York: Basic Books, 1974).

11. THE ROMANCE OF THE CLAN

1. James A. Michener, *Caravans: A Novel of Afghanistan* (New York: Random House Trade Paperbacks, 2003; originally published in 1963), 217.
2. Ibid., 271, 222.
3. Ibid., 242, 244–45.
4. William O. Douglas, *Beyond the High Himalayas* (Garden City, N.Y.: Doubleday, 1952), 264.
5. Khaled Hosseini, *The Kite Runner* (New York: Riverhead Books, 2003), 357.
6. "Ethnic Identity in Afghanistan," U.S. Naval Postgraduate School, accessed June 29, 2012, www.nps.edu/Programs/CCS/Ethnic_identity.html.
7. Michener, *Caravans*, 228.
8. On the conflict between "honor," "Islam," and the rule of law in the national self-conception of Afghanistan, see David B. Edwards, *Heroes of the Age: Moral Fault Lines on the Afghan Frontier* (Berkeley: University of California Press, 1996), 4.
9. Michener, *Caravans*, 289–92.
10. For an introduction to Korean history, see Carter J. Eckert, et. al., *Korea Old and New: A History* (Seoul: Ilchokak Publishers for the Korea Institute, Harvard University, 1990), and Ki-baik Lee, *A New History of Korea*, trans. Edward W. Wagner with Edward J. Shultz (Cambridge, Mass.: Harvard University Press for the Harvard-Yenching Institute, 1984). For a survey of premodern Korea, see Michael J. Seth, *A Concise History of Korea: From the Neolithic Period Through the Nineteenth Century* (Oxford, U.K.: Rowman and Littlefield, 2006). For the modern period, see Bruce Cummings, *Korea's Place in the Sun: A Modern History*, updated ed. (New York: W. W. Norton, 2005).
11. Hyung Il Pai, *Constructing "Korean" Origins: A Critical Review of Archaeology, Historiography, and Racial Myth in Korean State-Formation Theories*, Harvard East Asian Monographs 187, Harvard-Hallym Series on Korea (Cambridge, Mass.: Harvard University Press for the Harvard University Asia Center, 2000), 60.
12. Pai, *Constructing "Korean" Origins*, 115.
13. On this transformation, see Martina Deuchler, *The Confucian Transformation of Korea: A Study of Society and Ideology*, Harvard-Yenching Institute Monograph Series 36 (Cambridge, Mass.: Council on East Asian Studies, Harvard University, 1992).
14. For a review of the 1991 change in Korean family law, see Rosa Kim, "The Legacy of Institutionalized Gender Inequality in South Korea: The Family Law," *Boston College Third World Law Journal* 14, no. 1 (1994): 145–62, accessed June 29, 2012, http://lawdigitalcommons.bc.edu/twlj/vol14/iss1/7.
15. On the colonial period, in addition to the works cited above, see Peter Duus, *The Abacus and the Sword: The Japanese Penetration of Korea, 1895–1910* (Berkeley: University of California Press, 1995), and Michael E. Robinson, *Korea's Twentieth-Century Odyssey: A Short History* (Honolulu: University of Hawai'i Press, 2007).
16. Lee Tai-Yung, "The Legal Status of Korean Women," in *Legal System of Korea*, ed. International Cultural Foundation, Korean Culture Series 5 (Seoul: Si-sa-young-o-sa, 1982), 83–114, 93, 86. Recognizing the general fact of the modernization of Korean women's social position under Japanese colonial rule naturally is not intended to ignore or excuse the various depredations of the Japanese wartime government, most notoriously sexual slavery ("comfort women"). On the role of

Japanese colonial legal reforms in modernity, see Chulwoo Lee, "Modernity, Legality, and Power in Korea Under Japanese Rule," in *Colonial Modernity in Korea*, eds. Gi-Wook Shin and Michael Robinson (Cambridge, Mass.: Harvard University Asia Center, 1999), 21–51.

17. Mark E. Caprio, *Japanese Assimilation Policies in Colonial Korea: 1910–1945* (Seattle: University of Washington Press, 2009).

18. Robinson, *Korea's Twentieth-Century Odyssey*, 96. On the use of name-change policy as an instrument of social control, see Takashi Fujitani, *Race for Empire: Koreans as Japanese and Japanese as Americans During World War II* (Berkeley: University of California Press, 2011), 336.

19. Oral history of Pak Sŏngp'il, in Hildi Kang, *Under the Black Umbrella: Voices from Colonial Korea, 1910–1945* (Ithaca, N.Y.: Cornell University Press, 2001), 117–18. For other ingenious name selections, see 120–22.

20. Kajiyama Toshiyuki, "The Clan Records," in *The Clan Records: Five Stories of Korea*, trans. Yoshiko Dykstra (Honolulu: University of Hawai'i Press, 1995), 7–46, 15.

21. Richard E. Kim, "Lost Names," in *Lost Names: Scenes from a Korean Boyhood* (Berkeley: University of California Press, 1998; originally published in 1970), 87–115, 111.

22. On Morgan's life, see Daniel Noah Moses, *The Promise of Progress: The Life and Work of Lewis Henry Morgan* (Columbia: University of Missouri Press, 2009).

23. On Morgan's place in the history of the study of the Roman *gens*, see C. J. Smith, *The Roman Clan: The Gens from Ancient Ideology to Modern Anthropology* (Cambridge, U.K.: Cambridge University Press, 2006), 88–101.

24. Lewis Henry Morgan, *Ancient Society*, Classics of Anthropology, ed. Ashley Montagu (Tucson: University of Arizona Press, 1985; originally published in 1877), 63.

25. Morgan, *Ancient Society*, 62, 552.

26. Friedrich Engels, *The Origin of the Family, Private Property, and the State in the Light of the Researches of Lewis H. Morgan*, ed. and intro. Eleanor Burke Leacock (New York: International Publishers, 1972), 237 (quoting Morgan, *Ancient Society*, 552) (Engels's italics).

27. Ernest Gellner, "The Asiatic Trauma," in *State and Society in Soviet Thought* (Oxford, U.K.: Basil Blackwell, 1988), 39–68, 52.

28. Likewise, for a well-intended but naive theoretical justification for the communalist ideals of the cultural revolution of the American 1960s in terms of Morgan's evolutionary framework, see Gary Snyder, "Passage to More Than India," *Earth House Hold: Technical Notes & Queries to Fellow Dharma Revolutionaries* (New York: New Directions, 1969), 103–12.

29. George Bernard Shaw, *The Perfect Wagnerite: A Commentary on the Ring of the Niblungs* (London: Grant Richards, 1898), 28.

30. Ibid., 31, 32.

31. See generally Claude Lévi-Strauss, *Structural Anthropology*, 2 vols., trans. Claire Jacobson and Brooke Grundfest Schoepf (New York: Basic Books, 1963).

32. See Frank Usbeck, "'Fellow Peoples': The Influence of the German Image of Indians on German National Identity and Its Appropriation by National Socialism in German Periodicals, 1925–1945" (PhD diss., University of Leipzig, Germany, Institute for American Studies, 2010; to be published by Berghahn Books, New York/Oxford).

33. Claire Lamont, "Introduction," in Sir Walter Scott, *Waverley; Or, 'Tis Sixty Years Since*, ed. Claire Lamont (Oxford, U.K.: Oxford University Press, 1986), vii–xx, vii, citing Henry Cockburn, *Memorials of His Time* (1856), 281.

34. Scott, *Waverley*, 100.

35. On Scott, see John Sutherland, *The Life of Walter Scott: A Critical Biography* (Oxford, U.K.: Blackwell, 1995); on Scott and the law, see pages 30–32. See also David Stechern, *Das Recht in den Romanen von Sir Walter Scott* (Berlin/Münster, Germany: LIT Verlag, 2003).

36. Scott, *Waverley*, 92.

37. Ibid., 269–70 ("The Confusion of King Agramant's Camp").

38. Sutherland, *The Life of Walter Scott*, 31.

39. [Walter Scott], *Hints Addressed to the Inhabitants of Edinburgh, and Others, in Prospect of His Majesty's Visit* (Edinburgh: Printed for Bell and Bradfute, Manners and Miller, Archibald Constable and Co., William Blackwood, Waugh and Innes, and John Robertson, 1822), 6–7, 26. See generally John Prebble, *The King's Jaunt: George IV in Scotland, August 1822: 'One and twenty daft days'* (Edinburgh: Birlinn, 1988), 97–103.

40. *Bagehot: The English Constitution*, Cambridge Texts in the History of Political Thought, ed. Paul Smith (Cambridge, U.K.: Cambridge University Press, 2001), 143 ("Of Changes of Ministry").

41. J. W. Burrow, *A Liberal Descent: Victorian Historians and the English Past* (Cambridge, U.K.: Cambridge University Press, 1981).

42. Rabindranath Tagore called Chatterji "our master in this respect," "Mulk Raj Anand's Conversation with Rabindranath Tagore," in Bankim Chandra Chatterji, *Anandamath*, trans. and adpt. Basanta Koomar Roy (Delhi: Orient Paperbacks, 1992), 9–12, 12.

43. Salman Rushdie, *The Satanic Verses: A Novel* (New York: Random House Trade Paperbacks, 2008), 93–94.

44. Hisham Sharabi, *Neopatriarchy: A Theory of Distorted Change in Arab Society* (New York: Oxford University Press, 1988), 106. For a related call in the context of Qur'anic interpretation, see Fazlur Rahman, *Islam and Modernity: Transformation of an Intellectual Tradition* (Chicago: University of Chicago Press, 1982).

12. THE CLAN'S RETURN

1. Stephen Kurczy and Drew Hinshaw, "Libya's Tribes: Who's Who?" *The Christian Science Monitor*, February 24, 2011, accessed June 29, 2012, www.csmonitor.com /World/Backchannels/2011/0224/Libya-tribes-Who-s-who; David D. Kirkpatrick and Mona El-Naggar, "Qaddafi's Son Warns of Civil War as Libyan Protests Widen," *The New York Times*, February 20, 2011, accessed June 29, 2012, www .nytimes.com/2011/02/21/world/africa/21libya.html.

2. M. Al. Gathafi [Muammar al-Qaddafi], *The Green Book: The Solution to the Problem of Democracy; The Solution to the Economic Problem; The Social Basis of the Third Universal Theory* (Reading, U.K.: Ithaca Press, 2005), 21, 3.

3. Ibid., 59.

4. John Davis, *Libyan Politics: Tribe and Revolution* (London: I. B. Tauris, 1987), 259.

5. "Uprising in Libya: 'Survival Hinges on Tribal Solidarity'" (interview with

Hanspeter Mattes), Spiegel Online, February 23, 2011, accessed June 29, 2012, www.spiegel.de/international/world/0,1518,747234,00.html.

6. David D. Kirkpatrick, "Death of Rebel Leader Stirs Fears of Tribal Conflict," *The New York Times*, July 28, 2011, accessed June 29, 2012, www.nytimes.com/2011/07/29/world/africa/29libya.html.

7. See Abdulsattar Hatitah, "Libyan Tribal Map: Network of Loyalties That Will Determine Gaddafi's Fate," Asharq Alawsat, February 22, 2011, accessed June 29, 2012, www.asharq-e.com/news.asp?section=3&id=24257. On tribal conflict after Qaddafi's overthrow, see Frederic Wehrey, "Libya's Terra Incognita: Who and What Will Follow Qaddafi?" *Foreign Affairs*, February 28, 2011, accessed June 29, 2012, www.foreignaffairs.com/articles/67551/frederic-wehrey/libyas-terra-incognita.

8. Robert Kagan, *The World America Made* (New York: Alfred A. Knopf, 2012), 3.

9. Ibid., 6–7.

10. Ibid., 97, 99.

11. Hisham Sharabi, *Neopatriarchy: A Theory of Distorted Change in Arab Society* (New York: Oxford University Press, 1988), 46.

12. For a stimulating meditation on the future of each person's right to construct his or her own identity, see Thomas M. Franck, "Clan and Superclan: Loyalty, Identity and Community in Law and Practice," *American Journal of International Law* 90 (1996): 359–83.

BIBLIOGRAPHY

Abou-Zeid, Ahmed. "Honour and Shame Among the Bedouins of Egypt." In *Honour and Shame: The Values of Mediterranean Society*. Edited by J. G. Peristiany. Chicago: University of Chicago Press, 1966.

Adams, Herbert Baxter. "The Germanic Origin of New England Towns." *Johns Hopkins University Studies in Historical and Political Science*, ser. 1, no. 2. Baltimore: Johns Hopkins University, 1882.

Aelfric. "Passion of Saint Edmund." In *Old and Middle English, c. 890–c. 1400: An Anthology*. 2nd ed. Edited by Elaine Treharne. Malden, Mass.: Wiley-Blackwell, 2004.

Ahmed, Akbar S. *Islam Under Siege: Living Dangerously in a Post-Honor World*. Cambridge, U.K.: Polity Press, 2003.

———. *Resistance and Control in Pakistan*. Rev. ed. London: Routledge, 2004.

Ahmed, Akbar S., and David M. Hart, eds. *Islam in Tribal Societies: From the Atlas to the Indus*. London: Routledge and Kegan Paul, 1984.

Ambedkar, B. R. *The Essential Writings of B. R. Ambedkar*. Edited by Valerian Rodrigues. Oxford, U.K.: Oxford University Press, 2002.

———. "The Hindu Social Order—Its Essential Principles." In *Dr. Babasaheb Ambedkar: Writings and Speeches*. Vol. 3. Compiled by Vasant Moon. Bombay: Education and Employment Department, Government of Maharashtra, 1987.

The Anglo-Saxon Chronicle. Translated and edited by M. J. Swanton. New York: Routledge, 1998.

The Anglo-Saxon World: An Anthology. Translated with an introduction by Kevin Crossley-Holland. Oxford, U.K.: Oxford University Press, 1999.

Arumugam Servai v. State of Tamil Nadu. Criminal Appeal No. 958, with Criminal Appeal No. 959 (April 19, 2011). 2011 STPL(Web) 403 SC. Accessed June 29, 2012, www.stpl-india.in/SCJFiles/2011_STPL(Web)_403_SC.pdf.

Austen, Ian. "Afghan Family, Led by Father Who Called Girls a Disgrace, Is Guilty of Murder." *The New York Times*, January 29, 2012. Accessed June 29, 2012, www.nytimes.com/2012/01/30/world/americas/afghan-family-members-convicted-in-honor-killings.html.

Austin, Granville. *The Indian Constitution: Cornerstone of a Nation*. Oxford, U.K.: Oxford University Press, 2012.

[Bagehot, Walter]. *Bagehot: The English Constitution*. Cambridge Texts in the History of Political Thought. Edited by Paul Smith. Cambridge, U.K.: Cambridge University Press, 2001.

Bailey, Clinton. *Bedouin Law from Sinai and the Negev: Justice Without Government*. New Haven, Conn.: Yale University Press, 2009.

Barfield, Thomas J. *The Nomadic Alternative*. Englewood Cliffs, N.J.: Prentice-Hall, 1993.

Barmash, Pamela. *Homicide in the Biblical World*. Cambridge, U.K.: Cambridge University Press, 2005.

Barton, Roy Franklin. *Ifugao Law*. Berkeley: University of California Press, 1919.

Bass, Sadie. "How Many Different Ways Can You Spell 'Gaddafi'?" ABC News, September 22, 2009. Accessed June 29, 2012, http://abcnews.go.com/blogs/headlines/2009/09/how-many-different-ways-can-you-spell-gaddafi.

Bellow, Adam. *In Praise of Nepotism: A History of Family Enterprise from King David to George W. Bush*. New York: Anchor Books, 2003.

Benedict, Ruth. *The Chrysanthemum and the Sword: Patterns of Japanese Culture*. New York: Mariner Books, 2005. Originally published in 1946.

Berman, Harold J. *Law and Revolution: The Formation of the Western Legal Tradition*. Cambridge, Mass.: Harvard University Press, 1983.

Boehm, Christopher. "Ambivalence and Compromise in Human Nature." *American Anthropologist* 91 (1989): 921–39.

———. *Blood Revenge: The Anthropology of Feuding in Montenegro and Other Tribal Societies*. Lawrence: University Press of Kansas, 1984.

The Book of Settlements: Landnámabók. Translated with an introduction by Hermann Pálsson and Paul Edwards. Winnipeg: University of Manitoba Press, 2006.

"Building." High Court of Punjab and Haryana. Accessed June 29, 2012, http://highcourtchd.gov.in/index.php?trs=building.

Burrow, J. W. *A Liberal Descent: Victorian Historians and the English Past*. Cambridge, U.K.: Cambridge University Press, 1981.

Byock, Jesse L. *Feud in the Icelandic Saga*. Berkeley: University of California Press, 1982.

———. *Medieval Iceland: Society, Sagas, and Power*. Berkeley: University of California Press, 1988.

———. *Viking Age Iceland*. New York: Penguin Books, 2001.

Campbell, J. K. *Honour, Family, and Patronage: A Study of Institutions and Moral Values in a Greek Mountain Community*. New York: Oxford University Press, 1964.

Canuday, Jose Jowel. "Big War, Small Wars: The Interplay of Large-scale and Community Armed Conflicts in Five Central Mindanao Communities." In *Rido: Clan Feuding and Conflict Management in Mindanao*. Edited by Wilfredo Magno Torres III. Makati City, Philippines: Asia Foundation, 2007.

Caprio, Mark E. *Japanese Assimilation Policies in Colonial Korea: 1910–1945*. Seattle: University of Washington Press, 2009.

Carr, Jack L., and Janet T. Landa. "The Economics of Symbols, Clan Names, and Religion." *Journal of Legal Studies* 12 (1983): 135–56.

"Central List of Other Backward Classes." National Commission for Backward Classes. Accessed June 29, 2012, http://ncbc.nic.in/Centrallistifobc.html.

Chanock, Martin. *Law, Custom, and Social Order: The Colonial Experience in Malawi and Zambia*. Portsmouth, N.H.: Heinemann, 1998.

Chatterji, Bankim Chandra. *Anandamath*. Translated and adapted by Basanta Koomar Roy. Delhi: Orient Paperbacks, 1992.

Cheyne-Macpherson, William. *The Chiefs of Clan Macpherson*. Edinburgh: Oliver and Boyd, 1947.

Chowdhry, Prem. *Political Economy of Production and Reproduction: Caste, Custom, and Community in North India*. Oxford, U.K.: Oxford University Press, 2011.

Clark, Victoria. *Yemen: Dancing on the Heads of Snakes*. New Haven, Conn.: Yale University Press, 2010.

Cocks, R.C.J. *Sir Henry Maine: A Study in Victorian Jurisprudence*. Cambridge, U.K.: Cambridge University Press, 1988.

Collins, Kathleen. *Clan Politics and Regime Transition in Central Asia*. Cambridge, U.K.: Cambridge University Press, 2006.

Copnall, James. "Can Sudan's Oil Feed North and South?" BBC News, July 4, 2011. Accessed June 29, 2012, www.bbc.co.uk/news/world-africa-12128080.

Cummings, Bruce. *Korea's Place in the Sun: A Modern History*. Updated edition. New York: W. W. Norton, 2005.

Cunningham, Erin. "Long the Glue of Gaza, Clans Say Hamas Is Undermining Tribal Justice." *The Christian Science Monitor*, January 22, 2010. Accessed June 29, 2012, www.csmonitor.com/World/Middle-East/2010/0122/Long-the-glue-of-Gaza-clans-say-Hamas-is-undermining-tribal-justice.

Dasgupta, Probal. *The Otherness of English: India's Auntie Tongue Syndrome*. New Delhi: Sage Publications, 1993.

Davis, John. *Libyan Politics: Tribe and Revolution*. London: I. B. Tauris, 1987.

Deuchler, Martina. *The Confucian Transformation of Korea: A Study of Society and Ideology*. Harvard-Yenching Institute Monograph Series 36. Cambridge, Mass.: Council on East Asian Studies, Harvard University, 1992.

Dickinson, W. Croft. *Scotland from the Earliest Times to 1603*. 3rd ed. Revised and edited by Archibald A. M. Duncan. Oxford, U.K.: Clarendon Press, 1977.

Dictionary of the Middle Ages. 13 vols. Edited by Joseph R. Strayer. New York: Charles Scribner's Sons, 1982–1989.

Donner, Fred McGraw. *The Early Islamic Conquests*. Princeton, N.J.: Princeton University Press, 1981.

———. *Muhammad and the Believers: At the Origins of Islam*. Cambridge, Mass.: Belknap Press of Harvard University Press, 2010.

Doro, Monalinda Emperio. "Management and Resolution of Rido Among Meranao in Baloi, Lanao del Norte: Case Studies." In *Rido: Clan Feuding and Conflict Management in Mindanao*. Edited by Wilfredo Magno Torres III. Makati City, Philippines: Asia Foundation, 2007.

Douglas, William O. *Beyond the High Himalayas*. Garden City, N.Y.: Doubleday, 1952.

Duus, Peter. *The Abacus and the Sword: The Japanese Penetration of Korea, 1895–1910*. Berkeley: University of California Press, 1995.

Earle, Timothy. *How Chiefs Come to Power: The Political Economy in Prehistory*. Stanford, Calif.: Stanford University Press, 1997.

Ebert, Roger. "Eat, Pray, Love." rogerebert.com, August 11, 2010. Accessed June 29, 2012, http://rogerebert.suntimes.com/apps/pbcs.dll/article?AID-/20100811/reviews /100819999.

Eckert, Carter J., et. al. *Korea Old and New: A History.* Seoul: Ilchokak Publishers for the Korea Institute, Harvard University, 1990.

Edwards, David B. *Heroes of the Age: Moral Fault Lines on the Afghan Frontier.* Berkeley: University of California Press, 1996.

Egil's Saga. Translated by Bernard Scudder. Edited with an introduction by Svanhildur Óskarsdóttir. New York: Penguin Books, 2004.

Eickelman, Dale F. *The Middle East and Central Asia: An Anthropological Approach.* 4th ed. Upper Saddle River, N.J.: Prentice Hall, 2002.

Ekeh, Peter P. "Colonialism and the Two Publics in Africa: A Theoretical Statement." *Comparative Studies in Society and History* 17 (1975): 91–112.

Ellickson, Robert C. *Order Without Law: How Neighbors Settle Disputes.* Cambridge, Mass.: Harvard University Press, 1991.

Elmi, Afyare Abdi. *Understanding the Somalia Conflagration: Identity, Political Islam, and Peacebuilding.* London: Pluto Press, 2010.

Engels, Friedrich. *The Origin of the Family, Private Property, and the State, in the Light of the Researches of Lewis H. Morgan.* Edited with an introduction by Eleanor Burke Leacock. New York: International Publishers, 1972.

Ertman, Thomas. *Birth of the Leviathan: Building States and Regimes in Medieval and Early Modern Europe.* Cambridge, U.K.: Cambridge University Press, 1997.

"Ethnic Identity in Afghanistan." U.S. Naval Postgraduate School. Accessed June 29, 2012, www.nps.edu/Programs/CCS/Ethnic_identity.html.

Evans-Pritchard, E. E. *The Nuer: A Description of the Modes of Livelihood and Political Institutions of a Nilotic People.* New York: Oxford University Press, 1940.

Fairbank, John King, and Merle Goldman. *China: A New History.* 2nd ed. Cambridge, Mass.: Belknap Press of Harvard University Press, 2006.

Feaver, George. *From Status to Contract: A Biography of Sir Henry Maine, 1822–1888.* London: Longmans, Green, 1969.

——. "The Victorian Values of Sir Henry Maine." In *The Victorian Achievement of Sir Henry Maine: A Centennial Reappraisal.* Edited by Alan Diamond. Cambridge, U.K.: Cambridge University Press, 1991.

Filppula, Markku, Juhani Klemola, and Heli Paulasto. *English and Celtic in Contact.* New York: Routledge, 2008.

Fox, Richard G. *Kin, Clan, Raja, and Rule: State-Hinterland Relations in Preindustrial India.* Berkeley: University of California Press, 1971.

Fox, Robin. *Kinship and Marriage: An Anthropological Perspective.* Cambridge, U.K.: Cambridge University Press, 1967.

——. *The Tribal Imagination: Civilization and the Savage Mind.* Cambridge, Mass.: Harvard University Press, 2011.

Franck, Thomas M. "Clan and Superclan: Loyalty, Identity, and Community in Law and Practice." *American Journal of International Law* 90 (1996): 359–83.

Freedman, Maurice. *Chinese Lineage and Society: Fukien and Kwangtung.* Oxford, U.K.: Berg, 2007.

——. *Lineage Organization in Southeastern China.* London: Athlone Press, University of London, 1970.

Freud, Sigmund. *Totem and Taboo: Some Points of Agreement Between the Mental Life of Savages and Neurotics.* Edited and translated by James Strachey. New York: Norton, 1950. Originally published in 1913.

Freund, David M. P. *Colored Property: State Policy and White Racial Politics in Suburban America.* Chicago: University of Chicago Press, 2007.

———. "Marketing the Free Market: State Intervention and the Politics of Prosperity in Metropolitan America." In *The New Suburban History.* Edited by Kevin M. Kruse and Thomas J. Sugrue, 11–32. Chicago: University of Chicago Press, 2006.

Fried, Morton H. *The Evolution of Political Society.* New York: Random House, 1967.

Frisch, Hillel. "Modern Absolutist or Neopatriarchal State Building? Customary Law, Extended Families, and the Palestinian Authority." *International Journal of Middle East Studies* 29 (1997): 341–58.

Fujitani, Takashi. *Race for Empire: Koreans as Japanese and Japanese as Americans During World War II.* Berkeley: University of California Press, 2011.

Fukuyama, Francis. *The Origins of Political Order: From Prehuman Times to the French Revolution.* New York: Farrar, Straus and Giroux, 2011.

Garang, Ngor Arol. "Clashes Claim over 80 Lives in Warrap State." *Sudan Tribune,* May 10, 2011. Accessed June 29, 2012, www.sudantribune.com/Clashes-claims -over-80-lives-in,38850.

Gathafi, M. Al [Qaddafi, Muammar al-]. *The Green Book: The Solution to the Problem of Democracy; The Solution to the Economic Problem; The Social Basis of the Third Universal Theory.* Reading, U.K.: Ithaca Press, 2005.

Gellner, Ernest. "The Asiatic Trauma." In *State and Society in Soviet Thought.* Oxford, U.K.: Basil Blackwell, 1988.

Ghani, Ashraf, and Clare Lockhart. *Fixing Failed States: A Framework for Rebuilding a Fractured World.* New York: Oxford University Press, 2008.

Gilbert, Elizabeth. *Eat, Pray, Love: One Woman's Search for Everything Across Italy, India, and Indonesia.* New York: Penguin Books, 2006.

Ginat, Joseph. *Blood Revenge: Family Honor, Mediation, and Outcasting.* 2nd ed. Brighton, U.K.: Sussex Academic Press, 1997.

A Glossary of the Tribes and Castes of the Punjab and North-West Frontier Province: Based on the Census Report for Punjab, 1883. Compiled by H. A. Rose. 3 vols. Patiala, India: Languages Department Punjab, 1970. Originally published in 1883.

Gluckman, Max. *Custom and Conflict in Africa.* Oxford, U.K.: Basil Blackwell, 1970. Originally published in 1956.

Goody, Jack. *The European Family: An Historico-Anthropological Essay.* Oxford, U.K.: Blackwell, 2000.

Gore, M. S. *The Social Context of an Ideology: Ambedkar's Political and Social Thought.* New Delhi: Sage Publications, 1993.

Gregory of Tours. *History of the Franks.* Translated by Ernest Brehaut. New York: Norton, 1969. Originally published in 1916.

Greif, Avner. "Reputation and Coalitions in Medieval Trade: Evidence on the Maghribi Traders." *Journal of Economic History* 49 (1989): 857–82.

Guillaume, Alfred. *The Life of Muhammad: A Translation of Ibn Ishaq's Sirat Rasul Allah.* Oxford, U.K.: Oxford University Press, 1955.

Harding, Alan. *Medieval Law and the Foundations of the State.* Oxford, U.K.: Oxford University Press, 2002.

Hasluck, Margaret. *The Unwritten Law in Albania*. Cambridge, U.K.: Cambridge University Press, 1954.

Hastrup, Kirsten. "Kinship in Medieval Iceland." *Island of Anthropology: Studies in Past and Present Iceland*. Odense, Denmark: Odense University Press, 1990.

——. *A Place Apart: An Anthropological Study of the Icelandic World*. Oxford, U.K.: Clarendon Press, 1998.

Hatitah, Abdulsattar. "Libyan Tribal Map: Network of Loyalties That Will Determine Gaddafi's Fate." Asharq Alawsat, February 22, 2011. Accessed June 29, 2012, www.asharq-e.com/news.asp?section=3&id=24257.

Hirsi Ali, Ayaan. *Infidel*. New York: Free Press, 2007.

——. *Nomad: From Islam to America—A Personal Journey Through the Clash of Civilizations*. New York: Free Press, 2010.

Hitti, Philip K. *History of the Arabs: From the Earliest Times to the Present*. 10th ed. Revised preface by Walid Khalidi. New York: Palgrave MacMillan, 2002. Originally published in 1970; original edition published in 1937.

Hodgson, Marshall G. S. *The Venture of Islam: Conscience and History in a World Civilization*. Vol. 1. Chicago: University of Chicago Press, 1974.

Hosseini, Khaled. *The Kite Runner*. New York: Riverhead Books, 2003.

Hsu, Francis L. K. *Clan, Caste, and Club*. New York: D. Van Nostrand, 1963.

Hu, Hsien Chin. *The Common Descent Group in China and Its Functions*. New York: Viking Fund, 1948.

Hyde, Lewis. *The Gift: Imagination and the Erotic Life of Property*. New York: Vintage Books, 1983.

Ibn Khaldūn. *The Muqaddimah: An Introduction to History*. Translated with an introduction by Franz Rosenthal. Abridged and edited by N. J. Dawood. New introduction by Bruce B. Lawrence. Princeton, N.J.: Princeton University Press, 2005.

"Informal Justice: Rule of Law and Dispute Resolution in Palestine: National Report on Field Research Results." Project coordinator Dima al Khalidi. Birzeit, West Bank: Institute of Law, Birzeit University, 2006.

"Inside Gaza: The Challenge of Clans and Families." Middle East Report No. 71. Gaza, Jerusalem, and Brussels: International Crisis Group, December 20, 2007.

Iraq Tribal Study—Al-Anbar Governorate: The Albu Fahd Tribe, The Albu Mahal Tribe, and the Albu Issa Tribe. Directed by Lin Todd; contributing researchers: W. Patrick Lang, Jr.; R. Alan King; Andrea V. Jackson; Montgomery McFate; Ahmed S. Hashim; and Jeremy S. Harrington. Study Conducted Under Contract with the U.S. Department of Defense, June 18, 2006.

Jabbur, Jibrail S. *The Bedouins and the Desert: Aspects of Nomadic Life in the Arab East*. Translated by Lawrence I. Conrad. Edited by Suhayl J. Jabbur and Lawrence I. Conrad. Albany: State University of New York Press, 1995.

Jaffrelot, Christophe. *Dr. Ambedkar and Untouchability: Fighting the Indian Caste System*. New York: Columbia University Press, 2005.

Jóhannesson, Jón. *Íslendinga Saga: A History of the Old Icelandic Commonwealth*. Translated by Haraldur Bessason. Winnipeg: University of Manitoba Press, 2006.

Johnson, Allen W., and Timothy Earle. *The Evolution of Human Societies: From Foraging Group to Agrarian State*. 2nd ed. Stanford, Calif.: Stanford University Press, 2000.

Jok, Aleu Akechak, Robert A. Leitch, and Carrie Vandewint. "A Study of Customary Law in Contemporary Southern Sudan." World Vision International, 2004.

Jones, Seth G. "It Takes the Villages: Bringing Change from Below in Afghanistan." *Foreign Affairs* 89, no. 3 (May/June 2010): 120–27.

"Justice Katju—Media Debate: Justice Markandey Katju on the Role of Media in India." Law Resource India. Accessed June 29, 2012, http://indialawyers.wordpress .com/tag/justice.

Kagan, Robert. *The World America Made.* New York: Alfred A. Knopf, 2012.

Kang, Hildi. *Under the Black Umbrella: Voices from Colonial Korea, 1910–1945.* Ithaca, N.Y.: Cornell University Press, 2001.

Karlsson, Gunnar. *The History of Iceland.* Minneapolis: University of Minnesota Press, 2000.

Karsten, Rafael. *Blood Revenge, War, and Victory Feasts Among the Jibaro Indians of Eastern Ecuador.* Washington, D.C.: U.S. Government Printing Office, 1923.

Keer, Dhananjay. *Dr. Ambedkar: Life and Mission.* Bombay: Popular Prakashan, 1954.

Keiser, R. Lincoln. *Vice Lords: Warriors of the Streets.* New York: Holt, Rinehart and Winston, 1969.

"Kenyans 'Rearming for 2012 Poll.'" BBC News, October 7, 2009. Accessed June 29, 2012, http://news.bbc.co.uk/2/hi/africa/8293745.stm.

Khoury, Philip S., and Joseph Kostiner, eds. *Tribes and State Formation in the Middle East.* Berkeley: University of California Press, 1990.

Kim, Richard E. "Lost Names." In *Lost Names: Scenes from a Korean Boyhood.* Berkeley: University of California Press, 1998. Originally published in 1970.

Kim, Rosa. "The Legacy of Institutionalized Gender Inequality in South Korea: The Family Law." *Boston College Third World Law Journal* 14, no. 1 (1994): 145–62. Accessed June 29, 2012, http://lawdigitalcommons.bc.edu/twlj/vol14/iss1/7.

Kipling, Rudyard. "The Broken Men." In *Rudyard Kipling: Complete Verse.* New York: Anchor Press, 1940.

Kirkpatrick, David D. "Death of Rebel Leader Stirs Fears of Tribal Conflict." *The New York Times,* July 28, 2011. Accessed June 29, 2012, www.nytimes.com/2011/07/29 /world/africa/29libya.html.

Kirkpatrick, David D., and Mona El-Naggar. "Qaddafi's Son Warns of Civil War as Libyan Protests Widen." *The New York Times,* February 20, 2011. Accessed June 29, 2012, www.nytimes.com/2011/02/21/world/africa/21libya.html.

Koch, D. M. "Sudan: Anyuak and Cholo's Kingdoms Are Our National Heritage!" Anyuak Media, August 21, 2009. Accessed June 29, 2012, www.anyuakmedia .com/com_temp_09_08_22.html.

Krader, Lawrence. *Formation of the State.* Englewood Cliffs, N.J.: Prentice-Hall, 1968.

Krebs, Christopher B. *A Most Dangerous Book: Tacitus's Germania from the Roman Empire to the Third Reich.* New York: W. W. Norton, 2011.

Kurczy, Stephen, and Drew Hinshaw. "Libya's Tribes: Who's Who?" *The Christian Science Monitor,* February 24, 2011. Accessed June 29, 2012, www.csmonitor.com /World/Backchannels/2011/0224/Libya-tribes-Who-s-who.

Landa, Janet T. "The Enigma of the *Kula Ring*: Gift-Exchanges and Primitive Law and Order." *International Review of Law and Economics* 3 (1983): 137–60.

——. "A Theory of the Ethnically Homogeneous Middleman Group: An Institutional Alternative to Contract Law." *Journal of Legal Studies* 10 (1981): 349–62.

Larssen, Dagmar I. *SüdSüdOst Mekka: Pakistanische Muslime in Norwegen.* Berlin/ Münster, Germany: LIT Verlag, 2010.

Laws of Early Iceland, Grágás: The Codex Regius of Grágás, with Material from Other Manuscripts. Vol. 2. Translated and edited by Andrew Dennis, Peter Foote, and Richard Perkins. Winnipeg: University of Manitoba Press, 2000.

The Laws of Manu. Introduced and translated by Wendy Doniger, with Brian K. Smith. New York: Penguin Books, 1991.

Lee, Chulwoo. "Modernity, Legality, and Power in Korea Under Japanese Rule." In *Colonial Modernity in Korea.* Edited by Gi-Wook Shin and Michael Robinson, 21–51. Cambridge, Mass.: Harvard University Asia Center, 1999.

Lee, Ki-baik. *A New History of Korea.* Translated by Edward W. Wagner with Edward J. Shultz. Cambridge, Mass.: Harvard University Press for the Harvard-Yenching Institute, 1984.

Leland, John, and Namo Abdulla. "A Killing Set Honor Above Love." *The New York Times,* November 20, 2010. Accessed June 29, 2012, www.nytimes.com/2010/11 /21/world/middleeast/21honor.html.

Lévi-Strauss, Claude. *Structural Anthropology.* Translated by Claire Jacobson and Brooke Grundfest Schoepf. 2 vols. New York: Basic Books, 1963.

Lewis, Ioan M. *Blood and Bone: The Call of Kinship in Somali Society.* Lawrenceville, N.J.: Red Sea Press, 1994.

Lindholm, Charles. *Generosity and Jealousy: The Swat Pukhtun of Northern Pakistan.* New York: Columbia University Press, 1982.

——. *The Islamic Middle East: Tradition and Change.* Rev. ed. Malden, Mass.: Wiley-Blackwell, 2002.

Liu, Hui-Chen Wang. *The Traditional Chinese Clan Rules.* Monographs of the Association for Asian Studies VII. New York: J. J. Augustin for the Association for Asian Studies, 1959.

Liu, Xin. *In One's Own Shadow: An Ethnographic Account of the Condition of Post-Reform Rural China.* Berkeley: University of California Press, 2000.

Lives Together, Worlds Apart: Men and Women in a Time of Change. State of the World Population 2000. Nafis Sadik, executive director. New York: United Nations Population Fund, 2000. Accessed June 29, 2012, www.unfpa.org/swp/2000/english /index.html.

Llewellyn, Karl N., and E. Adamson Hoebel. *The Cheyenne Way: Conflict and Case Law in Primitive Jurisprudence.* Norman: University of Oklahoma Press, 1941.

Loeb, Vernon. "Clan, Family Ties Called Key to Army's Capture of Hussein: 'Link Diagrams' Showed Everyone Related by Blood or Tribe." *The Washington Post,* December 16, 2003, A27.

Maddison, Angus. *Contours of the World Economy, 1–2030 AD: Essays in Macro-Economic History.* Oxford, U.K.: Oxford University Press, 2007.

——. *Monitoring the World Economy, 1820–1992.* Paris: Development Centre of the Organisation for Economic Co-operation and Development, 1995.

"Mahsud." Program for Culture and Conflict Studies, U.S. Naval Postgraduate School. Accessed June 29, 2012, www.nps.edu/programs/ccs/Docs/Pakistan/Tribes/Mah sud.pdf.

Maine, Henry Sumner. *Ancient Law: Its Connection with the Early History of Society and Its Relation to Modern Ideas.* Introduction and notes by Frederick Pollock; preface to the Beacon Paperback edition by Raymond Firth. Gloucester, Mass.: Peter Smith, 1970. Originally published in 1861.

——. *Lectures on the Early History of Institutions.* New York: Henry Holt, 1875.

——. *Village-Communities in the East and West: Six Lectures Delivered at Oxford.* London: J. Murray, 1871.

Malik, Saurabh. "Runaway Couples; Evolve Compassionate Mechanism: HC." *The Tribune* (Chandigarh, India), June 24, 2008. Accessed June 29, 2012, www.tribune india.com/2008/20080625/main6.htm.

Mamdani, Mahmood. *Citizen and Subject: Contemporary Africa and the Legacy of Late Colonialism.* Princeton, N.J.: Princeton University Press, 1996.

Mandelbaum, David G. *Society in India.* 2 vols. Berkeley: University of California Press, 1970.

Mantena, Karuna. *Alibis of Empire: Henry Maine and the Ends of Liberal Imperialism.* Princeton, N.J.: Princeton University Press, 2010.

Marshall, Paul, and Nina Shea. *Silenced: How Apostasy and Blasphemy Codes Are Choking Freedom Worldwide.* New York: Oxford University Press, 2011.

Mauss, Marcel. *The Gift: The Form and Reason for Exchange in Archaic Societies.* Translated by W. D. Halls. New York: W. W. Norton, 1990.

McAuliffe, Jane Dammen, et al. *Encyclopaedia of the Qur'ān.* 6 vols. Leiden, The Netherlands: Brill, 2001–2006.

McFate, Montgomery. "Anthropology and Counterinsurgency: The Strange Story of Their Curious Relationship." *Military Review* 85, no. 2 (March–April 2005): 24–38.

——. "The Military Utility of Understanding Adversary Culture." *Joint Force Quarterly* 38, no. 3 (2005): 42–48.

McFaul, Michael. *Advancing Democracy Abroad: Why We Should and How We Can.* Hoover Studies in Politics, Economics, and Society. Lanham, Md.: Rowman & Littlefield in cooperation with the Hoover Institution at Stanford University, 2010.

McGirk, Tim. "On Bin Laden's Trail." *National Geographic,* December 2004. Accessed June 29, 2012, http://ngm.nationalgeographic.com/features/world/asia/pakistan /pashtun-text.html.

Meggit, Mervyn. *Blood Is Their Argument: Warfare Among Mae Enga Tribesmen of the New Guinea Highlands.* Palo Alto, Calif.: Mayfield, 1977.

The Message of the Qur'ān: The Full Account of the Revealed Arabic Text Accompanied by Parallel Transliteration. Translated by Muhammad Asad. Bristol, U.K.: Book Foundation, 2003.

Michener, James A. *Caravans: A Novel of Afghanistan.* New York: Random House Trade Paperbacks, 2003. Originally published in 1963.

Mill, John Stuart. *On Liberty.* Edited by David Bromwich and George Kateb. New Haven, Conn.: Yale University Press, 2003.

Miller, William Ian. *Bloodtaking and Peacemaking: Feud, Law, and Society in Saga Iceland.* Chicago: University of Chicago Press, 1990.

——. *Eye for an Eye.* Cambridge, U.K.: Cambridge University Press, 2006.

Mody, Perveez. *The Intimate State: Love-Marriage and the Law in Delhi.* New York: Routledge, 2008.

Moffat, Alistair. *The Highland Clans.* New York: Thames and Hudson, 2010.

Moore, Sally Falk. *Social Facts and Fabrications: "Customary" Law on Kilimanjaro, 1880–1980.* Cambridge, U.K.: Cambridge University Press, 1986.

Morgan, Lewis Henry. *Ancient Society.* Edited by Ashley Montagu. Tucson: University of Arizona Press, 1985. Originally published in 1877.

Morris, Colin. *The Discovery of the Individual: 1050–1220.* New York: Harper and Row, 1972.

Mortimer, Majlinda, and Anca Toader. "Blood Feuds Blight Albanian Lives." BBC News, September 23, 2005. Accessed June 29, 2012, http://news.bbc.co.uk/2/hi/europe /4273020.stm.

Moses, Daniel Noah. *The Promise of Progress: The Life and Work of Lewis Henry Morgan.* Columbia: University of Missouri Press, 2009.

Newton, Michael. *Warriors of the Word: The World of the Scottish Highlanders.* Edinburgh: Birlinn, 2009.

Njal's Saga. Translated with an introduction by Robert Cook. New York: Penguin Books, 2001.

Novak, William J. *The People's Welfare: Law and Regulation in Nineteenth-Century America.* Chapel Hill: University of North Carolina Press, 1996.

O'Carroll, Eoin. "Gaddafi? Kadafi? Qaddafi? What's the Correct Spelling?" *The Christian Science Monitor,* February 22, 2011. Accessed June 29, 2012, www.csmonitor .com/World/2011/0222/Gaddafi-Kadafi-Qaddafi-What-s-the-correct-spelling.

Pactus Legis Salicae. In *The Laws of the Salian Franks,* translated with an introduction by Katherine Fischer Drew. Philadelphia: University of Pennsylvania Press, 1991.

Pai, Hyung Il. *Constructing "Korean" Origins: A Critical Review of Archaeology, Historiography, and Racial Myth in Korean State-Formation Theories.* Harvard East Asian Monographs 187. Harvard-Hallym Series on Korea. Cambridge, Mass.: Harvard University Press for the Harvard University Asia Center, 2000.

Paul, Ron. "Political Power and the Rule of Law." *Texas Straight Talk,* February 5, 2007. Accessed June 29, 2012, http://paul.house.gov/index.php?option=com_con tent&task=view&id=1106&Itemid=69.

Prebble, John. *The King's Jaunt: George IV in Scotland, August 1822: "One and Twenty Daft Days."* Edinburgh: Birlinn, 1988.

Prohibition of Unlawful Assembly (Interference with the Freedom of Matrimonial Alliances) Bill, 2011. Available via lawcommissionofindia.nic.in/reports/cp-Honour %20Killing.pdf. Accessed February 24, 2012.

Qaddafi, Muammar al-. *See* Gathafi, M. Al.

Quran: The Final Testament: Authorized English Version, with the Arabic Text. Translated by Rashad Khalifa. 4th rev. ed. Capistrano Beach, Calif.: Islamic Productions, 2005.

Rabi, Uzi. *The Emergence of States in a Tribal Society: Oman under Sa 'id bin Taymur, 1932–1970.* Brighton, U.K.: Sussex Academic Press, 2006.

Rahman, Fazlur. *Islam and Modernity: Transformation of an Intellectual Tradition.* Chicago: University of Chicago Press, 1982.

Rahman, Tariq. "Images of the 'Other' in Pakistani Textbooks." *Pakistan Perspectives* (July–December 2002): 33–49. Accessed June 29, 2012, www.tariqrahman.net /language/images%20of%20the%20%27other%27.htm.

———. "Language-Teaching and Power in Pakistan." *Indian Social Science Review* 5, no. 1 (January–June 2003): 45–62. Accessed June 29, 2012, www.tariqrahman.net

/language/language-teaching%20&%20power%20%20in%20pakistan%20 (amended).htm.

Rainsford, Sarah. "The Turkish Peacemaker." *BBC News*, November 11, 2006. Accessed June 29, 2012, http://news.bbc.co.uk/2/hi/programmes/from_our_own_correspondent/6137236.stm.

Rich, George W. "Problems and Prospects in the Study of Icelandic Kinship." In *The Anthropology of Iceland*. Edited by E. Paul Durrenberger and Gísli Pálsson. Iowa City: University of Iowa Press, 1989.

Robinson, Glenn E. *Building a Palestinian State: The Incomplete Revolution.* Bloomington and Indianapolis: Indiana University Press, 1997.

———. "Palestinian Tribes, Clans, and Notable Families." *Strategic Insights* 7, no. 4 (September 2008).

Robinson, Michael E. *Korea's Twentieth-Century Odyssey: A Short History.* Honolulu: University of Hawai'i Press, 2007.

Ronfeldt, David. *In Search of How Societies Work: Tribes—The First and Forever Form.* RAND Pardee Center working paper WR-433-RPC. Santa Monica, Calif.: RAND, December 2006.

Rushdie, Salman. *The Satanic Verses: A Novel.* New York: Random House Trade Paperbacks, 2008.

Saeed, Abdullah, and Hassan Saeed. *Freedom of Religion, Apostasy, and Islam.* Aldershot, U.K.: Ashgate, 2004.

The Sagas of Icelanders: A Selection. Preface by Jane Smiley; introduction by Robert Kellogg. New York: Penguin Books, 2000.

Sahlins, Marshall D. "The Segmentary Lineage: An Organization of Predatory Expansion." *American Anthropologist*, n s. 63 (1961): 322–45.

———. *Tribesmen.* Englewood Cliffs, N.J.: Prentice-Hall, 1968.

Salimi, Abdulrahman al-. "A Comparison of Modern Religious Education in Arabia: Oman and Yemen." IjtihadReason, n.d. Accessed June 29, 2012, www.ijtihadreason.org/articles/modern-religious-education.php.

Salzman, Philip Carl. *Culture and Conflict in the Middle East.* Amherst, N.Y.: Humanity Books, 2008.

Sarhan, Afif, and Caroline Davies. "'My Daughter Deserved to Die for Falling in Love.'" *The Observer*, May 10, 2008. Accessed June 29, 2012, www.guardian.co.uk/world/2008/may/11/iraq.humanrights.

The Saxon Chronicle. Translated by J. Ingram. London: Longman, Hurst, Rees, Orne, and Brown, 1823.

Schacht, Joseph. *An Introduction to Islamic Law.* Oxford, U.K.: Clarendon Press, 1982.

Schatz, Edward. *Modern Clan Politics: The Power of "Blood" in Kazakhstan and Beyond.* Seattle: University of Washington Press, 2004.

Schwartz, Benjamin I. *The World of Thought in Ancient China.* Cambridge, Mass.: Belknap Press of Harvard University Press, 1985.

Scott, James C. *The Art of Not Being Governed: An Anarchist History of Upland Southeast Asia.* New Haven, Conn.: Yale University Press, 2009.

———. *Seeing Like a State: How Certain Schemes to Improve the Human Condition Have Failed.* New Haven, Conn.: Yale University Press, 1998.

[Scott, Walter.] *Hints Addressed to the Inhabitants of Edinburgh, and Others, in Prospect of His Majesty's Visit. By an Old Citizen.* Edinburgh: Printed for Bell and

Bradfute, Manners and Miller, Archibald Constable and Co., William Black-wood, Waugh and Innes, and John Robertson, 1822.

Scott, Walter. *Waverley; Or, 'Tis Sixty Years Since*. Edited by Claire Lamont. Oxford, U.K.: Oxford University Press, 1986.

Seth, Michael J. *A Concise History of Korea: From the Neolithic Period Through the Nineteenth Century*. Oxford, U.K.: Rowman and Littlefield, 2006.

Shakespeare, William. *Romeo and Juliet*. In *The Norton Shakespeare*, 2nd ed. Edited by Stephen Greenblatt. New York: W. W. Norton, 2008.

Sharabi, Hisham. *Neopatriarchy: A Theory of Distorted Change in Arab Society*. New York: Oxford University Press, 1988.

Shaw, George Bernard. *The Perfect Wagnerite: A Commentary on the Ring of the Niblungs*. London: Grant Richards, 1898.

Shoufani, Elias. *Al-Riddah and the Muslim Conquest of Arabia*. Toronto: University of Toronto Press, 1973.

Smith, C. J. *The Roman Clan: The Gens from Ancient Ideology to Modern Anthropology*. Cambridge, U.K.: Cambridge University Press, 2006.

Smith, William Robertson. *Kinship and Marriage in Early Arabia*. Cambridge, U.K.: Cambridge University Press, 1885.

Snyder, Gary. "Passage to More Than India." In *Earth House Hold: Technical Notes & Queries to Fellow Dharma Revolutionaries*. New York: New Directions, 1969.

Spruyt, Hendrik. *The Sovereign State and Its Competitors*. Princeton, N.J.: Princeton University Press, 1994.

Stack, Carol. *All Our Kin: Strategies for Survival in a Black Community*. New York: Basic Books, 1974.

Starr, S. Frederick. *Clans, Authoritarian Rulers, and Parliaments in Central Asia*. Washington, D.C.: Central Asia–Caucasus Institute and Silk Road Studies Program, 2006.

Stechern, David. *Das Recht in den Romanen von Sir Walter Scott*. Berlin/Münster, Germany: LIT Verlag, 2003.

Stephenson, Carl, and Frederick George Marcham, eds. and trans. *Sources of English Constitutional History*. New York: Harper and Brothers, 1937.

Strayer, Joseph R. *On the Medieval Origins of the Modern State*. Princeton, N.J.: Princeton University Press, 1998. Originally published in 1970.

Strong, Roy. *Coronation: A History of Kingship and the British Monarchy*. New York: HarperCollins, 2005.

Sturluson, Snorri. *Heimskringla: History of the Kings of Norway*. Translated and with an introduction by Lee M. Hollander. Austin: University of Texas Press for the American-Scandinavian Foundation, 1964.

Suri, Jeremi. *Liberty's Surest Guardian: American Nation-Building from the Founders to Obama*. New York: Free Press, 2011.

Sutherland, John. *The Life of Walter Scott: A Critical Biography*. Oxford, U.K.: Blackwell, 1995.

Tacitus. *The Agricola and the Germania*. Translated and introduced by H. Mattingly. Revised translation by S. A. Handford. New York: Penguin, 1970.

——. "Germany and Its Tribes" (*Germania*). Translated by Alfred John Church and William Jackson Brodribb. In *The Complete Works of Tacitus*. Edited and with an introduction by Moses Hadas. New York: Random House, 1942.

Tai-Yung, Lee. "The Legal Status of Korean Women." In *Legal System of Korea*. Edited by International Cultural Foundation. Korean Culture Series 5. Seoul: Si-sa-young-o-sa, 1982.

Terris, Robert, and Vera Inoue-Terris. "A Case Study of Third World Jurisprudence—Palestine: Conflict Resolution and Customary Law in a Neopatrimonial Society." *Berkeley Journal of International Law* 20 (2002): 462–95.

Thatcher, Margaret. "Interview for *Woman's Own*." Margaret Thatcher Foundation. Accessed June 29, 2012, www.margaretthatcher.org/document/106689.

Thomas, Mark G., Michael P. H. Stumpf, and Heinrich Härke. "Evidence for an Apartheid-like Social Structure in Early Anglo-Saxon England." *Proceedings of the Royal Society B* (2006): 2651–57.

[Þorgilsson, Ari.] *Íslendingabók*. In *Íslendingabók/The Book of the Icelanders; Kristni Saga/The Story of the Conversion*. Translated by Siân Grønlie. London: Viking Society for Northern Research, University College London, 2006.

Tiger, Lionel. "Zuckerberg: The World's Richest Primatologist." *The Wall Street Journal*, February 6, 2012. Accessed June 29, 2012, http://online.wsj.com/article/SB10001424052748703421204576327443487322026.html.

Tilly, Charles. *Coercion, Capital, and European States, AD 990–1992*. Cambridge, Mass.: Blackwell, 1992.

Tocqueville, Alexis de. *Democracy in America*. Translated by Henry Reeve; revised by Francis Bowen; revised and edited by Phillips Bradley. 2 vols. New York: Vintage Books, 1990.

Toshiyuki, Kajiyama. "The Clan Records." In *The Clan Records: Five Stories of Korea*, 7–46. Translated by Yoshiko Dykstra. Introduction by George Akita and Yong-ho Choe. Honolulu: University of Hawai'i Press, 1995.

Trautmann, Thomas R. *India: Brief History of a Civilization*. Oxford, U.K.: Oxford University Press, 2011.

——. *Lewis Henry Morgan and the Invention of Kinship*. Berkeley: University of California Press, 1987.

Trevor-Roper, Hugh. "The Invention of Tradition: The Highland Tradition of Scotland." In *The Invention of Tradition*. Edited by Eric Hobsbawm and Terence Ranger. Cambridge, U.K.: Cambridge University Press, 1983.

Unger, Roberto Mangabeira. *Law in Modern Society*. New York: Free Press, 1976.

United Nations Development Programme, Regional Bureau for Arab States. *Arab Human Development Report 2004: Towards Freedom in the Arab World*. New York: United Nations Development Programme, 2005.

U.S. Marine Corps/Marine Recruiting/Marines.com. "Principles & Values." Accessed June 29, 2012, www.marines.com/history-heritage/principles-values.

"Uprising in Libya: 'Survival Hinges on Tribal Solidarity.'" Interview with Hanspeter Mattes. Spiegel Online, February 23, 2011. Accessed June 29, 2012, www.spiegel.de/international/world/0,1518,747234,00.html.

Usbeck, Frank. "'Fellow Peoples': The Influence of the German Image of Indians on German National Identity and Its Appropriation by National Socialism in German Periodicals, 1925–1945." PhD diss., University of Leipzig, Germany, Institute for American Studies, 2010.

Watt, W. Montgomery. *Muhammad at Mecca*. Oxford, U.K.: Oxford University Press, 1953.

———. *Muhammad at Medina*. Oxford, U.K.: Clarendon Press, 1956.

———. *Muhammad's Mecca: History in the Qur'an*. Edinburgh: Edinburgh University Press, 1988.

Weale, Michael E., Deborah A. Weiss, Rolf F. Jager, Neil Bradman, and Mark G. Thomas. "Y Chromosome Evidence for Anglo-Saxon Mass Migration." *Molecular Biology and Evolution* 19 (2002): 1008–1021. Accessed June 29, 2012, www.ucl .ac.uk/mace-lab/publications/articles/2002/Weale-MBE-02-AS.pdf.

Wehrey, Frederic. "Libya's Terra Incognita: Who and What Will Follow Qaddafi?" *Foreign Affairs*, February 28, 2011. Accessed June 29, 2012, www.foreignaffairs .com/articles/67551/frederic-wehrey/libyas-terra-incognita.

Weir, Shelagh. A *Tribal Order: Politics and Law in the Mountains of Yemen*. Austin: University of Texas Press, 2007.

Weyrauch, Walter O., and Maureen Anne Bell. "Autonomous Lawmaking: The Case of the 'Gypsies.'" In *Gypsy Law: Romani Legal Traditions and Culture*. Edited by Walter O. Weyrauch. Berkeley: University of California Press, 2001.

Wilson, Isaiah, III. "Saving Westphalia: Countering Insurgency Through Tribal Democratization." In *Countering Insurgency and Promoting Democracy*. Edited by Manolis Priniotakis. New York: Council for Emerging National Security Affairs, 2007.

Wolpert, Stanley. *India*. 4th ed. Berkeley: University of California Press, 2009.

Wunsch, James S. "Foundations of Centralization: The Colonial Experience and the African Context." In *The Failure of the Centralized State: Institutions and Self-Governance in Africa*. Edited by James S. Wunsch and Dele Olowu. Boulder, Colo.: Westview Press, 1990.

Yan, Yunxiang. *The Individualization of Chinese Society*. Oxford, U.K.: Berg, 2009.

Yardley, Jim. "In India, Castes, Honor and Killings Intertwine." *The New York Times*, July 9, 2010. Accessed June 29, 2012, www.nytimes.com/2010/07/10/world/asia /10honor.html.

———. "Unelected Councils in India Run Villages with Stern Hand." *The New York Times*, June 4, 2011. Accessed June 29, 2012, www.nytimes.com/2011/06/05/world /asia/05india.html.

ACKNOWLEDGMENTS

I wish to thank many colleagues and institutions for their generous assistance. At the Rutgers School of Law–Newark, I am pleased to have had the support of Chancellor Steven Diner, Dean John Farmer, and Vice Dean Ronald Chen, as well as my many friends in the administration and on the faculty, above all George Thomas. I also have been fortunate in my students, and I thank especially those who took part in my course on the history of the common law, which first stimulated my thinking on the subjects I address here. I likewise thank my students and colleagues at Cardozo School of Law from the spring term of 2010 and my friends on the Cardozo faculty, particularly David Carlson and Alex Stein, and my students and colleagues at the University of Connecticut School of Law from the spring term of 2011, especially Richard Kay and Peter Siegelman.

The outlines for this book came into focus during a term spent as a Fulbright Scholar in Akureyri, Iceland. For their hospitality and for sharing their insights about Icelandic history and society, I thank Lára Jónsdóttir and Hjordis Bjartmars of the Fulbright Commission, Dean Sigurður Kristinsson of the University of Akureyri, Ágúst Þór Árnason, Giorgio Baruchello, Páll Björnsson, Andrew Brooks, Meredith Cricco, Adolf Fridriksson, Hrannar Hafberg, Dagmar Hannesdóttir, Margrét Heinreksdóttir, Anna Höskuldsdóttir, Rachael Johnstone, Elin Kjartansdóttir, Sigurður Líndal, Timothy Murphy, Oddur Olafsson, Kári Á Rógvi, and Jon Vidar Sigurdsson.

For encouraging my study of Islamic history, I am grateful among others to Sirin Hamsho, Aurangzeb Haneef, Shareda Hosein, Abdullah Saeed, Christian Sahner, and Sophia Shafi.

For his unstinting kindness and support in Germany, I thank the late Winfried Brugger of the University of Heidelberg, who is deeply missed.

In writing this book, I have relied extensively on the work of many specialists in the fields of law, history, political science, anthropology, and area studies. Their expertise has been both humbling and inspiring. I am able to acknowledge some of these scholars in my notes, which I hope will provide interested readers with a starting point for further reading.

Talks or presentations based on this work were given at the University of Akureyri, Brigham Young University, Cardozo School of Law, the University of Florida Levin College of Law, the University of Heidelberg, the University of Richmond School of Law, the Rutgers School of Law–Newark, Rutgers University–Newark, St. John's School of Law, Touro Law Center, the Witherspoon Institute, the University of Würzburg, and the Yale Law School Legal History Forum. Published work in preparation for this book has or will shortly appear in *Erasmus Law Review*, *Lögfrœðingur*, *The Review of Faith & International Affairs*, and Legal History Blog.

For their many suggestions, insights, assistance, and encouragement, I thank Ruiseart Alcorn, Michael Armstrong-Roche, Amy Bach, Elizabeth Bartlett, Lofty Becker, Al Bell, Avis and Iris Beneš, Ayelet Ben-yishai, Guyora Binder, Daniel Bonilla, Marie Borroff, Patricia Boulhosa, Donna Lee Bowen, Jonathan Boyarin, Giannina Braschi, John Brigham, Joel Cogan, Joe and Wanda Corn, Michael Curtis, Elizabeth Dale, Deven Desai, Gabriella Doob, Mark Fenster, Owen Fiss, William Forbath, Beth Gilson, Rupendra Guha Majumdar, Lucas Grosman, Roya Hakakian, George Handley, Steven Heller, Thomas Hilbink, James Eric Jones, Ben Karp, Stuart Klipper, Mehmet Kucukozer, Andrea Kuduk, David and Cathy Kuduk, Samuel Levine, Tanya Llewellyn, Rudolph Lohmeyer, Ramesh Manian, Daniel Markovits, Sean McCann, Natalia Mendieta, Ziya Meral, Matt Milford, Robin Miller, Sonia Mittal, María José Moore, Liliana Mosca, Mukhtiar Muhammad, Nicholas Parillo, Richard Pershan, Deborah Poritz, Vicki and Pierce Rafferty, Shelley Sadin, Norman Samuels, Sudha Setty, Keith

Sharfman, Jennifer Siegel, Ash Sogal, Kevin Stack, Jonathan Stein, Kirk Swinehart, Trysh Travis, and my parents, Bernard and Marijana Weiner.

This book could not have been written without the support and advice of my friend and agent, Tina Bennett, and my editors, Eric Chinski and Thomas LeBien.

Lastly, I wish to thank Jennifer Bryson for her guidance and personal example, and Mitchell Orenstein for twenty years of inestimable friendship and the exchange of ideas.

This book is dedicated to my wife, for reasons beyond expression.

INDEX